ON THE KABBALAH
AND ITS SYMBOLISM

ON THE KABBALAH
AND ITS SYMBOLISM

by

GERSHOM SCHOLEM

translated by

RALPH MANHEIM

Schocken Books · New York

First SCHOCKEN PAPERBACK edition 1969

10 9   83 84

The translation of this volume is based
upon the original edition published by
Rhein-Verlag, Zurich, under the title
Zur Kabbala and ihrer Symbolik, copyright
© 1960 by Rhein-Verlag, Zurich. All rights
reserved by Suhrkamp Verlag, Frankfurt am Main.

Manufactured in the United States of America
ISBN 0-8052-0235-8

Contents

v

ON THE KABBALAH
AND ITS SYMBOLISM

Introduction

THE Kabbalah, literally 'tradition,' that is, the tradition of things divine, is the sum of Jewish mysticism. It has had a long history and for centuries has exerted a profound influence on those among the Jewish people who were eager to gain a deeper understanding of the traditional forms and conceptions of Judaism. The literary production of the Kabbalists, more intensive in certain periods than in others, has been stored up in an impressive number of books, many of them dating back to the late Middle Ages. For many centuries the chief literary work of this movement, the *Zohar*, or 'Book of Splendor,' was widely revered as a sacred text of unquestionable value, and in certain Jewish communities it enjoys such esteem to this day. When Israel became an independent state, the Jews of Yemen, a remote and isolated principality in southern Arabia, immigrated almost to a man aboard the 'magic carpets,' as they called the airliners. They were obliged to abandon nearly all their belongings; but one object many had been unwilling to part with was their copy of the *Zohar*, which they have continued to study to this day.

But this world has been lost to European Jewry. Down to our own generation, students of Jewish history showed little understanding for the documents of the Kabbalah and ignored them almost completely. For in the late eighteenth century, when the Jews of Western Europe turned so resolutely to European culture, one of the first and most important elements of their old heritage to be sacrificed was the Kabbalah. Jewish mysticism with its intricate, introverted symbolism was felt to be alien and disturbing, and soon forgotten. The Kabbalists had attempted to penetrate and even to describe the mystery of the world as a reflection of the mysteries of divine life. The images into which their experience had crystallized were too deeply involved with the historical experience of the Jewish people, which in the nineteenth century seemed to have lost its relevance. For centuries the Kabbalah had been vital to the Jews' understanding of themselves. Now it vanished beneath the turmoil of modern life, so completely that for whole generations next to nothing was known of it. What remained resembled an overgrown field of ruins, where only very occasionally a learned traveler was surprised or shocked by some bizarre image of the sacred, repellent to rational thought. The key to the understanding of the Kabbalistic books seemed to have been lost. Scholars were perplexed and embarrassed by this world, which, instead of offering clear and simple concepts that could be developed, presented symbols of a very special kind, in which the spiritual experience of the mystics was almost inextricably intertwined with the historical experience of the Jewish people.

It is this interweaving of two realms, which in most other religious mysticisms have remained separate, that gave the Kabbalah its specific imprint. Small wonder that it seems strange to students of Christian mysticism, since it does not fit into the categories of 'mysticism' with which they are familiar. The more sordid, pitiful, and cruel the fragment of historical reality allotted to the Jew amid the storms of exile, the deeper and more precise the symbolic meaning it assumed, and the more radiant became the Messianic hope which burst through it and transfigured it. At the heart of this reality lay a great image of rebirth, the myth of exile and redemption, which assumed such vast dimensions with the Kabbalists and accounts for their prolonged historical influence. For in the books of the Kabbalists the personal element is almost negligible and so veiled in all manner of disguises that we must look very closely to find it. Very rarely did a Kabbalist speak of his own way to God. And the chief interest of the Kabbalah for us does not lie in such statements, but in the light it throws on the 'historical psychology' of the Jews. Here each individual was the totality. And this is the source of the fascination which the great symbols of the Kabbalah possess for a historian no less than a psychologist. In the Kabbalah the law of the Torah became a symbol of cosmic law, and the history of the Jewish people a symbol of the cosmic process.

In a generation that has witnessed a terrible crisis in Jewish history, the ideas of these medieval Jewish esoterics no longer seem so strange. We see with other eyes, and the obscure symbols strike us as worth clarifying. Research in this field involves an enormous responsibility. In digging up and evaluating the material, a scholar must make every effort to preserve a critical attitude. For long before historians became interested in Jewish mysticism, charlatans and cranks were drawn to it. This was of doubtful benefit to the study of the Kabbalah. The endeavor to understand what was here enacted at the heart of Jewry cannot dispense with historical criticism and clear vision. For even symbols grow out of historical experience and are saturated with it. A proper understanding of them requires both a 'phenomenological' aptitude for seeing things as a whole and a gift of historical analysis. One complements and clarifies the other; taken together, they promise valuable findings.

1. Religious Authority and Mysticism

THE problem to be dealt with in the ensuing pages is of central importance to the history of religions and can be considered under a number of aspects. We shall start from the assumption that a mystic, insofar as he participates actively in the religious life of a community, does not act in the void. It is sometimes said, to be sure, that mystics, with their personal striving for transcendence, live outside of and above the historical level, that their experience is unrelated to historical experience. Some admire this ahistorical orientation, others condemn it as a fundamental weakness of mysticism. Be that as it may, what is of interest to the history of religions is the mystic's impact on the historical world, his conflict with the religious life of his day and with his community. No historian can say—nor is it his business to answer such questions—whether a given mystic in the course of his individual religious experience actually found what he was so eagerly looking for. What concerns us here is not the mystic's inner fulfillment. But if we wish to understand the specific tension that often prevailed between mysticism and religious authority, we shall do well to recall certain basic facts concerning mysticism.

A mystic is a man who has been favored with an immediate, and to him real, experience of the divine, of ultimate reality, or who at least strives to attain such experience. His experience may come to him through sudden illumination, or it may be the result of long and often elaborate preparations. From a historical point of view, the mystical quest for the divine takes place almost exclusively within a prescribed tradition—the exceptions seem to be limited to modern times, with their dissolution of all traditional ties. Where such a tradition prevails, a religious authority, established long before the mystic was born, has been recognized by the community for many generations. Grounded in the specific experience of the community, this authority has been developed through an interchange between the community and those individuals who have interpreted its fundamental experience and so helped the community to express itself, who in a manner of speaking have made it articulate. There is then a scale of values that has been taken over from tradition; there is also a group of doctrines and dogmas, which are taken as authentic statements concerning the religious experience of a given community. And there is in addition a body of rites and customs, traditionally believed to transmit the values and express the mood and rhythm of religious life. Very different media can be invested with religious authority. They may be impersonal in character, a sacred book for example, or distinctly personal—in Catholicism, for example, it is the Pope who has the last word in deciding what is compatible with the Catholic tradition. There may also be mixtures and combinations of the two types, or authority may reside in the consensus of an assembly of priests or other religious persons, even where—as in Islam—these representatives of authority need not actually meet in order to formulate or lend weight to their decisions.

A mystic operates within the context of such traditional institutions and authority. If he accepts the context and makes no attempt to change the community, if he has no interests in sharing his novel experience with others and finds his peace in solitary immersion in the divine—then there is no problem, for there is nothing to bring him into conflict with others. There have assuredly been obscure mystics of this kind in all religions. The Jewish mysticism of recent centuries, in any case, has brought forth the 'hidden saint' (*nistar*), an enormously impressive type with a profound appeal for the common people. According to a tradition that goes back to Talmudic times there are, in every generation, thirty-six righteous men who are the foundations of the world. If the anonymity, which is part of their very nature, were broken, they would be nothing. One of them is perhaps the Messiah, and he remains hidden only because the age is not worthy of him. Especially among the Hasidim of Eastern Europe, later generations spun endless legends about these most obscure of men, whose acts, because they are performed so entirely beyond the ken of the community, are free from the ambiguities inseparable from all public action. In a truly sublime sense the 'hidden saint' makes religion a private affair, and because he is by definition barred from communication with other men, he is unaffected by the problems involved in all dealings with society.

But let us make no mistake. Inestimable as may be the worth of these mute, anonymous saints, the history of religions is not concerned with them. It is concerned with what happens when men attempt to enter into communication with each other. And it is generally recognized that in the case of mystics such communication presents a problem. From a historian's point of view, the sum of religious phenomena known as mysticism consists in the attempts of mystics to communicate their 'ways,' their illuminations, their experience, to others. If not for such attempts it would be impossible to regard mysticism as a historical phenomenon. And it is precisely in the course of such attempts that mysticism comes to grips with religious authority.

All mysticism has two contradictory or complementary aspects: the one conservative, the other revolutionary. What does this mean?

It has been said that mystics are always striving to put new wine into old bottles—just what a famous passage in the Gospels warns us not to do. It seems to me that this formulation is strikingly apt and of the utmost relevance to our problem. How can a mystic be a conservative, a champion and interpreter of religious authority? How is he able to do what the great mystics of Catholicism, such Sufis as Ghazzali, and most of the Jewish Kabbalists did? The answer is that these mystics seem to rediscover the sources of traditional authority. Perceiving the ancient foundations of this authority, they have no desire to change it. On the contrary, they try to preserve it in its strictest sense.

Sometimes this conservative function has been included in the very definition of mysticism—but this strikes me as questionable and one-sided. An American author, for example, has defined mysticism as 'the endeavor to secure consciousness of the presence of the Agency through which (or through Whom) the conservation of socially recognized values is sought.'[1]

The conservative function of mysticism is made possible by the

[1] K. Wright, *A Student's Philosophy of Religion*, New York, 1938, p. 287.

fact that the fundamental mystical experience has two aspects. In itself it has no adequate expression; mystical experience is fundamentally amorphous. The more intensely and profoundly the contact with God is experienced, the less susceptible it is of objective definition, for by its very nature it transcends the categories of subject and object which every definition presupposes. On the other hand, such experience can be interpreted in different ways, that is, clothed in different meanings. The moment a mystic tries to clarify his experience by reflection, to formulate it, and especially when he attempts to communicate it to others, he cannot help imposing a framework of conventional symbols and ideas upon it. To be sure, there is always some part of it that he cannot adequately and fully express. But if he does try to communicate his experience—and it is only by doing so that he makes himself known to us—he is bound to interpret his experience in a language, in images and concepts, that were created before him.

Because mystical experience as such is formless, there is in principle no limit to the forms it can assume. At the beginning of their path, mystics tend to describe their experience in forms drawn from the world of perception. At later stages, corresponding to different levels of consciousness, the world of nature recedes, and these 'natural' forms are gradually replaced by specifically mystical structures. Nearly all the mystics known to us describe such structures as configurations of lights and sounds. At still later stages, as the mystic's experience progresses toward the ultimate formlessness, these structures dissolve in their turn. The symbols of the traditional religious authority play a prominent part in such structures. Only the most universal formal elements are the same in different forms of mysticism.[1] For light and sound and even the name of God are merely symbolic representations of an ultimate reality which is unformed, amorphous. But these structures which are alternately broken down and built up in the course of the mystic's development also reflect certain assumptions concerning the nature of reality, which originated in, and derived their authority from, philosophical traditions, and then surprisingly (or perhaps not so surprisingly) found confirmation in mystical experience. This applies even to assumptions that may strike us as utterly fantastic, such as certain ideas of the Kabbalists, or the Buddhist theory of the identity of the skandhas with

[1] Cf. Mircea Eliade in *Eranos-Jahrbuch*, XXVI (1957), pp. 189–242.

the Buddha, no less than to the philosophico-theological hypotheses of Catholic mystics (concerning the Trinity for example), which all seem to be confirmed by mystical experience.

In general, then, the mystic's experience tends to confirm the religious authority under which he lives; its theology and symbols are projected into his mystical experience, but do not spring from it.[1] But mysticism has another, contrasting, aspect: precisely because a mystic is what he is, precisely because he stands in a direct, productive relationship to the object of his experience, he transforms the content of the tradition in which he lives. He contributes not only to the conservation of the tradition, but also to its development. Seen with new eyes, the old values acquire a new meaning, even where the mystic had no such intention or was not even aware of doing anything new. Indeed, a mystic's understanding and interpretation of his own experience may even lead him to question the religious authority he had hitherto supported.

For the same experience, which in one case makes for a conservative attitude, can in another case foster a diametrically opposite attitude. A mystic may substitute his own opinion for that prescribed by authority, precisely because his opinion seems to stem from the very same authority. This accounts for the revolutionary character of certain mystics and of the groups which accept the symbols in which mystics of this type have communicated their experience.

Occasionally a revolutionary mystic has laid claim to a prophetic gift and asserted a prophetic function in his efforts to reform his community. This brings up a question which we must briefly consider: can we and should we identify prophetic revelation and mystical experience? It is an old question, that has led to endless controversy. Personally I reject such an identification and am convinced that it can throw no light on our problem. Nevertheless, I should like to say a few words about the paradoxical phenomenon of medieval prophetology, which is particularly instructive in this connection.

How puzzling, not to say indigestible, the phenomenon of Biblical prophecy seemed to those schooled in the systematic thinking of the Greeks may be gathered from the fact that in the medieval philosophy of both the Arabs and the Jews there

[1] I owe this formulation to an article by G. A. Coe, 'The Sources of the Mystic Revelation,' *Hibbert Journal*, VI (1907–8), p. 367.

developed a theory of prophecy which amounts to an identification of the prophet with the mystic. Henry Corbin's illuminating analyses show, for example, that Shiite prophetology was essentially a hierarchy of mystical experience and illumination, rising from stage to stage.[1] The Biblical or Koranic concept of the prophet as bringer of a message is so reinterpreted as to denote the ideal type of the mystic, even when he is called a prophet. Such a prophet as Amos, whom God raised up from among the dressers of sycamore trees, to make him the bearer of His message, is transformed by philosophical prophetology into something entirely different: an enlightened one, who passes through successive stages of spiritual discipline and initiation until, at the end of a long preparation, he is favored with the gift of prophecy, considered as union with the 'active intellect,' that is, with a divine emanation or stage of revelation. Cautiously as the authors may express themselves, this theory of prophecy as union with the 'active intellect' always suggests something of the *unio mystica*, though not of the ultimate degree. In this respect there is no essential difference between so radically spiritualistic a doctrine as the prophetology of the Ismaili and a rationalistic theory like that of Maimonides.

But prophecy as it was originally understood is something entirely different. The prophet hears a clear message and sometimes beholds an equally plain vision, which he also remembers clearly. Undoubtedly a prophetic message of this sort lays direct claim to religious authority. In this it differs fundamentally from mystical experience. And yet, no one would think of denying the prophet's immediate experience of the divine. Plainly, we are dealing with two distant categories of experience, and I very much doubt whether a prophet can justifiably be called a mystic. For as we have said, the mystic's experience is by its very nature indistinct and inarticulate, while the prophet's message is clear and specific. Indeed, it is precisely the indefinable, incommunicable character of mystical experience that is the greatest barrier to our understanding of it. It cannot be simply and totally translated into sharp images or concepts, and often it defies any attempt to supply it— even afterward—with positive content. Though many mystics have attempted such 'translation,' have tried to lend their experience form and body, the center of what a mystic has to say

[1] *Eranos-Jahrbuch*, XXVI (1957), pp. 57–188.

always remains a shapeless experience, regardless of whether we choose to interpret it as *unio mystica* or as 'mere' communion with the divine. But it is precisely the shapeless core of his experience which spurs the mystic to his understanding of his religious world and its values, and it is this dialectic which determines his relation to the religious authority and lends it meaning.

The most radical of the revolutionary mystics are those who not only reinterpret and transform the religious authority, but aspire to establish a new authority based on their own experience. In extreme cases, they may even claim to be above all authority, a law unto themselves. The formlessness of the original experience may even lead to a dissolution of all form, even in interpretation. It is this perspective, destructive, yet not unrelated to the original impulse of the mystic, which enables us to understand the border-line case of the nihilistic mystic as an all too natural product of inner mystical upheavals even if he was rejected with horror by all those about him. All other mystics try to find the way back to form, which is also the way to the community; he alone, because in his experience the breakdown of all form becomes a supreme value, tries to preserve this formlessness in an undialectic spirit, instead of taking it, like other mystics, as an incentive to build up new form. Here all religious authority is destroyed in the name of authority: here we have the revolutionary aspect of mysticism in its purest form.

II

In connection with this relationship between mysticism and religious authority the following point is of crucial importance: where the authority is set forth in holy scriptures, in documents bearing a character of revelation, the question rises: what is the attitude of mysticism toward such an historically constituted authority? This question in itself might well take up an entire chapter. But I shall be able to treat it briefly, because it has been amply covered in Ignaz Goldziher's work on the exegesis of the Koran (1920) and in Henry Corbin's above-mentioned paper on Ismailian Gnosis,[1] while I myself have analyzed it in detail in connection with Jewish mysticism.[2]

What happens when a mystic encounters the holy scriptures of

[1] Cf. Corbin's above-mentioned article.
[2] Cf. Chapter 2 of the present book.

his tradition is briefly this: the sacred text is smelted down and a new dimension is discovered in it. In other words: the sacred text loses its shape and takes on a new one for the mystic. The question of meaning becomes paramount. The mystic transforms the holy text, the crux of this metamorphosis being that the hard, clear, unmistakable word of revelation is filled with *infinite* meaning. The word which claims the highest authority is opened up, as it were, to receive the mystic's experience. It clears the way to an infinite inwardness, where ever new layers of meaning are disclosed. Rabbi Pinhas of Koretz, a Hasidic mystic, expressed this with the utmost precision when he translated the formula *Rabbi Shim'on patah* ('Rabbi Simeon opened [his lecture] with the verse of Scripture'; it is with these words that Rabbi Simeon ben Yohai's mystical exegeses and lectures are introduced in the *Zohar*) literally as 'Rabbi Simeon *opened* the verse of Scripture.'

The holiness of the texts resides precisely in their capacity for such metamorphosis. The word of God must be infinite, or, to put it in a different way, the absolute word is as such meaningless, but it is *pregnant* with meaning. Under human eyes it enters into significant finite embodiments which mark innumerable layers of meaning. Thus mystical exegesis, this *new* revelation imparted to the mystic, has the character of a key. The key itself may be lost, but an immense desire to look for it remains alive. In a day when such mystical impulses seem to have dwindled to the vanishing point they still retain an enormous force in the books of Franz Kafka. And the same situation prevailed seventeen centuries ago among the Talmudic mystics, one of whom left us an impressive formulation of it. In his commentary on the Psalms, Origen quotes a 'Hebrew' scholar, presumably a member of the Rabbinic Academy in Caesarea, as saying that the Holy Scriptures are like a large house with many, many rooms, and that outside each door lies a key—but it is not the right one. To find the right keys that will open the doors—that is the great and arduous task.[1] This story, dating from the height of the Talmudic era, may give an idea of Kafka's deep roots in the tradition of Jewish mysticism. The rabbi whose metaphor so impressed Origen[2] still possessed

---

[1] Origen, *Selecta in Psalmos* (on Psalm I), in Migne, *Patrologia Graeca*, XII, 1080. This important passage is stressed by F. I. Baer in his Hebrew article in *Zion*, XXI (1956), p. 16.

[2] Origen calls this metaphor 'very ingenious.'

the Revelation, but he knew that he no longer had the right key, and was engaged in looking for it. Another formulation of the same idea is frequent in the books of the Lurianic Kabbalah:[1] every word of the Torah has six hundred thousand 'faces,' that is, layers of meaning or entrances, one for each of the children of Israel who stood at the foot of Mount Sinai. Each face is turned toward only one of them; he alone can see it and decipher it. Each man has his own unique access to Revelation. Authority no longer resides in a single unmistakable 'meaning' of the divine communication, but in its infinite capacity for taking on new forms.

But this mystical approach to Scripture embraces two clearly discernible attitudes, the one conservative, and the other revolutionary. The conservatives recognize the eternal validity of the historical facts recorded in such books as the Torah or the Koran. Precisely because they preserve these foundations of the traditional authority for all time, they are able to treat Scripture with the almost unlimited freedom that never ceases to amaze us in the writings of the mystics, a freedom even to despair, as in our metaphor of the wrong keys. Recognition of the unaltered validity of the traditional authority is the price which these mystics pay for transforming the meanings of the texts in their exegesis. As long as the framework is kept intact, the conservative and revolutionary elements in this type of mystic preserve their balance, or perhaps it would be better to say, their creative tension. One cannot but be fascinated by the unbelievable freedom with which Meister Eckhart, the author of the *Zohar*, or the great Sufi mystics read their canonical texts, from which their own world seems to construct itself.

But even where the religious authority of the same sacred book is recognized, a revolutionary attitude is inevitable once the mystic invalidates the literal meaning. But how can he cast aside the literal meaning while still recognizing the authority of the text? This is possible because he regards the literal meaning as simply nonexistent or as valid only for a limited time. It is *replaced* by a mystical interpretation.

The history of Judaism provides two classical examples of these two possible attitudes toward the sacred texts; both occurred after the establishment of the Biblical canon. I am referring to the attitude of the authors of the exegetic texts in the Dead Sea scrolls,

[1] Cf. Chapter 2.

probably dating from the pre-Christian era, and to that of Paul. It is not yet certain whether the Dead Sea scrolls should be regarded as mystical in the strictest sense. Our interpretation of these texts, and particularly of the personal element in them, is still so uncertain that the question will probably not be decided for some time to come.[1] But if it should turn out that the leaders of this sect were mystics (and not merely conservative reformers), this literature will provide an excellent example, indeed, the oldest known example, of a conservative attitude towards the sacred text, accompanied by the greatest freedom of exegesis. Even if the hymns which express the personal religion of this community (or perhaps even of one of its leaders) derive their ultimate inspiration from mystical illumination, the world they reflect remains entirely within the frame of the traditional authority; this exegesis is strictly conservative even when it actually transforms the authority. There can be no question of an abrogation of the authority; the aim is rather to restore it in all its harshness.

It is very different with Paul, the most outstanding example known to us of a revolutionary Jewish mystic. Paul had a mystical experience which he interpreted in such a way that it shattered the traditional authority. He could not keep it intact; but since he did not wish to forgo the authority of the Holy Scriptures as such, he was forced to declare that it was limited in time and hence abrogated. A purely mystical exegesis of the old words replaced the original frame and provided the foundation of the new authority which he felt called upon to establish. This mystic's clash with religious authority was clear and sharp. In a manner of speaking, Paul read the Old Testament 'against the grain.' The incredible violence with which he did so shows not only how incompatible his experience was with the meaning of the old books, but also how determined he was to preserve, if only by purely mystical exegeses, his bond with the sacred text. The result was the paradox that never ceases to amaze us when we read the Pauline Epistles: on the one hand the Old Testament is preserved, on the

---

[1] The smoothness and expressiveness of the translations of these texts are sometimes in diametric opposition to the roughness and obscurity of the Hebrew originals. The mystical lyricism, for example, which characterizes Theodor H. Gaster's impressive translation of one of the most important of these texts in *The Dead Sea Scriptures*, New York, 1956, pp. 109–202, cannot but arouse the envy of anyone who has read the Hebrew original.

other, its original meaning is completely set aside. The new authority that is set up, for which the Pauline Epistles themselves serve as a holy text, is revolutionary in nature. Having found a new source, it breaks away from the authority constituted in Judaism, but continues in part to clothe itself in the images of the old authority, which has now been reinterpreted in purely spiritual terms.

In either of these attitudes, the mystic rediscovers his own experience in the sacred text. Often it is hard to say whether the mystical meaning is actually there or whether he injects it. The genius of mystical exegeses resides in the uncanny precision with which they derive their transformation of Scripture into a *corpus symbolicum* from the exact words of the text. The literal meaning is preserved but merely as the gate through which the mystic passes, a gate, however, which he opens up to himself over and over again. The *Zohar* expresses this attitude of the mystic very succinctly in a memorable exegesis of Genesis 12 : 1. God's words to Abraham, *Lekh lekha*, are taken not only in their literal meaning, 'Get thee out,' that is, they are not interpreted as referring only to God's command to Abraham to go out into the world, but are also read with mystical literalness as 'Go to thee,' that is, to thine own self.

III

The conservative character so frequent in mysticism hinges largely on two elements: the mystic's own education and his spiritual guide—a matter of which I shall speak later on. As to the mystic's education, he almost always bears within him an ancient heritage. He has grown up within the framework of a recognized religious authority, and even when he begins to look at things independently and to seek his own path, all his thinking and above all his imagination are still permeated with traditional material. He cannot easily cast off this heritage of his fathers, nor does he even try to. Why does a Christian mystic always see Christian visions and not those of a Buddhist? Why does a Buddhist see the figures of his own pantheon and not, for example, Jesus or the Madonna? Why does a Kabbalist on his way of enlightenment meet the prophet Elijah and not some figure from an alien world? The answer, of course, is that the expression of their experience is immediately transposed into symbols from their own world, even if the objects of this experience are essentially the same and not, as some students of mysticism, Catholics in particular, like to suppose, fundamentally different. While recognizing different degrees and stages of mystical experience and still more numerous possibilities of interpretation, a non-Catholic tends to be extremely skeptical toward these repeated attempts which Catholics have made in line with their doctrine to demonstrate that the mystical experiences of the various religions rest on entirely different foundations.[1]

Here it may be worth our while to ask what happens when mysticism has no ties with any religious authority. This problem of the secularized interpretation of amorphous mystical experiences has been raised repeatedly since the Enlightenment. The situation is somewhat obscured by the fact that certain authors, disregarding or rejecting all traditional authority, describe their mystical experience in resolutely secular terms, yet clothe their interpretation of the same experience in traditional images. This is the case with Rimbaud and more consistently with William Blake. They regard themselves as Luciferian heretics, yet their imagination is shot through with traditional images, either of the official Catholic Church (Rimbaud) or of subterranean and esoteric, hermetic and spiritualist origin (Blake). Even in such revolutionaries, who seek their authority essentially in themselves and in a secular interpretation of their visions, tradition asserts its power. This secular mysticism takes a particularly interesting form in the Anglo-Saxon countries, where, after Blake, we encounter such figures as Walt Whitman, Richard Bucke, and Edward Carpenter, who in their interpretation of their experience recognized no authority whatsoever.

Perhaps the best example of a purely naturalistic interpretation of an overwhelming mystical experience is provided by the work, still widely read in North America, of the Canadian physician

---

[1] Perhaps the most illuminating expression of this view—that mystical experience has not one, but several essentially different objects—is provided by R. C. Zaehner's stimulating and controversial work, *Mysticism, Sacred and Profane: An Enquiry into Some Varieties of Praeternatural Experience*, Oxford (1957). Though exceedingly useful for certain purposes, the classification of mystical phenomena as natural, praeternatural, and supernatural, which in the last thirty years has found wide currency in scholarship of Catholic inspiration, remains highly questionable.

Richard Maurice Bucke, Walt Whitman's friend and the executor of his will. In 1872 Bucke experienced an overpowering mystical illumination; in the years that followed he tried to clarify its meaning and also to arrive at an understanding of all the great mystical experiences that struck him as authentic. He recorded his findings in a book which he entitled *Cosmic Consciousness*.[1] The book makes it clear that authentic mystical experience can be interpreted, even by the 'mystic' himself, in a purely immanent, naturalistic way, without the slightest reference to religious authority. But even here the scientific and philosophical theories accepted by the author play a determining role, just as the corresponding theories of the Buddhists, Neoplatonists, or Kabbalists shape their interpretations of their experience. The scientific theory which provided this late-nineteenth-century author with his basic concepts was Darwinism. In line with Darwinian theory, he regarded mystical experience as a stage in the development of human consciousness toward greater universality. Just as the coming of a new biological species is announced by mutations, which make their appearance in isolated members of the old species, the higher form of consciousness, which Bucke terms 'cosmic consciousness,' is today present only in a few human specimens—this heightened consciousness that will ultimately spread to all mankind is what is now termed mystical experience. Past generations put a religious interpretation on it—a historically understandable error. The mystic's claim to authority is legitimate, but must be interpreted in a different way: it is the authority of those whose consciousness has achieved a new stage of development. Of course Bucke's theories strike us today as naïve and scientifically untenable. Nevertheless, I find them extremely illuminating as one more indication that mystical experience is essentially amorphous and can therefore be interpreted in any number of ways.

Still, such secular mysticism is an exception. Most mystics, as we have seen, are strongly influenced by their education, which in a perfectly natural way imbues them with the traditional attitudes and symbols. But the community did not consider this a sufficient safeguard. By its very nature mysticism involves the danger of an uncontrolled and uncontrollable deviation from traditional

---

[1] Cf. Richard Maurice Bucke, *Cosmic Consciousness: A Study in the Evolution of the Human Mind*. The book first appeared in 1901; I have used the eighteenth printing, New York, 1956.

authority. The religious training of the group still leaves room for all manner of spiritual adventures, contrary to the recognized ideas and doctrines and likely to bring about a clash between the mystic and the religious authority of his group. This is no doubt one of the many reasons for the widespread belief that a mystic requires a spiritual guide, or *guru*, as he is called in India. On the face of it the function of the *guru* is primarily psychological. He prevents the student who sets out to explore the world of mysticism from straying off into dangerous situations. For confusion or even madness lurk in wait; the path of the mystic is beset by perils. It borders on abysses of consciousness and demands a sure and measured step. The Yogis, the Sufis, and the Kabbalists, no less than the manuals of Catholic mysticism, stress the need for such a spiritual guide, without whom the mystic runs the risk of losing himself in the wilderness of mystical adventure. The guide should be capable of preserving the proper balance in the mystic's mind. He alone is familiar with the practical applications of the various doctrines, which cannot be learned from books. And he has an additional function, which has been very little discussed but is nevertheless of great importance; he represents traditional religious authority. He molds the mystic's interpretation of his experience, guiding it into channels that are acceptable to established authority. How does he accomplish this? By preparing his student for what he may expect along the way and at the goal. He provides at the outset the traditional coloration which the mystical experience, however amorphous, will assume in the consciousness of the novice.

Let us consider, for example, the *Spiritual Exercises* of Ignatius of Loyola, an invaluable manual of Catholic mysticism. From the start it impregnates the consciousness of the novice with the images of Christ's Passion. It shows exactly what the novice has to expect at every step, and sets out to produce the phenomenon it promises. It is the same, to take an example from Jewish mysticism, with the Hasidic-Kabbalistic analysis of the stages of meditation and ecstasy, contained in a famous treatise emanating from the Habad school of White Russian Hasidism.[1] It informs the traveler on the path of 'active' contemplation in detail of the stages through which he must pass if his mystical career is to con-

[1] *Kuntras ha-Hithpa'aluth* by Rabbi Baer, son of Rabbi Shne'ur Zalman of Ladi, printed in the volume *Likkute Be'urim*, Warsaw, 1868.

form to the strict Jewish conceptions of the pure fear and pure love of God, and if he is to be safeguarded against uncontrollable emotional excesses. It provides the traditional Kabbalistic symbols with which this path of the Jewish mystic toward the experience of the divine can be described or interpreted, thus making certain that the path will conform, especially at its most dangerous turning points, to the dictates of authority.

To keep mysticism within the framework of constituted authority, compromises were often necessary. As one might expect, they vary in the extreme, according to the requirements of the various religious groups. As a highly instructive example of such a compromise, I should like to discuss here the Kabbalistic conception of the *gilluy Eliyahu*, the 'Revelation of the Prophet Elijah.' It provides an example of how the conservative and the 'progressive' aspects of mysticism can merge to form a single eloquent symbol.

When the first Kabbalists appeared on the scene of Jewish history, in Languedoc at the end of the twelfth century, they did not claim to have spoken directly with God. They took a compromise position. On the one hand, they wished to communicate something which obviously had not come to them through the traditional and generally accepted channels. But on the other hand, as orthodox Jews, they could not claim for their own mystical experience the same rank as for the revelation underlying the religious authority of Judaism. All monotheistic religions possess a distinct conception, one might call it a philosophy, of their own history. In this view, the first revelation expressing the fundamental contents of a religion is the greatest, the highest in rank. Each successive revelation is lower in rank and less authoritative than the last. Such a conception forbids a true believer to place a new revelation on a level with the great revelations of the past and obviously creates a serious problem for the mystic, since he imputes enormous value to his fresh, living experience. This situation necessitated compromise solutions which were inevitably reflected in the religious terminology. In Rabbinical Judaism, from which Kabbalistic mysticism developed, a number of different revelations were recognized as authentic and each in its own way authoritative, namely, the revelations of Moses, of the Prophets, of the Holy Spirit (which spoke in the authors of the Psalms and other parts of the Bible), of the receivers of the

'Heavenly Voice' (*bath kol*, believed to have been audible in the Talmudic era), and finally the 'revelation of the Prophet Elijah.' Each of these stages represents a lesser degree of authority than the stage preceding it. The principle remained in force: each generation can claim only a certain level of experience. But mystics could still make a place for their experience within the traditional framework, provided they defined it in accordance with this descending scale of values.

This was why the Kabbalists claimed no more for themselves than the seemingly so modest rank of receivers of a 'revelation of the Prophet Elijah.' In this connection it should be borne in mind that in such experience the auditive factor was paramount and the visual factor only secondary, since, primarily, no doubt under the influence of the mystical theory of prophecy referred to above, the Jewish mystics accorded far more importance to the hearing of a voice than to visions of light.

Since the beginnings of Rabbinical Judaism the Prophet Elijah has been a figure profoundly identified with the central preoccupations of Jewry: it is he who carries the divine message from generation to generation, he who at the end of time will reconcile all the conflicting opinions, traditions, and doctrines manifested in Judaism.[1] Men of true piety meet him in the market place no less than in visions. Since he was conceived as the vigilant custodian of the Jewish religious ideal, the Messianic guardian and guarantor of the tradition, it was impossible to suppose that he would ever reveal or communicate anything that was in fundamental contradiction with the tradition. Thus by its very nature the interpretation of mystical experience as a revelation of the Prophet Elijah tended far more to confirm than to question the traditional authority.

It is extremely significant that the first Kabbalists said to have attained this rank were Rabbi Abraham of Posquières and his son Isaac the Blind. Abraham ben David (d. 1198) was the greatest Rabbinical authority of his generation in southern France, a man deeply rooted in Talmudic learning and culture. But at the same time he was a mystic, who formulated his experience in distinctly conservative terms.[2] He himself relates in his writings that

---

[1] Cf. the article 'Elijahu' in *Encyclopaedia Judaica*, VI (1930), pp. 487–95.

[2] Cf. the chapter on Abraham ben David in my *Reshith ha-Kabbalah* (The Beginnings of the Kabbalah), Jerusalem, 1948, pp. 66–98.

the Holy Spirit appeared to him in his house of study; but the Kabbalists said it was the Prophet Elijah who had appeared to to him. This interpretation alone could guarantee that no conflict would arise between the Rabbi's traditional knowledge and the translation of his mystical experience into new conceptions. And when his son, a pure contemplative mystic without any outstanding claim to Rabbinical authority, carried on in his father's mystical path, the same claim was raised for him. The doctrines formulated by him and his school were looked upon as a legitimate completion of Rabbinical doctrine, whose adherents were in no danger of conflict with traditional authority. Yet tremendous forces were at work in this mysticism, and the symbols in which the new revelation was communicated disclose an intense and by no means undangerous conflict with traditional authority.

This was at the very beginning of Kabbalism. The same phenomenon is to be met with in a central figure of its later development, Isaac Luria in the sixteenth century. Luria represents both aspects of mysticism in their fullest development. His whole attitude was decidedly conservative. He fully accepted the established religious authority, which indeed he undertook to reinforce by enhancing its stature and giving it deeper meaning. Nevertheless, the ideas he employed in this seemingly conservative task were utterly new and seem doubly daring in their conservative context. And yet, for all their glaring novelty, they were not regarded as a break with traditional authority. This was possible because the authority of the Prophet Elijah was claimed for them—a claim that was widely recognized thanks to Luria's impressive personality and piety. Thus Luria's source of inspiration became a new authority in its own right. But though defined in traditional categories, this new authority, once accepted, brought about profound changes in Judaism, even when its advocates claimed to be doing nothing of the sort. In line with the prevailing view that each new revelation is lower in rank than the last, Luria was reticent about the source of his inspiration. But this reticence should not mislead us. The mystical experience that was his source is still as authentic as any, and as high in rank as any earlier phenomenon in the world of Rabbinical Judaism.

IV

In connection with the conservative interpretation and function of mysticism there is another important point. I have said that a mystic's background and education lead him to translate his experience quite spontaneously into traditional symbols. This brings us back to the problem of symbolism. Of course the question of interpreting symbols presents an abundance of aspects. To stress a single one of these aspects in the present context is not to minimize the importance of other aspects in other contexts. Symbols, by their very nature, are a means of expressing an experience that is in itself expressionless. But this psychological aspect is not the whole story. They also have a function in the human community. We may indeed go so far as to say that it is one of the main functions of religious symbols to preserve the vitality of religious experience in a traditional, conservative milieu.[1] The richness of meaning that they seem to emanate lends new life to tradition, which is always in danger of freezing into dead forms— and this process continues until the symbols themselves die or change.

The mystic who lends new symbolic meaning to his holy texts, to the doctrines and ritual of his religion—and this is just what almost all mystics have done and what accounts largely for their importance in the history of religions—discovers a new dimension, a new depth in his own tradition. In employing symbols to describe his own experience and to formulate his interpretations of it, he is actually setting out to confirm religious authority by reinterpreting it, regardless of whether he looks upon the traditional conceptions as symbols or attempts to elucidate them with the help of new symbols. But by thus opening up the symbolic dimensions, he transforms religious authority, and his symbolism is the instrument of this transformation. He bows to authority in pious veneration, but this does not prevent him from transforming it, sometimes radically. He uses old symbols and lends them new meaning, he may even use new symbols and give them an old

---

[1] For a discussion of the function of symbolism in religion, see the symposium *Religious Symbolism*, ed. F. Ernest Johnson, New York, 1955. However, I cannot by any means support the view, here put forward by Professor Abraham Heschel, that Rabbinical Judaism is a religion constituted outside the categories of symbolism.

meaning—in either case we find dialectical interrelationship between the conservative aspects and the novel, productive aspects of mysticism.

Another question arises: is it correct to distinguish these two attitudes toward authority as conscious and unconscious? Are we justified in saying that the religious authority is a conscious power in the mind of the mystic, while his conflict with it is rooted in the unconscious layers of his experience? Something can be said in favor of this view. Undoubtedly there have been mystics in whom the dividing line between conscious and unconscious coincided with the dividing line between their conservative and revolutionary tendencies. But this should not lead us to oversimplify. Usually these dividing lines are not so clear. Often enough the conflict takes place quite openly and the mystic is perfectly conscious of it. In such cases the mystic knows that he must oppose the existing authority, that he has been chosen to found a new authority or to do away with authority altogether.

This was the case with the great leaders of the Anabaptists, whose mystical inspiration is undeniable, and of the Quakers, to cite only these two striking examples from the history of Christianity. And in Judaism the same is true of the Sabbatian and Hasidic leaders. The psychological and historical categories are by no means identical. Often mystics have done their utmost to express themselves within the framework of established authority, and were driven to open conflict with it only when they met with too much opposition within their community. But if they had been free to choose, they would have avoided these conflicts which were not of their seeking. In certain cases it can be shown that the mystics began to put an increasingly radical interpretation on their ideas only after such a conflict had been forced upon them.

The *Journal* of John Wesley, founder of Methodism, provides an excellent example of such a case. Seldom has it been described so clearly how a mystic, caught up in the dialectic of his experience, struggled with all his might to avoid being drawn into conflict with the established religious authority. This conflict with the Anglican Church was forced upon Wesley, not from within but from without, but then he accepted it with full awareness and fought his battle to a finish. As far as the available documents allow us to judge, the situation of Valentinus, the outstanding

Gnostic leader, seems to have been much on the same order. And we find a similar development in the history of the Hasidim, whose first leaders had no thought of clashing with the Rabbinical authority. When the conflict was forced upon them, some of them gave free rein to their spiritualist mysticism; but after a time the movement and its Rabbinical adversaries arrived at a compromise, shaky at first but gradually gaining in stability. As far as I can see, our understanding of these matters is furthered very little by a distinction between conscious and unconscious processes.

But under what circumstances does such a conflict arise? What are the decisive factors? What kind of mysticism invites conflict with authority, and what kind does not? To these questions, unfortunately, we have no satisfactory answer. Such conflicts are largely unpredictable and do not hinge essentially on the personality or doctrines of the mystic. They depend entirely on historical circumstances. But the relationship between religion and historical conditions is constantly changing and cannot be reduced to any simple common denominator. A sound answer would require a knowledge of all the historical factors and of the specific conditions under which the mystics embarked on their activities. Yet perhaps there is one exception to this statement: those mystics who may be characterized as innately radical—a specific personal quality that is by no means limited to mystics. There are plenty of men who incline by nature to the radical formulation of their ideas, who chafe at authority of any kind and have no patience whatever with the folly of their fellow men. They need not necessarily be mystics to enter into opposition to established authority. But if they do become mystics, this radical tendency becomes particularly marked, as in the case of George Fox at the inception of the English Quaker movement.

Only in the rare and extreme case of nihilistic mysticism do mystical doctrines *as such* imply conflict. Otherwise, doctrines which have been expressed with the utmost force at certain times and places without leading to any conflict whatsoever may, under other historical conditions, foment violent struggles. Of course the dialectic of symbolism, of which we have spoken, is always present; but whether it results in open conflict with authority depends on extraneous factors. Of this the history of Catholic mysticism contains famous examples, and a historian of mysticism can derive little benefit from the attempts of the apologists to prove that two doctrines, one of which has been accepted by the Church, while the other has been condemned as heretical, only appear to be similar, but are in reality fundamentally different. This is amply illustrated by the history of quietist mysticism in Christianity.[1] For it was not the doctrines of quietism as originally formulated by its representatives in the Spanish Church that had changed when Madame Guyon was condemned; what had changed was the historical situation. One of the most dramatic conflicts in the history of the Church shows how such a struggle can arise against the will of the leading participants, if a historical situation that has no bearing whatever on mystical doctrines makes it seem desirable.

We find the same situation in Hasidism. When Israel Baal-Shem, the eighteenth-century founder of Polish Hasidism, put forward the mystical thesis that communion with God (*devekuth*) is more important than the study of books, it aroused considerable opposition and was cited in all the anti-Hasidic polemics as proof of the movement's subversive and anti-Rabbinical tendencies. But the exact same theory had been advanced two hundred years before by a no lesser mystical authority, by Isaac Luria himself in Safed, without arousing the slightest antagonism. It was not the thesis that had changed, but the historical climate.

In the above we have outlined the attitude of the mystics toward authority. As to the efforts of the authorities to contain the strivings of the mystics within the traditional framework, we have shown that they usually do their best to place obstacles in the path of the mystic. They give him no encouragement, and if in the end the obstacles frighten the mystic and bring him back to the old accustomed ways—so much the better from the standpoint of authority.

All great institutional religions have shown a marked distaste for lay mystics, that is, the unlearned mystics who, fired by the intensity of their experience, believe they can dispense with the traditional and approved channels of religious life. The less educated the candidate for mystical illumination, the less he knew of

---

[1] In this connection it is interesting to compare two so different accounts as those of Heinrich Heppe, *Geschichte der quietischen Mystik in der katholischen Kirche*, Berlin, 1875, and Ronald A. Knox, *Enthusiasm: A Chapter in the History of Religion with Special Reference to the XVII and XVIII Centuries*, Oxford, 1950.

theology, the greater was the danger of a conflict with authority. Quite regardless of their specific content, all manuals of mysticism written from the standpoint of traditional authority illustrate this point. The Jewish authorities, for example, tried to avoid conflicts by restricting the right to engage in mystical practice and speculation to fully trained Talmudic scholars. All Kabbalistic manuals quote Maimonides' warning: 'No one is worthy to enter Paradise [the realm of mysticism] who has not first taken his fill of bread and meat,'[1] i.e., the common fare of sober Rabbinical learning.

Such warnings, it must be admitted, were none too effective. The history of the great religions abounds in lay mysticism and in movements growing out of it. In the history of Christianity lay mysticism is exemplified by such movements as the Gnostics, the Brethren of the Free Spirit, the Spanish Alumbrados, and the Protestant sects of the last four centuries. The Church, it is true, branded all such movements as heresies. But in Judaism this was not always the case. Although many of the great Kabbalists fully met the requirements of Maimonides' conservative warning, there were always Kabbalists who were not so well versed in Rabbinical knowledge or who, in any case, had no complete Talmudic schooling. A case in point is the most celebrated of all the Jewish mystics of recent centuries, Israel Baal-Shem, the founder of Polish Hasidism. His 'knowledge' in the traditional sense of the word was very meager; he had no teacher of flesh and blood to guide him on his way—the only spiritual guide he ever alluded to was the Prophet Ahijah of Shiloh, with whom he was in constant spiritual and visionary contact. In short, he was a pure lay mystic and lay mysticism was a vital factor in the development of the movement he founded. Yet this movement (though at the price of a compromise) won the recognition of the traditional authority. Other movements, in which lay mysticism played an important part—the Sabbatians, for example—were unable to gain such recognition and were forced into open conflict with Rabbinical authority.

Especially in monotheistic religions the religious authorities had still another method of avoiding conflicts with the mystics of the community. This was to charge them with social responsi-

---

[1] Maimonides, *Mishneh Torah, Hilkhoth Yesode ha-Torah*, IV, 13.

bility. They put pressure on the mystics to mingle with the simple folk, to participate in their activities, instead of remaining among themselves in communities of the 'enlightened.' In Christianity, where since the beginnings of monasticism mystics have always been able to band together, this trend has not always been as clear as in Judaism. Since Talmudic times we find a decided disinclination to let mystics organize communities of their own. Time and time again the rabbis insisted that mystical experience, the 'love of God,' must be confirmed by activity in the human community, that it was not enough for an individual to pour out his soul to God. Here I shall not speak in detail of this tendency. Suffice it to say that it has been highly effective in 'taming' mystics and holding them within the limits imposed by traditional authority.

In diametrical and irreconcilable opposition to all such attempts to relieve the tension between mysticism and religious authority stands the extreme case of mystical nihilism, in which all authority is rejected in the name of mystical experience or illumination. At first glance the nihilist mystic seems to be the most free, the most faithful to his central insight; for having attained the highest goal of mystical experience, namely, the dissolution of all form, he extends his mystical insight to his relation with the real world, that is to say, he rejects all values and the authority which guarantees the validity of values. Yet from the standpoint of history, he is the most constrained and unfree of mystics, for historical reality as embodied in the human community prevents him, far more than it does any other mystic, from openly proclaiming his message. This explains no doubt why the documents of nihilistic mysticism are extremely rare. Because of their subversive character the authorities suppressed and destroyed them; where they have come down to us, it is because their authors resorted to an ambiguity of expression that makes our interpretation of the texts questionable. This explains, for example, why the nihilistic character of certain mystical doctrines, such as those of the Ismailis and the Druses in particular but also of such groups as the Bektashi order of dervishes, is still a matter of discussion. On the other hand, the intentional ambiguity of such writings has caused them, time and time again, to be suspected of mystical nihilism.

For want of the original sources of second-century gnostic

nihilism, which have not come down to us,[1] it seems to me that we possess no more impressive record of an unmistakably nihilistic mysticism than the Polish *Book of the Words of the Lord*, in which the disciples of Jacob Frank (1726–91) set down their master's teachings after his own spoken words.[2] I have elsewhere analyzed the circumstances which made possible this eruption of mystical nihilism within so firmly organized and authoritarian a community as Rabbinical Judaism.[3] Messianism and mysticism played equal parts in crystallizing these ideas, which sprang from the radical wing of the Sabbatian movement.[4]

What interests us here is the way in which the mystical experience of man's contact with the primal source of life could find its expression in a symbol implying the negation of all authority. An illumination concerning Messianic freedom in redemption crystallizes around the symbol of Life. In his mystical experience the mystic encounters Life. This 'Life,' however, is not the harmonious life of all things in bond with God, a world ordered by divine law and submissive to His authority, but something very different. Utterly free, fettered by no law or authority, this 'Life' never ceases to produce forms and to destroy what it has produced. It is the anarchic promiscuity of all living things. Into this bubbling caldron, this continuum of destruction, the mystic plunges. To him it is the ultimate human experience. For Frank, anarchic destruction represented all the Luciferian radiance, all the positive tones and overtones, of the word 'Life.' The nihilistic

---

[1] Valuable source material on which to base an analysis of the nihilistic possibilities of gnostic mysticism are provided by Hans Jonas in *Gnosis und spätantiker Geist*, I, Göttingen, 1933; but we are wholly dependent on quotations and reports transmitted by the Catholic adversaries of Gnosticism. Complete original texts have not been preserved. Cf. also Herbert Liboron, *Die karpokratianische Gnosis*, Leipzig, 1938.

[2] Thus far extensive quotations and notes from this book are to be found solely in Alexander Kraushar's two-volume work, *Frank i Frankiści Polscy*, Cracow, 1895. The manuscripts used by Kraushar were lost during the second World War when the Polish libraries were almost entirely destroyed. An incomplete manuscript of these copious notes was found only recently in the Cracow University library.

[3] Cf. my article, 'Le mouvement sabbataiste en Pologne,' *Revue de l'histoire des religions*, CLIII–CLIV (1953–4), especially the last section, CLIV, pp. 42–77.

[4] Cf. the detailed account in my two-volume Hebrew work, *Shabbetai Zevi*, Tel Aviv, 1957.

mystic descends into the abyss in which the freedom of living things is born; he passes through all the embodiments and forms that come his way, committing himself to none; and not content with rejecting and abrogating all values and laws, he tramples them underfoot and desecrates them, in order to attain the elixir of Life. In this radical interpretation of a symbol, the life-giving element of mystical experience was combined with its potential destructiveness. It goes without saying that from the standpoint of the community and its institutions, such mysticism should have been regarded as demonic possession. And it is indicative of one of the enormous tensions that run through the history of Judaism that this most destructive of all visions should have been formulated in its most unrestrained form by one who rebelled against the Jewish law and broke away from Judaism.

V

It seems to me that a statement which has come down to us from Rabbi Mendel Torum of Rymanóv (d. 1814),[1] one of the great Hasidic saints, throws a striking light on this whole problem of the relationship between authority and mysticism. Let me try to interpret this statement. The revelation given to Israel on Mount Sinai is, as everyone knows, a sharply defined set of doctrines, a summons to the human community; its meaning is perfectly clear, and it is certainly not a mystical formula open to infinite interpretation. But what, the question arises, is the truly divine element in this revelation? The question is already discussed in the Talmud.[2] When the children of Israel received the Ten Commandments, what could they actually hear, and what did they hear? Some maintained that all the Commandments were spoken to the children of Israel directly by the divine voice. Others said that only the first two Commandments: 'I am the Lord thy God' and 'Thou shalt have no other gods before me' (Exod. 20 : 2–3) were communicated directly. Then the people were overwhelmed, they could no longer endure the divine voice. Thus they had been obliged to receive the remaining Commandments through Moses. Moses alone was able to withstand the divine voice, and it was he

---

[1] Quoted by Ahron Markus, in *Der Chassidismus*, Pleschen, 1901, p. 239, from *Torath Menahem*, a collection of some sermons of the Rabbi of Rymanóv.

[2] Makkoth, 24a.

who repeated in a human voice those statements of supreme authority that are the Ten Commandments.

This conception of Moses as interpreter of the divine voice for the people was developed much more radically by Maimonides,[1] whose ideas Rabbi Mendel of Rymanóv carried to their ultimate conclusion. In Rabbi Mendel's view not even the first two Commandments were revealed directly to the whole people of Israel. All that Israel heard was the *aleph* with which in the Hebrew text the first Commandment begins, the *aleph* of the word *anokhi*, 'I.' This strikes me as a highly remarkable statement, providing much food for thought. For in Hebrew the consonant *aleph* represents nothing more than the position taken by the larynx when a word begins with a vowel. Thus the *aleph* may be said to denote the source of all articulate sound, and indeed the Kabbalists always regarded it as the spiritual root of all other letters, encompassing in its essence the whole alphabet and hence all other elements of human discourse.[2] To hear the *aleph* is to hear next to nothing; it is the preparation for all audible language, but in itself conveys no determinate, specific meaning. Thus, with his daring statement that the actual revelation to Israel consisted only of the *aleph*, Rabbi Mendel transformed the revelation on Mount Sinai into a mystical revelation, pregnant with infinite meaning, but without specific meaning. In order to become a foundation of religious authority, it had to be translated into human language, and that is what Moses did. In this light every statement on which authority is grounded would become a human interpretation, however valid and exalted, of something that transcends it.[3] Once

---

[1] Maimonides, *Guide to the Perplexed*, II, 33. Maimonides puts forward the opinion that wherever, in passages dealing with the revelation on Mount Sinai, the children of Israel are said to have heard words, it is meant that they heard the (inarticulate) sound of the voice, but that Moses heard the words (in their meaningful articulation) and communicated them.

[2] This view is expressed by Jacob Kohen of Soria at the beginning of his Kabbalistic explanation of the Hebrew alphabet, which I have published in *Madda'e ha-Yahaduth*, II (1927), especially p. 203.

[3] This opinion, as my friend Ernst Simon has called to my attention, is expressed with great precision and in a form suggesting the language of the mystics, by Franz Rosenzweig in a letter of 1925 to Martin Buber. Rosenzweig denies that the revelation on Mount Sinai gave laws. "The only immediate content of revelation . . . is revelation itself; with *va-yered* [he came down, Exod. 19 : 20] it is essentially complete, with *va-yedabber* [he spoke, Exod. 20 : 1] interpretation sets in, and all the more so with *'anokhi* [the "I" at the

in history a mystical experience was imparted to a whole nation and formed a bond between that nation and God. But the truly divine element in this revelation, the immense *aleph*, was not in itself sufficient to express the divine message, and in itself it was more than the community could bear. Only the prophet was empowered to communicate the meaning of this inarticulate voice to the community. It is mystical experience which conceives and gives birth to authority.

---

beginning of the Ten Commandments].' Cf. Franz Rosenzweig, *Briefe*, Berlin, 1935, p. 535; English translation in F. Rosenzweig, *On Jewish Learning*, ed. N. N. Glatzer, New York, 1955, p. 118.

2. The Meaning of the Torah in Jewish Mysticism

JEWISH mysticism is the sum of the attempts made to put a mystical interpretation on the content of Rabbinical Judaism as it crystallized in the period of the Second Temple and later. Obviously the process of crystallization had to be fairly far advanced before such a development could set in. This is equally true of the type of Judaism which centered round the law and which Philo of Alexandria undertook to interpret, and of the more highly developed Talmudic Judaism on which the endeavors of the medieval Kabbalists were based. Here it is not my intention to discuss the historical problems involved in the development of Jewish mysticism and specifically of the Kabbalah; I have done so elsewhere, particularly in my *Major Trends in Jewish Mysticism*. Suffice it to say that the subject I wish to discuss occupies a central position in Jewish mysticism.

In a religious system based on divine revelation and the acceptance of sacred books that define its content, questions concerning the nature of such revelation as set forth in the sacred books are unquestionably of the utmost importance. In times of crisis, moreover—and mysticism as a historical phenomenon is a product of crises—these questions become particularly urgent. Mystics are men who by their own inner experience and their speculation concerning this experience discover new layers of meaning in their traditional religion. When their experience and speculation did not lead them to break with the traditional institutions of their religion, it was inevitable that they should come to grips with two questions: how were they to find their own experience reflected and anticipated in the sacred texts? And: how could their view of the world be brought into harmony with the view accepted by their own tradition?[1] It is generally known that allegorical interpretations arise spontaneously whenever a conflict between new ideas and those expressed in a sacred book necessitates some form of compromise. What is true of allegorical interpretation is still more applicable to the specifically mystical interpretation of such texts.

Here it is not my intention to discuss mystical exegesis in its concrete application to the Bible. Vast numbers of books have been written by Jewish mystics attempting to find their own ideas in, or read them into, the Biblical texts. A large part of the enormous Kabbalistic literature consists of commentaries on Books of the Bible, especially the Pentateuch, the Five Scrolls, the Psalms, the Song of Songs, the Book of Ruth, and Ecclesiastes. Many productive minds among the Kabbalists found this a congenial way of expressing their own ideas, while making them seem to flow from the words of the Bible. It is not always easy, in a given case, to determine whether the Biblical text inspired the exegesis or whether the exegesis was a deliberate device, calculated to bridge the gap between the old and the new vision by reading completely new ideas into the text. But this perhaps is to take too rationalistic a view of what goes on in the mind of a mystic. Actually the thought processes of mystics are largely unconscious, and they may be quite unaware of the clash between old and new which is of such passionate interest to the historian. They are thoroughly steeped in the religious tradition in which they have grown up, and many notions which strike a modern reader as fantastic distortions of a text spring from a conception of Scripture which to the mystic seems perfectly natural. For one thing that can be said with certainty about Kabbalists is this: they are, and do their best to remain, traditionalists, as is indicated by the very word Kabbalah, which is one of the Hebrew words for 'tradition.'

Thus it is important for us to understand the basic assumptions underlying the concrete exegesis of the mystics. This is the problem we shall now discuss. In our pursuit of it we are not dependent on conjectures or inferences drawn from the exegeses, for the

[1] Cf. Chapter 1, in which this question is discussed in detail.

mystics have left us extremely precise and illuminating formulations of their ideas. Mystical speculation on the nature of the
Torah goes hand in hand with the development of certain general
principles. Some of the mystics' ideas have a very peculiar history
and are not common to all Kabbalists but characteristic only of
certain trends. It is not uninteresting to observe the relationship
between these different ideas and the basic principles from which
they developed.

A great deal has been written about the allegorical exegesis of
Philo of Alexandria and the assumptions on which it is based.
At this point there is no need to say more. In discussing the specific conceptions of the Kabbalists with regard to the meaning of
the Torah, we inevitably come across certain striking parallels to
passages in Philo. Only recently so outstanding a scholar as Y. F.
Baer attempted to demonstrate a profound structural kinship and
even identity between the conceptions of Philo and those of the
Kabbalists, and to interpret both as perfectly legitimate developments of the strictly Rabbinical conception underlying the
Halakhah.[1] But this parallelism, as far as I can see, does not spring
from any historical influence of Philo upon the medieval Kabbalists, although there have been numerous attempts—to my mind
all unsuccessful—to demonstrate such a line of filiation.[2] Insofar
as such parallels actually exist, they are based on similarity of purpose. As we shall see, the Kabbalists formulated their purpose

[1] Cf. Y. F. Baer's Hebrew article in *Zion*, XXIII–XXIV (1959), pp.
143 ff., especially up to p. 154, where reference is made to the first version of
the present chapter, published in *Diogenes*, Nos. 14–15 (1956). Baer, who
attempts to prove that logos and Torah are identical in Philo, goes still
further than Erwin Goodenough (*By Light, Light: the Mystic Gospel of Hellenistic Judaism*, New Haven, 1935, who speaks of no such identification in his
chapter on the Torah in Philo, pp. 72–94. Cf. also Harry A. Wolfson, *Philo*,
I, pp. 115–43; Edmund Stein, *Die allegorische Exegese des Philo aus Alexan-
dreia*, 1929.

[2] Recently such an attempt has been made by Samuel Belkin in his Hebrew
work, *The Midrash ha-Ne'elam and its Sources in the Old Alexandrian Midrashim*, Jerusalem, 1958 (special edition from the Yearbook *Sura*, III, pp.
25–92). Belkin tries to prove that this important part of the *Zohar* is a midrash based on Alexandrian sources closely related to Philo. His undertaking
does not stand up to criticism; cf. the penetrating critique of his work by
R. Zwi Werblowsky in *Journal of Jewish Studies*, X, p. 276, note 3 (1959–60),
pp. 25–44, 112–35. The rejoinder by Joshua Finkel, 'The Alexandrian
Tradition and the Midrash ha-Ne'elam' in *The Leo Jung Jubilee*, New York,
1962, pp. 77–103, is wide of the mark.

with incomparable clarity and penetration, and one can easily be misled by reading Philo in the light of their sharp formulations. Similarity of purpose and hence in the fundamental structure of the mystical ideas about the nature of the Holy Scriptures accounts also for the parallels between certain Kabbalistic statements about the Torah and those of Islamic mystics about the Koran or of Christian mystics about their Biblical canon. Only a study of the historical conditions under which specific Kabbalistic ideas developed can tell us whether there was any historical connection between the speculation of the Jewish Kabbalists and that of non-Jews on the nature of the Holy Scriptures. I believe that I can demonstrate such an influence in at least one case, in connection with the doctrine of the fourfold meaning of Scripture.

But before I turn to our central problem, one more preliminary remark is in order. Most if not all Kabbalistic speculation and doctrine is concerned with the realm of the divine emanations or *sefiroth*, in which God's creative power unfolds. Over a long period of years, Kabbalists devised many ways of describing this realm. But throughout their history it remained the principal content of their vision, and always they spoke of it in the language of symbols, since it is not accessible to the direct perception of the human mind. Insofar as God reveals himself, He does so through the creative power of the *sefiroth*. The God of whom religion speaks is always conceived under one or more of these aspects of His Being, which the Kabbalists identified with stages in the process of divine emanation. This Kabbalistic world of the *sefiroth* encompasses what philosophers and theologians called the world of the divine attributes. But to the mystics it was divine life itself, insofar as it moves toward Creation. The hidden dynamic of this life fascinated the Kabbalists, who found it reflected in every realm of Creation. But this life as such is not separate from, or subordinate to, the Godhead, rather, it is the revelation of the hidden root, concerning which, since it is never manifested, not even in symbols, nothing can be said, and which the Kabbalists called *en-sof*, the infinite. But this hidden root and the divine emanations are one.

Here I need not go into the paradoxes and mysteries of Kabbalistic theology concerned with the *sefiroth* and their nature. But one important point must be made. The process which the Kabbalists described as the emanation of divine energy and divine light was also characterized as the unfolding of the divine *language*. This gives rise to a deep-seated parallelism between the two most important kinds of symbolism used by the Kabbalists to communicate their ideas. They speak of attributes and of spheres of light; but in the same context they speak also of divine names and the letters of which they are composed. From the very beginnings of Kabbalistic doctrine these two manners of speaking appear side by side. The secret world of the godhead is a world of language, a world of divine names that unfold in accordance with a law of their own. The elements of the divine language appear as the letters of the Holy Scriptures. Letters and names are not only conventional means of communication. They are far more. Each one of them represents a concentration of energy and expresses a wealth of meaning which cannot be translated, or not fully at least, into human language. There is, of course, an obvious discrepancy between the two symbolisms. When the Kabbalists speak of divine attributes and *sefiroth*, they are describing the hidden world under ten aspects; when, on the other hand, they speak of divine names and letters, they necessarily operate with the twenty-two consonants of the Hebrew alphabet, in which the Torah is written, or as they would have said, in which its secret essence was made communicable. Several ways of resolving this glaring contradiction were put forward. One explanation was that since letters and *sefiroth* are different configurations of the divine power, they cannot be reduced to a mechanical identity. What is significant for our present purposes is the analogy between Creation and Revelation, which results from the parallel between the *sefiroth* and the divine language. The process of Creation, which proceeds from stage to stage and is reflected in extra-divine worlds and of course in nature as well, is not necessarily different from the process that finds its expression in divine words and in the documents of Revelation, in which the divine language is thought to have been reflected.

These considerations take us to the very heart of our subject. There is a necessary relationship between the mystical meaning of the Torah and the assumptions concerning its divine essence. The Kabbalists do not start from the idea of communicable meaning. Of course the Torah means something to us. It communicates something in human language. But this, as we shall see, is only the most superficial of the various aspects under which it can be considered. In the following we shall see what these aspects are.

The Kabbalistic conceptions of the true nature of the Torah are based on three fundamental principles. They are not necessarily connected, although in our texts they often appear together, but it is not difficult to see how a relation can be established between them. These principles may be identified as

1. The principle of God's name;
2. The principle of the Torah as an organism;
3. The principle of the infinite meaning of the divine word.

Historically and presumably also psychologically, they do not all have the same origin.

II

The conception of God's name as the highest concentration of divine power forms a connecting link between two sets of ideas, the one originally associated with magic, the other pertaining to mystical speculation as such. The idea of the magic structure and nature of the Torah may be found long before the Kabbalah, in a relatively early midrash, for example, where in commenting on Job 28 : 13: 'No man knoweth its order,' Rabbi Eleazar declares: 'The various sections of the Torah were not given in their correct order. For if they had been given in their correct order, anyone who read them would be able to wake the dead and perform miracles. For this reason the correct order and arrangement of the Torah were hidden and are known only to the Holy One, blessed be He, of whom it is said (Isa. 44 : 7): "And who, as I, shall call, and shall declare it, and set it in order for me".'[1]

Obviously this statement carries a strong magical accent and implies a magical view of the Torah. It is well known that in the Hellenistic period and later the Torah was put to magical use both by Jews and non-Jews: divine names gleaned from the Torah were

---

[1] *Midrash Tehillim*, ed. Buber, p. 33. The author of this statement is Eleazar ben Pedath, a teacher of the third century, whose interest in esoteric ideas is also apparent in other utterances; cf. W. Bacher, *Die Agada der paläs-tinensischen Amoräer*, II, Strassburg, 1896, p. 31. Bacher already refused 'to doubt the authenticity of this statement, which sounds like an early anticipation of the later so-called "practical Kabbalah".'

used for purposes of incantation. Often the methods of combination by which such magical names were derived from the Torah are unintelligible to us. Certain Hebrew and Aramaic texts of the late Talmudic and post-Talmudic periods indicate the specific use to which such magical names, allegedly taken from the Torah and the Book of Psalms, were put. The introduction to one of these works—*Shimmushe torah*, literally, the Theurgic Uses of the Torah —relates how Moses went up to heaven to receive the Torah, how he conversed with the angels, and how finally God gave him not only the text of the Torah as we know it, but also the secret combinations of letters which represent another, esoteric aspect of the Torah.[1] This book came to the knowledge of the first Kabbalists in Provence and in Spain about the year 1200. Moses ben Nahman (Nahmanides), one of the most prominent among the early Kabbalists, refers to it in the preface to his famous commentary on the Torah. 'We possess,' he writes,

an authentic tradition showing that the entire Torah consists of the names of God and that the words we read can be divided in a very different way, so as to form [esoteric] names. . . . The statement in the Aggadah to the effect that the Torah was originally written with black fire on white fire[2] obviously confirms our opinion that the writing was continuous, without division into words, which made it possible to read it either as a sequence of [esoteric] names ['*al derekh ha-shemoth*] or in the traditional way as history and commandments. Thus the Torah as given to Moses was divided into words in such a way as to be read as divine commandments. But at the same time he received the oral tradition, according to which it was to be read as a sequence of names.

In view of this esoteric structure of the Torah, says Nahmanides, the Masoretic tradition concerning the writing of the Bible and especially the scrolls of the Torah must be observed with the utmost care. Every single letter counts, and a scroll of the Torah must be rejected for use in the synagogue if there is so much as a

[1] This preface has been published several times separately under the title 'The Source of Wisdom.' The text of the book itself has been preserved only in manuscript. A German translation in August Wünsche, *Aus Israels Lehrhallen, kleine Midraschim*, I, Leipzig, 1907, pp. 127–33, especially p. 132.

[2] Likewise an utterance of Simeon ben Lakish, a Palestinian teacher very much inclined to esoteric mysticism. It has come down to us in several versions, first in the Palestinian Talmud, Shekalim, VI, end of *Halakhah* I. I shall deal further on with the mystical interpretation of this statement by one of the earliest Kabbalists.

single letter too few or too many. This conception is very old. As early as the second century, Rabbi Meir, one of the most important teachers of the Mishnah, relates:

When I was studying with Rabbi Akiba, I used to put vitriol in the ink and he said nothing. But when I went to Rabbi Ishmael, he asked me: My son, what is your occupation? I answered: I am a scribe [of the Torah]. And he said to me: My son, be careful in your work, for it is the work of God; if you omit a single letter, or write a letter too many, you will destroy the whole world. . . .[1]

The passage from Nahmanides clearly indicates the influence of the magical tradition, which was of course far older than the Kabbalah. From here it was only a short step to the still more radical view that the Torah is not only made up of the names of God but is as a whole the one great Name of God. This thesis is no longer magical, but purely mystical. It makes its first appearance among the Spanish Kabbalists, and the development from the old to the new view seems to have taken place among the teachers of Nahmanides. Commenting on a passage in the *Midrash Genesis Rabbah* to the effect that the word 'light' occurs five times in the story of the first day of Creation, corresponding to the five books of the Torah, Ezra ben Solomon, an older contemporary of Nahmanides, who frequented the same Kabbalistic circle in the Catalonian city of Gerona, writes: 'How far-reaching are the words of this sage; his words are true indeed, for the five books of the Torah are *the Name* of the Holy One, blessed be He.'[2] The mystical light that shines in these books is thus the one great Name of God. The same thesis is to be found in the writings of several members of the Gerona group of Kabbalists, and was finally taken over by the author of the *Zohar*, the classical book of Spanish Kabbalism.[3]

I believe that Nahmanides himself was perfectly familiar with this new idea, but that he was reluctant to express so radically

---

[1] Erubin 13a. Baer has stressed the implications of this passage for a mystical interpretation of the Torah, *loc. cit.*, p. 145.

[2] Ezra ben Solomon, Commentary on the Talmudic Aggadoth, in Vatican MS Cod. Hebr. 294, Fol. 34a.

[3] Cf. Azriel, *Perush Aggadoth*, ed. Tishby, p. 76; Pseudo-Nahmanides, *Sefer ha-'emunah vehabittahon*, XIX; *Zohar*, II, 87b; III, 80b, 176a. In III, 36a, we read: 'The entire Torah is a single holy mystical Name.'

mystical a thesis in a book intended for a general public un-
schooled in Kabbalistic doctrine. To say that the Torah was in
essence nothing but the great Name of God was assuredly a daring
statement that calls for an explanation. Here the Torah is interpreted as a mystical unity, whose primary purpose is not to convey a specific meaning, but rather to express the immensity of
God's power, which is concentrated in His 'Name.' To say that
the Torah is a name does not mean that it is a name which might
be pronounced as such, nor has it anything to do with any rational
conception of the social function of a name. The meaning is,
rather, that in the Torah God has expressed His transcendent
Being, or at least that part or aspect of His Being which can be
revealed to Creation and through Creation. Moreover, since even
in the ancient Aggadah the Torah was regarded as an instrument
of Creation, through which the world came into existence,[1] this
new conception of the Torah must be regarded as an extension
and mystical reinterpretation of the older conception. For the
instrument which brought the world into being is far more than a
mere instrument, since, as we have seen above, the Torah is the
concentrated power of God Himself, as expressed in His Name.
But this idea has a further implication. Another early Midrash says
that God 'looked into the Torah and created the world.'[2] The
author of these words must have thought that the law which
governs Creation as such, hence the cosmos and all nature, was
already prefigured in the Torah, so that God, looking into the
Torah, could see it, although to us this aspect of the Torah
remains concealed. This conception is actually formulated by
Philo, who explains the fact that the Mosaic Law begins with a
record of the Creation of the world by saying that 'Moses wished
to set forth the genesis of the great world state [*megalopolis*], since
his own laws were the best possible copy of the structure of all
nature.'[3] In the minds of the Kabbalists these ancient notions
handed down in the Aggadic tradition fused into a single idea. The
Name contains power, but at the same time embraces the secret

---

[1] *Mishnah Aboth*, III, 14; *Sifre* to Deut. 48, ed. Finkelstein, p. 114; *Genesis Rabbah*, I, 1. Cf. Leo Baeck, *Aus drei Jahrtausenden*, Tübingen, 1958, pp. 162 ff. and Baer, *loc. cit.*, p. 142.

[2] *Genesis Rabbah*, I, 1. The antecedents or parallels to this passage in Plato and Philo have often been discussed.

[3] Philo, *Vita Mosis*, II, 51.

laws and harmonious order which pervade and govern all existence. In addition the Kabbalists were able to read in the esoteric
and apocalyptic books of the Talmudic period that heaven and
earth were created by the Name of God.[1] It was only natural
to combine statmeents of this kind with the notion of the
Torah as the instrument of Creation, that is, the Great Name of
God.

This basic idea of the Torah as the Name of God was the source
of certain other Kabbalistic developments. It goes without saying
that such an assertion about the Torah does not refer to the document written in ink on a scroll of parchment, but to the Torah as
a pre-existential being, which preceded everything else in the
world. This follows, for example, from the Aggadah according to
which the Torah was created two thousand years before the
Creation of the world.[2] For the Kabbalists this 'Creation of the
Torah' was the process by which the divine Name or the divine
sefiroth of which we have spoken above emanated from God's
hidden essence. The Torah, as the Kabbalists conceived it, is consequently not separate from the divine essence, not created in the
strict sense of the word; rather, it is something that represents the
secret life of God, which the Kabbalistic emanation theory was
an attempt to describe. In other words, the secret life of God is
projected into the Torah; its order is the order of the Creation.
This most secret aspect of the Torah, or one might say, the Torah
in its occult form, is sometimes referred to in the Kabbalistic
literature of the thirteenth century as *torah kedumah*, the primordial
Torah, and is sometimes identified with God's *hokhmah* (*sophia*),
His 'wisdom,' the second emanation and manifestation of the
divine power, which sprang from the hidden 'nothingness.'[3] We
shall see in the course of our discussion how certain Kabbalists
conceived the state of the Torah when it was still contained in the
mystical unity of God's wisdom. There were Kabbalists for whom
this conception of the Torah as the Name of God meant simply

[1] Hekhaloth Rabbathi, IX. Cf. my book, *Jewish Gnosticism, Merkabah
Mysticism, and Talmudic Tradition*, New York, 1960.

[2] *Genesis Rabbah*, VIII, 2, ed. Theodor, p. 57.

[3] *Sophia* as the primordial Torah in the letter of Ezra ben Solomon,
published by me in *Sefer Bialik*, 1934, p. 159; other interpretations in Azriel,
Perush Aggadoth, p. 77, and the passages there cited by Tishby, the editor.
Also in the commentary of Pseudo-Abraham ben David on *Yetsirah*, I, 2, we
read: 'The primordial Torah is the name of God.'

that it was identical with God's wisdom or that it was a partial aspect of this same wisdom. But there were also other opinions.[1]

One of the most important variants of this theory occurs in Joseph Gikatila, a leading Spanish Kabbalist who wrote at the end of the thirteenth century and was no doubt familiar with parts of the *Zohar*. In his view, the Torah is not itself the name of God but the explication of the Name of God. To him the Name meant exactly what it had meant for the Jewish tradition, namely the tetragrammaton, which is the one and only true name of God. He writes: 'Know that the entire Torah is, as it were, an explication of, and commentary on, the tetragrammaton YHWH. And this is the true meaning of the Biblical term "God's Torah" [*torath YHWH*'.][2] In other words, the phrase *torath YHWH* does not mean the Torah which God gave but the Torah which explains YHWH, the name of God. Here Torah is understood as *hora'a*, a didactic exposition. But Gikatila's idea goes still further. In what sense is the Torah an 'explication' of the name of God? In the sense, he replies in several passages,[3] that the Torah was woven from the name of God. Gikatila seems to have been the first to employ this notion of a fabric, *'ariga*, to illustrate the recurrence of the Name in the text of the Torah. He writes for example: 'Behold the miraculous way in which the Torah was woven from God's wisdom.' And in another passage:

The whole Torah is a fabric of appellatives, *kinnuyim*—the generic term for the epithets of God, such as compassionate, great, merciful, venerable—and these epithets in turn are woven from the various names of God [such as *El*, *Elohim*, *Shaddai*]. But all these holy names are connected with the tetragrammaton YHWH and dependent upon it. Thus the entire Torah is ultimately woven from the tetragrammaton.[4]

These words, it seems to me, throw considerable light on Gikatila's thesis. The Torah is the Name of God, because it is a

---

[1] Azriel's own interpretation, *loc. cit.*, is unclear. He also says here that 'each single one of God's *sefiroth* is named Torah,' because as an attribute of God it also gives instruction concerning the ideal conduct of man, which represents a striving to imitate the attributes of God, which are manifested precisely in the *sefiroth*.

[2] Gikatila, *Sha'are 'Orah*, Offenbach, 1715, 51a.

[3] Also in his three books *Sha'are 'Orah*, *Sha'are Tsedek*, and *Ta'ame Mitsvoth*, the latter preserved only in manuscript. This thesis does not yet appear in Gikatila's earlier *Ginnath 'Egoz*.

[4] *Sha'are 'Orah*, 2b.

living texture, a *'textus'* in the literal sense of the word, into which the one true name, the tetragrammaton, is woven in a secret, indirect way, but also directly as a kind of leitmotiv. The nucleus in any case is the tetragrammaton. If Gikatila had been asked exactly how this weaving was done, he would doubtless have answered with his teacher Abraham Abulafia that the basic elements, the name YHWH, the other names of God, and the appellatives, or *kinnuyim*, or rather, their consonants, went through several sets of permutations and combinations in accordance with the formulas set forth by the Talmudists, until at length they took the form of the Hebrew sentences of the Torah, as we read them now. The initiates, who know and understand these principles of permutation and combination, can proceed backward from the text and reconstruct the original texture of names. All these metamorphoses of names have a twofold function. They serve on the one hand to give the Torah its aspect as a communication, a message of God to man, accessible to human understanding. On the other hand, they point to the secret operation of the divine power, recognizable only by the garment woven from the Holy Names when they serve certain specific purposes in the work of Creation.

In conclusion it should be said that this conception of the Torah as a fabric woven of names provided no contribution to concrete exegesis. It was, rather, a purely mystical principle and tended to remove the Torah from all human insight into its specific meanings, which are, after all, the sole concern of exegesis. But this did not trouble the Kabbalists. To them the fact that God expressed Himself, even if His utterance is far beyond human insight, is far more important than any specific 'meaning' that might be conveyed. So considered, the Torah is an absolute and has primacy over all human interpretations, which, however deep they may penetrate, can only approximate the absolute 'meaninglessness' of the divine revelation.

Certain Kabbalists, such as Menahem Recanati (c. 1300), went still further. Starting from an old saying: 'Before the world was created, only God and His Name existed,'[1] they taught that the name here referred to was not only the tetragrammaton YHWH, but the totality of the manifestations of the divine power—this, they said, was the mystical meaning of the true name of God.

[1] *Pirke Rabbi Eliezer*, III.

From here it was only one more step to saying that God Himself is the Torah, 'for the Torah is not something outside Him, and He is not outside the Torah.'[1] Recanati ascribes this quotation to the Kabbalists, and indeed a similar statement occurs in Gikatila's work on the mystical foundations of the Commandments: 'His Torah is in Him, and that is what the Kabbalists say, namely, that the Holy One, blessed be He, is in His Name and His Name is in Him, and that His Name is His Torah.'[2] Elsewhere in the same book he elucidates this statement, drawing upon an old formula from the hymns of the *merkabah* mystics: 'It is an important principle that the ancients expressed in the words: "Thy Name is in Thee and in Thee is Thy Name." For the letters of His Name are He Himself. Even though they move away from Him, they remain firmly rooted [literally: fly away and remain with him].'[3] He explains this by saying that the letters are the mystical body of God, while God, in a manner of speaking, is the soul of the letters. This comparison between God and His Torah on the one hand and soul and body on the other leads us to the second principle, which will be discussed in the following.

III

The principle that the Torah is a living organism falls in with several lines of Kabbalistic thought. The reference to body and soul in the passage we have just quoted from Gikatila suggests such a conception, and the notion that the Torah is woven of holy names is merely a metaphoric way of saying that it is a living fabric. But the idea of the Torah as a living organism is older than Gikatila. It has been formulated with penetrating clarity by the earliest Spanish Kabbalists. In his commentary on the Song of Songs, Ezra ben Solomon of Gerona writes that the Torah contains not so much as one superfluous letter or point, 'because in its divine totality it is an edifice hewn from the Name of the Holy One, blessed be He.'[4] The nature of this divine edifice, *binyan*

[1] Recanati, *Ta'ame ha-Mitsvoth*, Basel, 1581, 3a. The statement God Himself is called Torah occurs also in the *Zohar*, II, 60a.

[2] MS Jerusalem, 8° 597, Fol. 21b. This manuscript contains Gikatila's work under the (plagiaristic?) authorship of Isaac ben Farhi or Perahia. We possess many manuscripts of Gikatila's important work under this name.

[3] *Ibid.*, Fol. 228b: *ki 'othiyoth porhoth ve-'omdoth bo.*

[4] MS Leiden, Warner 32, Fol. 23a.

elohi, may be gathered from a long discussion of this point by Ezra's younger contemporary, Azriel of Gerona, in his Kabbalistic commentary on the Talmudic Aggadah. He too starts from the assumption that the Torah is the Name of God and that it is a living body with a soul. The peculiarities in the Masoretic writing of the Torah, the different types of sections, paragraphs, etc., suggest to him a comparison with a complete, self-contained organism.

Just as in the body of a man there are limbs and joints, just as some organs of the body are more, others less, vital, so it seems to be with the Torah. To one who does not understand their hidden meaning, certain sections and verses of the Torah seem fit to be thrown into the fire; but to one who has gained insight into their true meaning they seem essential components of the Torah. Consequently, to omit so much as one letter or point from the Torah is like removing some part of a perfect edifice.[1] Thence it also follows that in respect of its divine character no essential distinction can be drawn between the section of Genesis 36, setting forth the generations of Esau [a seemingly superfluous passage], and the Ten Commandments, for it is all *one* whole and *one* edifice.'[2]

Here we have a clear combination of the two principles. The Torah is a name, but this name is constructed like a living organism. Not only is the Name that is the root of all things an absolute, but, as manifested in the Torah, it breaks down into the different parts of an organic being. The only difference is that a common organism includes vital organs and others that are not vital, while in the Torah any such distinction is only apparent, for an authentic mystic discovers secret meanings even in the parts that seem quite unimportant; indeed, it is precisely from such passages that he may glean key words or symbols for profound insights or doctrines, as, for example, the *Zohar* and the Lurianic Kabbalah did from the thirty-sixth chapter of Genesis.

This conception of the Torah as a mystical organism is already attested in Philo's account of the Jewish sect of the Therapeutae in Egypt: 'For the entire Torah (*nomothesia*) seems to these people something akin to a living being; the literal sense is the body, while the soul is the secret sense underlying the written word.'[3] And on

---

[1] Cf. above the statement by Rabbi Ishmael and Note 1, p. 39.

[2] Azriel, *Perush Aggadoth*, p. 37.

[3] Philo, *De vita contemplativa*, ed. Conybeare, p. 119.

several occasions Philo bases his own developments on a similar conception.[1] A direct line of influence from the Therapeutae of Egypt or from Philo to the Kabbalists strikes me as very unlikely. Quite independently of one another, mystics took similar attitudes toward the Holy Scriptures and expressed them in related images.

This conception of the Torah as an organism is also fundamental to the *Zohar*, which appeared fifty years after Azriel's work. Here we read for example:

He who labors in the Torah upholds the world and enables each part to perform its function. For there is not a member in the human body that does not have its counterpart in the world as a whole. For as man's body consists of members and parts of varying rank, all acting and reacting upon one another so as to form one organism, so is it with the world at large: it consists of a hierarchy of created things, which, when they properly act and react upon each other, together form one organic body.[2]

Another metaphor for the same idea, this time based on the image of the tree, occurs elsewhere in the *Zohar*[3] and is expressed still more strikingly in one of the Hebrew works of Moses de Leon, whom I regard as the author of the main part of the *Zohar*. 'For the Torah,' he writes,

is called the Tree of Life. . . . Just as a tree consists of branches and leaves, bark, sap and roots, each one of which components can be termed tree, there being no substantial difference between them, you will also find that the Torah contains many inner and outward things, and all form a single Torah and a tree, without difference between them. . . . And although among the sages of the Talmud one forbids what the other allows, one declares a thing to be ritually clean which another terms impermissible, one says this and another that, nevertheless it is necessary to know that the whole is one unity.[4]

[1] Cf. E. Goodenough, *By Light, Light*, pp. 83–4. Baer presumes that in Philo this conception of the Torah as an organism may go back to the similar metaphor of the logos as a *zoön* in Plato's *Phaedrus* (264 C), and that Philo no longer, like Plato, interpreted this logos as 'discourse', but as God's word. From Philo this idea of the organism was then taken over by Origen, whose words (*De principiis*, IV, 2, 4, ed. Kötschau, p. 312) to some extent anticipate the position of the *Zohar*: 'Scripture is like a man and has flesh [according to the literal meaning], soul [according to the allegorical interpretation] and spirit [in accordance with the mystery].'

[2] *Zohar*, I, 134b.   [3] *Zohar*, III, 202a.

[4] Moses de Leon, *Sefer ha-Rimmon*, MS British Museum, Margoliouth No. 759, Fol. 100b.

The author of the *Tikkune Zohar*, who wrote only a few years after the completion of the main body of the *Zohar*, also declares: 'The Torah has a head, a body, a heart, a mouth and other organs, in the same way as Israel.'[1] Here we have a parallel between the two mystical organisms: the Torah and Israel. The *Zohar* itself speaks of each of these organisms in different passages, and they are not brought into direct relation. A parallel between them seems first to have been drawn by the author of the *Tikkunim*. The mystical organism of the Torah, which embodies the name of God, is thus correlated with the mystical body of the Community of Israel, which the Kabbalists regarded not only as the historical organism of the Jewish people, but also as an esoteric symbol for the *Shekhinah*, its members being, as it were, the 'members of the *Shekhinah*.'[2] Later Kabbalists, as we shall see, draw still more explicit conclusions from this correlation.

But there is still another symbolism in which the idea of an organism is expressed, and in which certain particularly daring views about the nature of the revelation contained in the Torah first made their appearance. In order to understand these ideas, we must bear in mind the very old traditional distinction between the 'written Torah' and the 'oral Torah.' According to the exoteric usage of the Talmudic sources, the written Torah is the text of the Pentateuch. The oral Torah is the sum total of everything that has been said by scholars or sages in explanation of this written corpus, by the Talmudic commentators on the Law and all others who have interpreted the text. The oral Torah is the tradition of the Congregation of Israel, it performs the necessary role of completing the written Torah and making it more concrete. According to Rabbinical tradition, Moses received both Torahs at once on Mount Sinai, and everything that any subsequent scholar finds in the Torah or legitimately derives from it, was already included in this oral tradition given to Moses. Thus in Rabbinical Judaism the two Torahs are one.[3] The oral tradition and the written word complete one another, neither is conceivable

---

[1] *Tikkune Zohar*, Tikkun 21, Fol. 52b.

[2] Cf. Chapter 3, pp. 103–9.

[3] On these two concepts, cf. W. Bacher, *Die älteste Terminologie der jüdischen Schriftauslegung*, I, Leipzig, 1899, pp. 89 and 197; H. L. Strack, *Einleitung in den Talmud*, 5th ed., München, 1921, pp. 4 ff. On their position in the theology of orthodox Judaism, cf. the highly interesting monograph of S. Kaatz, *Die mündliche Lehre und ihr Dogma*, Leipzig, 1922.

without the other. From the outset these two conceptions played a significant part in the thinking of the Kabbalists, who connected them with the mystical symbolism of the *sefiroth*. The written Torah was looked upon chiefly as a symbol of the giving sphere of the Godhead, identified primarily with the *sefirah Tif'ereth*, while the oral Torah was seen as a symbol of the receptive sphere, which is at once that of the *Shekhinah* and of the 'Congregation of Israel.' In their active association, these two *sefiroth* manifest the action of God, and similarly the whole revelation of the Torah is given only in this unity of the written and the oral Torah. The forms in which the written and the oral Torah are given here on earth—e.g., the scroll of the Torah and the collections of Talmudic traditions—point back to those deeper spheres from which essentially they arose. In the above-cited passage from the *Tikkune Zohar*, the author goes on to identify the heart of the organism with the written Torah, the mouth with the oral Torah.

Speculations concerning these two aspects of the Torah are contained in the earliest books of the Kabbalists, the *Book Bahir*, for example.[1] But the most interesting discussion of the relationship between them occurs in a fragment which may be attributable to one of the very first Provençal Kabbalists, namely, Isaac the Blind. This fragment, which has come down to us only in manuscript, provides a mystical commentary on the beginning of the *Midrash Konen*, dealing with cosmogony.[2] This midrash repeats the above-mentioned conception that the pre-existent Torah was written in black fire on white fire, which, as we have seen above, Nahmanides already took as an indication of the mystical status of the Torah. Here the Torah seems to burn before God in black fiery letters on white fire, and it is this conception which inspired Rabbi Isaac, probably before Nahmanides, to write the following:

In God's right hand were engraved all the engravings [innermost forms] that were destined some day to rise from potency to act. From the emanation of all [higher] *sefiroth* they were graven, scratched, and molded into the *sefirah* of Grace (*hesed*), which is also called God's right hand, and this was done in an inward, inconceivably subtle way. This

[1] In the *Book Bahir*, 97 and 137, the last *sefirah* is called 'the treasury of the oral Torah', in which all commandments are contained. Cf. also 99 (according to the amended text): 'The written Torah [which is called "light"] needs the oral Torah, which is a lamp [that bears the "light"], in order to resolve the difficulties and to explain its secrets.'

[2] In Jellinek, *Beth ha-Midrash*, II, Leipzig, 1853, pp. 23–34.

formation is called the concentrated, not yet unfolded Torah, and also the Torah of Grace. Along with all the other engravings [principally] two engravings were made in it. The one has the form of the written Torah, the other the form of the oral Torah. The form of the written Torah is that of the colors of white fire, and the form of the oral Torah has colored forms as of black fire. And all these engravings and the not yet unfolded Torah existed potentially, perceptible neither to a spiritual nor to a sensory eye, until the will [of God] inspired the idea of activating them by means of primordial wisdom and hidden knowledge. Thus at the beginning of all acts there was pre-existentially the not yet unfolded Torah [*torah kelulah*], which is in God's right hand with all the primordial forms [literally: inscriptions and engravings] that are hidden in it, and this is what the Midrash implies when it says that God took the primordial Torah (*torah kedumah*), which stems from the quarry of 'repentance' and the source of original wisdom,[1] and in one spiritual act emanated the not yet unfolded Torah in order to give permanence to the foundations of all the worlds.

The author goes on to relate how from the not yet unfolded Torah, which corresponds to the *sefirah* of Grace, there sprang the written Torah, which corresponds to the *sefirah* of Divine Compassion, which is *tif'ereth*, and the oral Torah, corresponding to the power of divine judgment in *malkhuth*, the last *sefirah*. He interprets the fiery organism of the Torah, which burned before God in black fire on white fire, as follows: the white fire is the written Torah, in which the form of the letters is not yet explicit, for the form of the consonants and vowel points was first conferred by the power of the black fire, which is the oral Torah. This black fire is like the ink on the parchment. 'And so the written Torah can take on corporeal form only through the power of the oral Torah, that is to say: without the oral Torah, it cannot be truly understood.' Essentially only Moses, master of all the Prophets, penetrated in unbroken contemplation to that mystical written Torah, which in reality is still hidden in the invisible form of white light. Even the other Prophets gained only a fleeting glimpse of it in momentary intuitions.[2]

[1] Primordial wisdom is the second *sefirah*. 'Repentance' (literally 'return' in Hebrew) is a name for the third, because all things 'return' to its womb in the end.

[2] In the preceding I have followed the difficult text of 'Rabbi Isaac the Old' in MS 584/699 of the Enelow Memorial Collection in the Jewish Theological Seminary of New York. The manuscript forms a single codex, which a bookseller has arbitrarily broken into two parts.

The mystical symbolism of this profoundly meaningful passage conceals the view that, strictly speaking, there is no written Torah here on earth. A far-reaching idea! What we call the written Torah has itself passed through the medium of the oral Torah, it is no longer a form concealed in white light; rather, it has emerged from the black light, which determines and limits and so denotes the attribute of divine severity and judgment. Everything that we perceive in the fixed forms of the Torah, written in ink on parchment, consists, in the last analysis, of interpretations or definitions of what is hidden. *There is only an oral Torah:* that is the esoteric meaning of these words, and the written Torah is a purely mystical concept. It is embodied in a sphere that is accessible to prophets alone. It was, to be sure, revealed to Moses, but what he gave to the world as the written Torah has acquired its present form by passing through the medium of the oral Torah. The mystical white of the letters on the parchment is the written Torah, but not the black of the letters inscribed in ink.[1] In the mystical organism of the Torah the two spheres overlap, and there is no written Torah, free from the oral element, that can be known or conceived of by creatures who are not prophets.

IV

This principle of the Torah as an organism is closely connected with the third principle, which we can now proceed to discuss. This is the principle of the manifold, not to say infinite, meanings of the Torah. Often the different members of the Torah, seen as an organism, were not regarded as organs of equal rank and importance, but as different levels of meaning within the Torah. They guide the mystical student of the holy texts from the outward meanings to increasingly deeper layers of understanding. Thus the idea of the organism becomes identified with the conception of a living hierarchy of meanings and levels of meaning.

In this connection the Kabbalists adopted a line of thought

[1] The theory formulated in this early fragment must already have provided the foundation of the Kabbalistic treatise of Jacob ben Jacob Kohen of Soria concerning the forms of the letters, which is based on this distinction—which first derives meaning from the context we have been discussing—between an 'esoteric white form' and an 'exoteric black form'; cf. my edition of this treatise in *Madda'e ha-Yahaduth*, II (1927), pp. 203–4.

which they found in the Jewish philosophers of the Middle Ages, who in turn had taken it from the philosophical tradition of the Arabs. I am referring to the idea of the two levels of meaning—inward and outward—in the sacred texts. This dualism was equally welcome on the one hand to the esoteric rationalism of the philosophers and reformers, to which in our generation Leo Strauss has devoted several significant works,[1] and, on the other, to the religious interests of the mystics, who undertook to rediscover their own world in the depths of the Holy Scriptures. Here I need not go into detail about the Islamic groups, notably such esoteric sects as the Ismaili, which stressed the inner, allegorical, or mystical meaning of the Koran in contrast to the outward or literal sense, which in the higher stages of initiation lost all meaning. The Arabic authors refer to the adherents of these trends as *batiniyya*, or advocates of the inner meaning, that is to say, esoterics or spiritualists. It is interesting to note that the terms used by many Jewish philosophers to denote these two levels of meaning (*hitson* and *penimi*, outward and inward) never occur in this context in the older Jewish sources, but are literal translations of the corresponding Arabic terms. Thus it is evident that this terminology originated in Islam, whence it was taken over by the Jewish philosophers, who proceeded to identify the inner meaning with the philosophical interpretation of the text, which was not strictly speaking mystical. A mystical interpretation arose only when this terminology was taken over by the Spanish Kabbalists and finally by the author of the *Zohar*, who translated it into Aramaic. In many passages of the *Zohar* the principle is developed that the Torah is at once hidden and manifest, esoteric and exoteric, *'oraitha sethim ve-galya*.[2] The author finds this dualism not only in the Torah, but in every conceivable sphere of existence, beginning with God and embracing every realm and aspect of Creation.

On the other hand, it should not be forgotten that in the Spanish Kabbalistic period the climate was such as to favor an

[1] Cf. in particular the subtle investigations of Leo Strauss in *Persecution and the Art of Writing*, Glencoe, Ill., 1952.

[2] Cf. *Zohar*, II, 230b (the exact same formulation already occurs in Gikatila, *Ginnath 'Egoz*, Hanau, 1615, 3b), III, 75a and 159a. The same formula occurs in the shift from the philosophical to the Kabbalistic use of the terms 'exoteric' and 'esoteric' in Isaac ben Latif, *Ginze ha-Melekh*, ed. Jellinek, XXV, printed in Stern's *Kokhbe Yitzhak*, XXXII, Vienna, 1865, p. 9.

easy flow of ideas between the Christian and the Jewish communities. Two different branches stemming from the same root meet in the doctrine of the Torah as it finally took shape in the *Zohar*. The ancient root is undoubtedly Philo of Alexandria, to whom we may ultimately attribute all these distinctions between literal meaning and spiritual meaning, which were taken over by the Church Fathers and the Christian Middle Ages, and also by Islam (which derived them from Oriental Christian sources). Though it is perfectly possible that such ideas had also been preserved by Jewish groups which we have thus far been unable to identify, their historically visible expression is undoubtedly attributable to Christian and Islamic influence.

The question arises: was there a historical link between the Zoharic doctrine of different levels of meaning and the similar, but older, theory of the fourfold meaning of Scripture that had been developed by the Christian authors of the early Middle Ages?[1] Some seventy years ago Wilhelm Bacher tried, in a valuable article on the Biblical exegesis of the *Zohar*, to demonstrate a line of historical filiation.[2] But since he had no clear idea of the various literary strata of which the *Zohar* consists, he could not formulate his findings with the precision which in my opinion present-day scholarship has made possible.

But before we look into the conceptions underlying the *Zohar*, one more remark is in order. As we have said above, many Jewish philosophers identified the inner meaning of the Torah with philosophical allegory. And indeed many of their allegorical explanations smack strongly of Philo. Philosophical ideas are rediscovered in the Bible. But allegory in this sense was by no means the cornerstone of Kabbalistic exegesis, which was strictly symbolic. What Kabbalistic exegesis discovers behind the literal meaning of the Bible or of the Talmudic interpretations of the Bible was something very different. What the Kabbalists looked for in the Bible was not primarily philosophical ideas, but a symbolic description of the hidden process of divine life, as it unfolds in the manifestations and emanations of the *sefiroth*. Their primary

---

[1] Ernst von Dobschütz, 'Vom vierfachen Schriftsinn. Die Geschichte einer Theorie,' *Harnack = Ehrung, Beiträge zur Kirchengeschichte . . . Adolf von Harnack . . . dargebracht*, Leipzig, 1921, pp. 1–13.

[2] W. Bacher, 'L'Exégèse biblique dans le Zohar,' *Revue des Etudes Juives*, XXII (1891), pp. 33–46.

interest in the Bible may be termed theosophical. As for allegory proper, we find very different attitudes among the Kabbalists. So outstanding an authority as Nahmanides deliberately avoided the allegorical interpretations of the philosophers in his commentary on the Torah. He was well aware of the danger that might accrue to the observance of Jewish ritual from a pure spiritualization of the Torah such as a consistent application of the allegorical method would imply. He expressly warned against this danger in a passage in his commentary on Deuteronomy 29 : 29, which for some reason is lacking in our editions.[1] The danger, in his opinion, was not present in the mystical interpretation of the Biblical text, where the symbol became meaningful only through the actual enactment of the commandment. But not all the Kabbalists were so reserved toward allegory. Many regarded it as a legitimate instrument. The author of the *Zohar*, though interested primarily in a mystical and symbolic description of the hidden world of the Godhead, did not refrain from interpreting certain Bible passages allegorically. Thus the Book of Jonah and also the stories of the Patriarchs in Genesis become allegorical accounts of the destiny of the human soul—though this does not prevent the author from giving a purely mystical (and more far-reaching) interpretation of these same stories of the Patriarchs. Once the esoteric interpretation of Scripture had assumed two different aspects—the one allegorical, the other mystical—the way lay open to the doctrine of the four levels of meaning. While, for example, Joseph ibn Aqnin, contemporary of Maimonides, speaks, throughout his commentary on the Song of Songs, of three such levels of interpretation—literal, Aggadic, and philosophico-allegorical—the Kabbalists added a fourth, that of the theosophical mystery in the sense defined above. This level the *Zohar* terms *raza de-mehemanutha*—understanding according to the 'mystery of faith.'

This conception of the essentially fourfold meaning of the Torah made its appearance at roughly the same time, toward the end of the thirteenth century, in the work of three Kabbalistic

---

[1] Philo already referred at length to the dangers of radical spiritualization of the Torah in a much discussed passage, *De migratione Abrahami*, 89–94. Cf. also the long passage attacking such pure allegorization of the Commandments in Moses de Leon's *Sefer ha-Rimmon*, which I have quoted in *Major Trends in Jewish Mysticism*, New York, 1954, pp. 397–8.

authors who probably belonged to the same group or were at least in contact with one another. They are Moses de Leon, who was also the author of the main part of the *Zohar*, Bahya ben Asher, and Joseph Gikatila. Their definitions of the four levels of meaning differ in some degree. But the conception found its most significant development in the Zoharic literature; and it was this trend which also exerted the most lasting influence on later Jewish mysticism.

The earliest reference to the four levels is to be found in the *Midrash ha-Ne'elam* to the Book of Ruth, one of the earliest works of the author of the *Zohar*. In it he writes: 'The words of the Torah are likened to a nut. How is this to be understood? Just as a nut has an outer shell and a kernel, each word of the Torah contains outward fact (*ma'aseh*), *midrash*, *haggadah*, and mystery (*sod*), each of which is deeper in meaning than the preceding.'[1] This passage is remarkable in several ways. It makes use of no specific term or formula such as was later used to designate the four levels. *Haggadah* seems to refer to some allegorical or tropic form of interpretation, while by *midrash* is meant the hermeneutic method by which the halakhists, or legalists, of the Talmud derived their definitions from the Biblical text. The comparison of the Torah with a nut is not new in Jewish literature. It was already employed by the German and French Hasidim of the early thirteenth century, especially in connection with the *merkabah* (chariot) described in Chapter I of Ezekiel. The metaphor was particularly apt, because the nut was said to possess not only a hard outward shell, but also two finer inward coverings which protected the kernel. The same figure, it is interesting to note, was used in the twelfth century by Joachim of Floris, the famous Calabrian monk, in his *Enchiridion in Apocalypsim*.[2]

[1] *Zohar Hadash*, Jerusalem, 1953, 83a. Bacher failed to take note of this earliest work of the *Zohar* complex.

[2] Ch. J. Huck, *Joachim von Floris und die joachitische Literatur*, 1938, p. 291: *si ad nucis dulcedinem pervenire volumus, primo necesse est, ut amoveatur exteria cortex, secunda testa, et ita tercio loco perveniatur ad nucleam.* Cf. also p. 148 of the same work. Moses de Leon uses the metaphor in diverse contexts: for the meaning of the Torah, for the meaning of the *merkabah* and the dangerous demonic realms surrounding it; cf. his *Ha-Nefesh ha-Hakhamah*, Basel, 1608, 21, quire O, Fol. I c–d. Even the community of mystics is solemnly apostrophized in *Zohar*, I, 154b, as those who have 'penetrated to the kernel.' In I, 19b, II, 15b, and other passages of the *Zohar* the nut is the symbol of the *merkabah*, which here means Kabbalistic knowledge of the world.

Essentially the same set of meanings, though formulated more explicitly, are set forth in a famous passage of the *Zohar*, which became a *locus classicus* for the Kabbalists.

Verily the Torah lets out a word and emerges a little from her sheath, and then hides herself again. But she does this only for those who know and obey her. For the Torah resembles a beautiful and stately damsel, who is hidden in a secluded chamber of her palace and who has a secret lover, unknown to all others. For love of her he keeps passing the gate of her house, looking this way and that in search of her. She knows that her lover haunts the gate of her house. What does she do? She opens the door of her hidden chamber ever so little, and for a moment reveals her face to her lover, but hides it again forthwith. Were anyone with her lover, he would see nothing and perceive nothing. He alone sees it and he is drawn to her with his heart and soul and his whole being, and he knows that for love of him she disclosed herself to him for one moment, aflame with love for him. So is it with the word of the Torah, which reveals herself only to those who love her. The Torah knows that the mystic [*hakim libba*, literally, the wise of heart] haunts the gate of her house. What does she do? From within her hidden palace she discloses her face and beckons to him and returns forthwith to her place and hides. Those who are there see nothing and know nothing, only he alone, and he is drawn to her with his heart and soul and his whole being. Thus the Torah reveals herself and hides, and goes out in love to her lover and arouses love in him. Come and see: this is the way of the Torah. At first, when she wishes to reveal herself to a man, she gives him a momentary sign. If he understands, well and good; if not, she sends to him and calls him a simpleton. To the messenger she sends to him the Torah says: tell the simpleton to come here that I may speak to him. As it is written [Prov. 9 : 47]: 'Whoso is simple, let him turn in hither, she saith to him that wanteth understanding.' When he comes to her, she begins from behind a curtain to speak words in keeping with his understanding, until very slowly insight comes to him, and this is called *derashah*.[1] Then through a light veil she speaks allegorical words [*millin de hida*] and that is what is meant by *haggadah*.[2] Only then, when he has become familiar

---

[1] *Derashah* means here the mode of interpretation practiced by the Talmudists, by which they derived the exoteric oral doctrine from the words of Scripture in accordance with certain fixed norms.

[2] The same use of *hida* for allegory, usual in medieval Hebrew, occurs also in Moses de Leon at the end of his *Mishkan ha-'Eduth*, MS Cambridge, 54a: 'In the words of the wise men there are *Haggadoth*, some of which are allegories [*hida*], while others should be understood literally, without any allegory.'

with her, does she reveal herself to him face to face and speak to him of all her hidden secrets and all her hidden ways, which have been in her heart from the beginning. Such a man is then termed perfect, a 'master,' that is to say, a 'bridegroom of the Torah' in the strictest sense, the master of the house, to whom she discloses all her secrets, concealing nothing. She says to him: do you see now how many mysteries were contained in that sign I gave you on the first day, and what its true meaning is? Then he understands that to those words indeed nothing may be added and nothing taken away. And then for the first time he understands the true meaning of the words of the Torah, as they stand there, those words to which not a syllable or a letter may be added and from which none may be taken away. And therefore men should take care to pursue the Torah [that is, study it with great precision], in order to become her lovers as has been related.[1]

This fine simile, shot through with figures from the chivalric tradition of the Middle Ages, offers an excellent development on the short sentence, from the midrash to Ruth, referring to the Torah as a nut. It makes use of the same terminology, except that here the *ma'aseh*, the outward fact, is replaced by the more customary term *peshat*, designating the literal or simple meaning, which is preserved even in the mystical transfiguration, though it has been made transparent by the mystical light shining through it. A further step is taken in another Zoharic passage (III, 202a), where the different levels of meaning are expressly represented as parts of the organism of the Torah, which is the Tree of Life. Here, however, the old term *haggadah* is replaced by the new term *remez*, which in medieval Hebrew had come (under Arabic influence) to designate allegory. Here, in addition to the abovementioned four levels of meaning, a fifth is mentioned, namely *gematria*, or interpretation through the numerical value of the Hebrew letters, which elsewhere is not regarded as an independent level of meaning.

At this stage the author of the *Zohar* had not yet conceived of a concise formula in which to sum up the whole conception. The above-cited passages were written between 1280 and 1286. But after completing the main part of the *Zohar* in pseudoepigraphical

[1] *Zohar*, II, 99a–b. An excellent investigation of the history of this important parable in late Kabbalistic literature is to be found in F. Lachover's essay, 'The Gate to the Tower' in *'Al gevul ha-yashan ve-he-hadash*, Jerusalem, 1951, pp. 29–78.

form as a collection of the dialogues and lectures of Rabbi Simeon ben Yohai and his pupils in the second century, Moses de Leon wrote a number of Kabbalistic works in Hebrew under his own name. In these he develops a number of ideas that were first set forth in the *Zohar*. We know that before 1290 he wrote a lost work entitled *Pardes*, which literally means 'paradise.' This title is based on a pun, which became widely known and was much used in subsequent Hebrew literature. This pun is based on the famous story in the Talmud about four great rabbis who engaged in esoteric studies in the second century. These four were said to have 'entered Paradise.' They were the Rabbis Akiba, Ben Zoma, Ben Azzai, and Aher. 'One saw and died, the second saw and lost his reason, the third laid waste the young plants [that is, became an apostate and seduced the young]. Only Rabbi Akiba entered in peace and came out in peace.'[1] The exact meaning of *pardes* in this passage has long been an object of speculation. I have discussed the matter elsewhere[2] and there is no need to go into it here. In any event, Moses de Leon employed this highly suggestive term, so rich in shades of meaning, as a cipher for the four levels of interpretation. Each consonant of the word PaRDeS denotes one of the levels: P stands for *peshat*, the literal meaning, R for *remez*, the allegorical meaning, D for *derasha*, the Talmudic and Aggadic interpretation, S for *sod*, the mystical meaning. The *pardes* into which the four ancient scholars entered thus came to denote speculations concerning the true meaning of the Torah on all four levels. In a work written not much later, Moses de Leon took up this image once again and combined it with the above-mentioned notion of the Torah as a nut composed of shell and kernel. A few years later, roughly between 1295 and 1305, an anonymous author, probably a student of Moses de Leon or a member of his circle, wrote the latest of the Zoharic books, namely, *Ra'ya Mehemna*, 'The True Shepherd,' and *Tikkune Zohar*, a work containing seventy interpretations of the first section of the Torah (Gen. 1–5). This author took over the term *pardes*, denoting the four levels of meaning, and it is from this source that all subsequent writers derived it.

In his commentary on Genesis 2 : 10 ff., dealing with the four

[1] Hagigah 14b; cf. *Major Trends*, p. 52.
[2] In Section II of my book *Jewish Gnosticism, Merkabah Mysticism, and Talmudic Tradition*, New York, 1960.

rivers that flow from the garden of Eden, or Paradise, the anonymous author gives a new turn to the old Talmudic anecdote about
the four rabbis. In this version one went into the river Pishon,
which name is here interpreted as *pi shone halakhoth*, that is to say,
'a mouth that learns the exact meaning of the *Halakhah*.' Here
Pishon stands for the literal meaning. The second went into the
river Gihon, which name is taken as a reference to allegory. The
third went into the river Hiddekel, which name is interpreted as a
combination of the two words *had* and *kal*, 'sharp' and 'deft,'
hence a reference to the sharpness and deftness of the Talmudic
interpretation, *derashah*. The fourth went into the Euphrates,
which is related to the innermost kernel, the marrow whence
flows the seed of life, which, in other words, discovers and develops ever new mysteries. Ben Zoma and Ben Azzai arrived only
at the shell and inner coverings of the Torah; there they remained
and incurred harm in these realms. Only Rabbi Akiba penetrated
to the marrow of the Torah; he alone entered and emerged
safe and sound.[1] The author of the *Ra'ya Mehemna* has still
another variant. In several passages he employs the catch-
word *pardes*, but he replaces *remez*, allegory, by *re'iyoth*, insights.[2]

The author of the *Tikkunim* identifies the *Shekhinah*, God's
presence, conceived as the last of the ten emanations, or *sefiroth*,
with the Torah in its total manifestations, embracing all its meanings and levels of meaning. Thus he calls the *Shekhinah*, 'the paradise of the Torah,' *pardes ha-Torah*.[3] Like Moses de Leon, he combines this conception with the motif of the nut: 'The *Shekhinah* in
exile is called *pardes* [because it is clothed as it were in the four
levels of meaning], but itself is the innermost kernel. Accordingly,
we also call it nut, and King Solomon said when he entered this
Paradise [of mystical speculation]: "I went down into the garden

---

[1] *Zohar*, I, 26b. The passage is not from the main part, but from the
Tikkune Zohar.

[2] The word must be read *re'iyyoth* and not *re'ayoth*, 'proofs,' which does not
fit into the context. Bacher's assumption that *re'ayoth*, as he read, is in our
editions a corruption of the correct term *remez* is refuted by the fact that the
same interpretation of the word *pardes* occurs in two other passages which
escaped him, *Zohar Hadash*, 102d and 107c. These passages also belong to
the *Tikkune Zohar*.

[3] *Zohar Hadash* (*Tikkunim* section), 102d.

of nuts" (Song of Songs 6 : 11).'[1] The exact meaning of the '*Shekh-inah* in exile' in this connection will be made clear later on in our investigation. In his *Book of the Rational Soul*, written in 1290, Moses de Leon himself connected the idea of the *pardes* with the first principle discussed above, namely, the principle of the Torah as the name of God. He says:

Under the title *Pardes* I have written a book about the mystery of the four ways, which the title in itself denotes, insofar as it refers to the four who entered the *pardes*, which is nothing other than *peshat, remez, derashah*, and *sod*. In this book I have commented at length on these matters in connection with the mystery of the stories and facts related in the Torah, in order to show that they all refer in a mystical sense to eternal life and that there is nothing in the Torah that is not contained in the mystery of His Name.[2]

The same fundamental principle of the fourfold interpretation of Scripture is used by Bahya ben Asher throughout his compendious commentary on the Torah, written about 1291 in Saragossa. Bahya does not use the term *remez*, but calls this allegorical method of interpretation, which for him is identical with an interpretation according to the principles of medieval philosophy, 'the rational way,' *derekh ha-sekhel*. The word *pardes*, however, was not yet known to him, for though he was familiar with certain sections of the main part of the *Zohar*, the later parts, in which the term occurs, had not yet been written when he began his commentary.

Still another way of defining four such levels of meaning is to be found in the fragmentary Kabbalistic commentary on Maimonides' *Guide to the Perplexed*. This text has been attributed to Joseph Gikatila and seems at all events to have been written toward the end of the thirteenth century.[3] The author says: 'The

---

[1] *Tikkun*, No. 24, Fol. 68a–b. Here the shells, *kellippin*, are already related directly to the demonic forces and their power, from which the *Shekhinah* is freed only on the Sabbath, when she puts on sefirothic garments.

[2] Moses de Leon, at the end of his *Sefer ha-Nefesh ha-Hakhamah*, Basel, 1608.

[3] Georges Vajda, who has devoted a penetrating investigation to some parts of this text, doubts the justification of the traditional attribution of this text to Gikatila; cf. *Mélanges offerts à Etienne Gilson*, Paris, 1959, p. 656. Undoubtedly the question is deserving of further investigation. Not only are the printed pieces attributed to Gikatila, but also the largely unpublished fragments preserved in the Oxford MS, Neubauer, 1911.

Torah can be interpreted in three or even more ways.' He calls these ways or methods *perush*, *be'ur*, *pesher*, and *derash*. *Perush* is for him the strict grammatical meaning, analogous to what was termed *peshat* above. *Pesher*, 'interpretation,' signifies a deeper penetration into the literal sense. *Derash* embraces both allegory and the Talmudic method of deducing the *Halakhah* from the words of Scripture and allegory. He calls the mystical meaning *be'ur*. Literally this means simply explanation, but by a mystical play on words in the Kabbalistic manner it is related to the Hebrew word *be'er*, or well, for the Torah is likened to a well of fresh water, whence spring ever new levels of hidden meaning. A very similar idea occurs in the *Ra'ya Mehemna*, whose author had read at least some of Gikatila's earlier writings. Here again the Torah is an inexhaustible well, which no pitcher (*kad*) can ever empty. The Hebrew word *kad* has the numerical value 24; to the author this means that even the twenty-four books of the traditional Biblical canon cannot exhaust the mystical depth of the Torah, the depth and fulness of the hidden essence of the Godhead, which is manifested through the books of the Bible.[1]

It is significant in this connection that in its attitude toward allegory the *Zohar* preserved all the aristocratic esotericism of the rationalist philosophers, The *Midrash ha-Ne'elam* shows a particular leaning toward allegorical interpretations. A highly remarkable passage is devoted to the interpretation of the well-known Aggadah about the Messianic banquet at which Israel will feast on leviathan.[2] The author is fully in agreement with Maimonides' philosophical interpretation of this banquet,[3] and uses it verbatim. Quite in the spirit of the philosophers, he justifies the crude figurative mode of expression employed by the rabbis, on the ground that the hope of this banquet and similar rewards helps the simple-minded populace to bear the miseries of exile. One of the speakers is made to say expressly that the popular faith should not be destroyed, but should on the contrary be reinforced.[4]

---

[1] *Zohar*, II, 114b, and Gikatila's commentary on Maimonides, in the second part of Saul Kohen's 'Questions Addressed to Abarbanel,' Venice, 1574, 21a.

[2] Baba bathra, 74b–75a; cf. L. Ginzberg, *The Legends of the Jews*, V, pp. 43–6.

[3] *Hilkhoth Teshuvah*, VIII, 4.

[4] *Zohar*, I, 135b–136a. It is interesting and not without a certain ironical significance that for popular faith the author uses the term *mehemanutha*

This fourfold aspect of the Torah bears a marked similarity to the conceptions of certain Christian authors of the early Middle Ages, such as Bede (eighth century). These ideas became widespread among the Christian authors of the late Middle Ages. They speak in this connection of history, allegory, tropology (which with them means moral homiletics), and anagogy (which usually meant the eschatological interpretation of Scripture). But here again the classifications vary. The strictly mystical interpretation is sometimes identified with *anagogia* and sometimes on the other hand *allegoria* and *anagogia* become one.[1] Famous in this connection are the pedagogic verses of unknown origin, quoted by Nicholas of Lyra in the fourteenth century:

> *Littera gesta docet, quid credas allegoria,*
> *Moralis quid agas, quo tendas anagogia.*

Did the Kabbalists derive this conception from the Christians? This question has been answered in various ways. In his above-mentioned article, Wilhelm Bacher assumed the existence of such a historical connection, while recently Perez Sandler has tried to prove that the Kabbalistic doctrine of the *pardes* developed independently.[2] Though of course it is possible that the Kabbalists arrived at their theory of the four levels of meaning without outside influence, by simply dividing the allegorical interpretation into its two aspects, the one philosophical, the other theosophico-mystical, I am inclined to agree with Bacher. The simultaneous appearance of the idea in three Kabbalistic authors, all living in Christian Spain and all working with the same theory of the four levels though their classifications differed, suggests that they had somewhere come across this idea of four meanings and adopted it. One is almost forced to conclude that they were influenced by Christian hermeneutics. The *Zohar*'s account of the four levels shows a striking resemblance to the Christian conception. On the other hand, Gikatila (or Pseudo-Gikatila) would have had no good reason for distinguishing two varieties of literal meaning if

[1] Cf. for details the article of E. von Dobschütz, cited above.

[2] P. Sandler, 'Le-ba'yath Pardes,' in the Jubilee Volume for Elias Auerbach, Jerusalem, 1955, pp. 222–35.

---

dekola, which in many other passages of the *Zohar* is employed in a mystical sense, to mean not 'what all believe,' but the world-permeating power of faith, the system of the *sefiroth*.

he had not been interested a priori in bringing out a fourfold meaning of the Torah.[1]

The crystallization of this idea of the four levels in the hierarchical organism of the Torah was not the only contribution of the *Zohar* to the question that concerns us here. Another important thesis put forward in it is that every word, indeed, every letter, has seventy aspects, or literally, 'faces.' This notion did not originate with the Kabbalists. It is found in the late midrash *Numbers Rabbah* and was cited as early as the twelfth century by Abraham ibn Ezra, the famous Bible commentator, in the introduction to his commentary on the Pentateuch.[2] It does not occur in the Talmud but was developed from a Talmudic theme. Seventy is the traditional number of the nations inhabiting the earth. The Talmud states that every commandment that issued from God's mouth in the Revelation on Mount Sinai was divided and could be heard in all seventy languages.[3] A link between this and the later notion of the seventy aspects appears clearly in a passage of the *Alphabet of Rabbi Akiba*, a semi-mystical treatise of the early post-Talmudic period, which has never before been considered in this connection. In it we read: 'All the treasures of wisdom were given over to the angelic prince of wisdom Seganzagael, and all were disclosed to Moses on Mount Sinai, so that during the forty days that he spent there he was instructed in the

[1] Here it seems worth pointing out that this relationship between Kabbalistic theory and the similar Christian conception was already noticed by Pico della Mirandola, the first Christian humanist to take a deep interest in the Kabbalah. In his *Apologia*, written in 1487, he writes: 'Just as with us there is a fourfold method of Biblical exegesis, the literal, the mystical or allegorical, the tropic and the anagogic, so also among the Hebrews. They call the literal meaning *peshat*, the allegorical *midrash*, the tropic *sekhel*, and the anagogic, the most sublime and divine of all, *kabbalah*.' Cf. *Opera*, Basel, 1557, pp. 178–9. The Hebrew terms are exactly the same as those employed by Bahya ben Asher, whose work must consequently have been used by Pico. The erroneous identification of *midrash* with allegory and of *sekhel*, which in Bahya actually means allegory, with tropology, shows that Pico's knowledge of these sources was very limited. The same mistake is repeated, in a more pronounced form, in the Apology for Pico, written by the Franciscan monk Archangelus of Borgo Novo. He cites the literature of the Midrash under the head of allegory, but such works as those of Maimonides and Gersonides are classified as tropology; cf. *Apologia fratris Archangeli de Burgonovo . . . pro defensione doctrinae Cabalae*, Bologna, 1564, 8b.

[2] *Numbers Rabbah*, XIII, 15.

[3] Shabbath 88b.

Torah in all seventy aspects of the seventy languages.'[1] Later the
seventy languages were dropped and the new formula was born.
The *Zohar* makes liberal use of it. The different aspects are the
secrets that can be discovered in every word. 'In every word
shine many lights.'[2] This thesis was indeed advanced by an early
twelfth-century author, held in high esteem by the Kabbalists of
Spain. Abraham bar Hiyya writes: 'Every letter and every word
in every section of the Torah have a deep root in wisdom and
contain a mystery from among the mysteries of [divine] understanding, the depths of which we cannot penetrate. God grant that
we may know some little of this abundance.'[3] The meaning of the
holy text cannot be exhausted in any finite number of lights and
interpretations, and the number seventy stands here of course for
the inexhaustible totality of the divine word. Moreover, the light
and the mystery of the Torah are one, for the Hebrew word *'or*,
light, and the Hebrew word *raz*, mystery, have the same numerical value, 207. When God said, 'Let there be light,' he meant, as
the author of the *Midrash ha-Ne'elam* puts it,[4] the mystery that
shines in the Torah. And it was this hidden primordial light of
Creation, which was so noble that it could not be abased to the
use of creatures, that God enclosed in the Torah. In his mystical
meditations on Scripture the Kabbalist catches a ray, 'light of the
inexhaustible light.' A striking application of this notion to the
Zohar itself is to be found in the work of the famous Kabbalist
Hayim Vital (d. 1620). The word *zohar* means literally radiance.
According to him, the radiance of the Torah's divine light is
reflected in the mysteries of this book. But when these mysteries
are shrouded in the literal meaning, their light is darkened. The
literal meaning is darkness, but the Kabbalistic meaning, the
mystery, is the *zohar* that shines in every line of Scripture.[5]

This devaluation of the simple literal meaning is no invention
of the later Kabbalists. It is clearly stressed in certain passages of
the *Zohar* itself.

Rabbi Simeon said: Alas for the man who regards the Torah as a
book of mere tales and profane matters. If this were so, we might even

[1] *'Othiyoth de-Rabbi Akiba*, ed. Wertheimer, Jerusalem, 1914, p. 12.
[2] *Zohar*, III, 202a.
[3] Abraham bar Hiyya, *Megillath ha-Megalle*, Berlin, 1924, p. 75.
[4] *Zohar*, I, 140a; *Zohar Hadash*, 8b.
[5] Vital, *Ets ha-Da'ath*, Zolkiev, 1871, 46–7.

today write a Torah dealing in such matters and still more excellent. In regard to earthly things, the kings and princes of the world [in their chronicles?] possess more valuable materials. We could use them as a model for composing a Torah of this kind. But in reality the words of the Torah are higher words and higher mysteries. When even the angels come down into the world [to fulfil a mission] they don the garment of this world, and if they did not, they could not survive in this world and the world could not endure them. And if this is true even of the angels, how much truer it is of the Torah, with which He created them and all the worlds and through which they all subsist. When she descends into the world, how could the world endure it if she did not don earthly garments? The tales of the Torah are only her outward garments. If anyone should suppose that the Torah herself is this garment and nothing else, let him give up the ghost. Such a man will have no share in the world to come. That is why David [Ps. 119 : 18] said: 'Open thou mine eyes, that I may behold wondrous things out of thy Torah,' namely, that which is beneath the garment of the Torah. Come and behold: there are garments that everyone sees, and when fools see a man in a garment that seems beautiful to them, they do not look more closely. But more important than the garment is the body, and more important than the body is the soul. So likewise the Torah has a body, which consists of the commandments and ordinances of the Torah, which are called *gufe torah*, 'bodies of the Torah.'[1] This body is cloaked in garments, which consist of worldly stories. Fools see only the garment, which is the narrative part of the Torah; they know no more and fail to see what is under the garment. Those who know more see not only the garment but also the body that is under the garment. But the truly wise, the servants of the Supreme King, those who stood at the foot of Mount Sinai, look only upon the soul, which is the true foundation of the entire Torah, and one day indeed it will be given them to behold the innermost soul of the Torah.

The Torah, the author adds, needs an outward garment of narratives, just as wine, if it is to keep, needs a jar. But it is always necessary to penetrate to the secret that lies beneath them.'[2]

The last and most radical step in the development of this principle of the infinite meaning of the Torah was taken by the Palestinian school of Kabbalists who flourished in the sixteenth

---

[1] This is a pun: the literal meaning of *gufe torah* is indeed 'bodies of the Torah,' but in the Talmud the words mean 'important doctrines of the Torah.'

[2] *Zohar*, III, 152a.

century in Safed. They started from the old conception that the souls of Israel who went out of Egypt and received the Torah at Mount Sinai numbered 600,000. According to the laws of transmigration and the distribution of the sparks into which the soul disintegrates, these 600,000 primordial souls are present in every generation of Israel.

Consequently, there are 600,000 aspects and meanings in the Torah. According to each one of these ways of explaining the Torah, the root of a soul has been fashioned in Israel. In the Messianic age, every single man in Israel will read the Torah in accordance with the meaning peculiar to his root. And thus also is the Torah understood in Paradise.[1]

This mystical idea that each individual soul has its own peculiar way of understanding the Torah was stressed by Moses Cordovero of Safed (d. 1570). He said that each of these 600,000 holy souls has its own special portion of the Torah, 'and to none other than he, whose soul springs from thence, will it be given to understand it in this special and individual way that is reserved to him.'[2] With the help of the *Zohar*, the Safed Kabbalists developed the further idea that the Torah, which in its visible form contains only some 340,000 letters, is, in some mysterious way, made up of 600,000. Each individual in Israel possesses a letter in this mystical Torah, to which his soul is attached, and he reads the Torah in the particular way predetermined by this upper root of his in the Torah. Menahem Azariah of Fano, one of the great Italian Kabbalists (c. 1600), says in his treatise on the soul that the Torah as originally engraved on the first tablets (those that were broken) contained these 600,000 letters and that only on the second tablets did it assume its shorter form, which, however, thanks to a secret way of combining letters, still indicates the original number of 600,000 letters which form the mystical body of the Torah.[3]

[1] Isaac Luria, *Sefer ha-Kavvanoth*, Venice, 1620, 53b. More on the subject in Vital, *Sha'ar Gilgulim*, XVII, Jerusalem, 1912, 17b; in Nathan Shapira, *Megalle 'Amukoth*, Cracow, 1637, IX, and in Naphtali Bacharach, *'Emek ha-Melekh*, Amsterdam, 1648, 42a.

[2] Cordovero, *Derisha be-'inyane Mal'akhim*, ed. Ruben Margolioth, Jerusalem, 1945, p. 70.

[3] M. A. Fano, *Ma'amar ha-Nefesh*, Pyotrkow, 1903, III, 6, Fol. 17a.

V

We have examined the three basic principles that may be said to govern the Kabbalists' general view of the Torah. But this is by no means the end of the matter. In certain Kabbalistic works these principles take a new turn and open far-reaching perspectives. The Kabbalists did not shrink back from daring inferences in such matters. All these new developments had their starting point in two questions which came quite naturally to the mind of a pious but speculatively inclined Jew: 1. What would have been the content of the Torah, which must be regarded as the highest manifestation of divine wisdom, if not for the fall of man? Or in a more radical formulation: If the Torah was pre-existent, if it preceded Creation, what was its nature before the fall? 2. What will be the structure of the Torah in the Messianic Age when man is restored to his pristine state?—Essentially the two questions are one, namely, what is the relation of the Torah to the fundamental history of man? Small wonder that this question should have greatly preoccupied certain Kabbalists. Widely re-echoed by later Kabbalistic writers, their ideas on the subject were to exert a profound influence on the subsequent development of Jewish mysticism, both in its orthodox and in its heretical aspects.

Even if the author of the main body of the *Zohar* did not himself raise such questions, they assumed central importance in the minds of his younger contemporary, who wrote the *Ra'ya Mehemna*, 'The Faithful Shepherd' (a work on the esoteric reasons of the commandments of the Torah) and the *Tikkune Zohar*. His books reveal two trains of thought that are relevant in this connection.

The one has to do with the two different aspects of the Torah, which in these books are termed *torah de-beri'ah*, 'the Torah in the state of creation,' and *torah de-'atsiluth*, 'the Torah in the state of emanation.' The latter is characterized by the words of the Psalmist (19 : 8): 'The Torah of the Lord is perfect,' meaning that it is self-contained in its divine character and still intact. The *torah de-beri'ah* on the other hand is characterized by the verse from Proverbs (8 : 22): 'The Lord created me in the beginning of his way.' This is the Torah as it appeared when God departed from His hidden essence and revealed Himself in created works and worlds.[1] And in another passage: 'There is a Torah which cannot be said to be creation; it is His emanation.' Only to this uncreated *torah de-'atsiluth* applies the mystical thesis that God and the Torah are one.[2] The author does not develop this idea in detail except in passages where it is connected with the second question, which he discusses frequently and at far greater length. Thus we read in a third passage that the created Torah, *torah de-beri'ah*, is the outer garment of the *Shekhinah*.[3] If man had not succumbed to sin, the *Shekhinah* might have dispensed with such a covering. As it is, she needs a covering, like a man who must hide his poverty. Thus every sinner may be likened to a man who robs the *Shekhinah* of her garments; but a man who carries out the commandments of the Torah is as one who clothes the *Shekhinah* in her garments, who causes her to appear in the earthly world. From this it follows that what the author calls *torah de-beri'ah* is the Torah as it is really manifested and can really be enacted, that is, the Torah of the Talmudic tradition. It contains positive and negative commandments and draws a clear dividing line between good and evil, clean and unclean, permitted and forbidden, sacred and profane. This idea of the garment of the Torah recurs over and over again in this latest section of the *Zohar*, though with very divergent shades of meaning. It is based on the identification of the *Shekhinah* (who is also the Queen or Matrona) with the Torah as it was revealed to men. It is stated several times, for example, that the color of her garments after the fall of man, but in particular during the period of exile, is black in token of mourning. But in other passages the color black is related to the literal meaning of the Torah, which is the first layer of meaning to be discerned in it. Thus in a passage in the *Ra'ya Mehemna*, speaking of the Matrona as the Torah, the author declares that through his good deeds and also of course through his deeper insight, a righteous man illumines the *Shekhinah*, 'stripping her of the somber garments of literal meaning and casuistry and adorning her with radiant garments, which are the mysteries of the Torah.'[4]

In other passages a different symbolism is applied to these two aspects of the Torah, the one factual and pragmatic, the other contemplative and mystical. We have seen that the Torah was likened

---

[1] *Tikkune Zohar*, Preface, 6b.   [2] *Ibid.*, No. 22, Fol. 64a.

[3] *Zohar*, I, 23a–b. This piece belongs to the *Tikkune Zohar*.

[4] III, 215b (*Ra'ya Mehemnv*).

to the Tree of Life in Paradise. But the Bible speaks of two trees in Paradise, each of which was now related to a different sphere of the divine realm. The Tree of Life was identified (even before the *Zohar*) with the written Torah, while the Tree of Knowledge of good and evil was identified with the oral Torah. In this connection the written Torah, it goes without saying, is considered as an absolute, while the oral Torah deals with the modalities of the Torah's application in the earthly world. This conception is not as paradoxical as it may seem at first sight. For the Kabbalists, the written Torah was indeed an absolute, which as such cannot be fully and directly apprehended by the human mind. It is the tradition which first makes the Torah accessible to the human understanding, by showing the ways and means by which it can be applied to Jewish life. For an orthodox Jew—and we must not forget that in their own minds the Kabbalists were orthodox Jews—the written Torah alone, without the tradition, which is the oral Torah, would be open to all sorts of heretical misinterpretation. It is the oral Torah that determines a Jew's actual conduct. It is easy to see how the oral Torah came to be identified— as it was by all the early Kabbalists—with the new mystical conception of the *Shekhinah*, which was regarded as the divine potency that governs the Congregation of Israel and is manifested in it. We have already discussed a number of daring inferences which one of the earliest Kabbalists drew from this symbolism of the two manifestations of the Torah.

The author of the *Ra'ya Mehemna* and the *Tikkunim*, however, gave this symbolism a new turn that was fraught with consequences. For him the Tree of Knowledge of good and evil came to symbolize that part of the Torah which distinguished good and evil, clean and unclean, etc. But at the same time this tree suggested to him the power that evil can gain over good in times of sin and especially in times of exile. Thus the Tree of Knowledge became the tree of restrictions, prohibitions, and delimitations, whereas the Tree of Life was the tree of freedom, symbolic of an age when the dualism of good and evil was not yet (or no longer) conceivable, and everything bore witness to the unity of divine life, as yet untouched by any restrictions, by the power of death, or any of the other negative aspects of life, which made their appearance only after the fall of man. These restrictive, limitative aspects of the Torah are perfectly legitimate in the world of sin, in the unredeemed world, and in such a world the Torah could not have assumed any other form. Only after the fall and its far-reaching consequences did the Torah take on the material and limited aspect in which it appears to us today. It is quite in keeping with this view that the Tree of Life should have come to represent the utopian aspect of the Torah.[1] From this standpoint it was perfectly plausible to identify the Torah as Tree of Life with the mystical Torah and the Torah as Tree of Knowledge of good and evil with the historical Torah. Here, of course, we have a striking example of the typological exegesis to which the author of the *Ra'ya Mehemna* and the *Tikkunim* was so given.

But we must go one step further. The author connects this dualism of the trees with the two different sets of tablets that were given to Moses on Mount Sinai. According to an old Talmudic tradition, the venom of the serpent, which had corrupted Eve and through her all mankind, lost its strength through the Revelation on Mount Sinai, but regained it when Israel began to worship the golden calf. The Kabbalistic author interprets this in his own way. The first tablets, which had been given before Israel sinned with the golden calf but which apart from Moses no one had read, came from the Tree of Life. The second tablets, which were given after the first had been broken, came from the Tree of Knowledge. The meaning is clear: the first tablets contained a revelation of the Torah in keeping with the original state of man, when he was governed by the principle embodied in the Tree of Life. This was a truly spiritual Torah, bestowed upon a world in which Revelation and Redemption coincided, in which everything was holy and there was no need to hold the powers of uncleanness and death in check by prohibitions and restrictions. In this Torah the mystery was fully revealed. But the utopian moment soon vanished. When the first tablets were broken, 'the letters engraved on them flew away,' that is, the purely spiritual element receded; since then it has been visible only to mystics, who can perceive it even beneath the new outer garments in which it appeared on the second tablets.[2] On the second tablets the Torah appears in a historical garment and as a historical power. To be sure, it still has

---

[1] Cf. 'Zum Verständnis der messianischen Idee im Judentum,' in *Eranos-Jahrbuch*, XXVIII (1960), pp. 221-3.

[2] *Zohar*, I, 26b (*Tikkunim*), II, 117b; III, 124b, 153a, 255a (all from the *Ra'ya Mehemna*); *Tikkune Zohar*, Nos. 56 and 60; *Zohar Hadash*, 106c.

its hidden depths, its infinite mystery. The good is still translucent, while evil must be fenced in and combated by all the prohibitions that are conceived as its counterparts. This is the hard shell of the Torah, indispensable in a world governed by the powers of evil. But the shell must not be mistaken for the whole. In enacting the commandments, a man can break through the outer shell and penetrate to the kernel. This conception also helps us to dispel in part the ambiguity of certain statements about the hierarchical order of the Bible, the Mishnah, the Talmud, and the Kabbalah, which are frequent in the *Ra'ya Mehemna* and the *Tikkunim* and which have baffled not a few readers of these texts. It would be a mistake to term these passages antinomistic or anti-Talmudic.[1] The author is far from wishing to do away with the Talmudic law, to which he accorded full validity and legitimacy as the historical form in which the Torah was given. The detailed discussions of elements of the *Halakhah* in these books are purely positive in character and show no sign of hostility. But there can be no doubt that the author expected the utopian and purely mystical aspect of the Torah to be made fully manifest and to enter into full force on the day of Redemption. The true essence of the Torah is one; and it is that essence which is embodied in the concept of the *torah de-'atsiluth*. But the garment or outward form it has taken in a world where it is necessary to combat the power of evil is absolutely legitimate and indispensable. The strong emphasis which the author lays on these somber aspects of the Torah in its Talmudic form—he is given to parallels, which seem almost ironic and critical, between the bondage of the Israelites in their Egyptian exile and the hermeneutical exertions by which the Talmudic scholars derive the content of the oral Torah from the written Torah[2]—shows the extent of his preoccupation with the mystical and utopian aspect of the Torah. The exile of the *Shekhinah*, which began in principle with the fall, took on its full meaning with the historical exile of the Jewish people. And that is why in these

[1] In his *History of the Jews* Heinrich Graetz interprets these passages in this way. Y. F. Baer shows much deeper insight into their meaning in his Hebrew essay on the historical background of the *Ra'ya Mehemna*, *Zion*, V (1940), pp. 1–44. He was the first to point out the connection between these ideas and those of the Franciscan Spirituals of the thirteenth century.

[2] Cf. such passages as I, 27a–28a; III, 124b, 153a–b, 229b; 254a–b; *Tikkune Zohar*, No. 21, Fol. 48a–b; *Tikkunim* in *Zohar Hadash*, 97c–99d. The *Zohar* passages quoted in the beginning all belong to the same source.

books two intrinsically so different concepts—sin and exile—are often combined and almost identified.

The Kabbalists of the Safed school in the sixteenth century developed this idea in a very interesting way. They tried to answer the question of what the Torah was before the fall and how this original Torah could be reconciled with the concrete historical Torah. These ideas are excellently formulated in the writings of Moses Cordovero, from which they were taken over by many other authors. He too starts from the assumption that the Torah in its innermost essence is composed of divine letters, which themselves are configurations of divine light. Only in the course of a process of materialization do these letters combine in various ways. First they form names, that is, names of God, later appellatives and predicates suggesting the divine, and still later they combine in a new way, to form words relating to earthly events and material objects. Our present world took on its crude material character in consequence of the fall of man, and the Torah underwent a parallel change. The spiritual letters became material when the material character of the world made this change necessary. On the strength of this theory Cordovero found an answer to the two questions: what was the nature of the Torah before the fall? and: what will be its nature in the Messianic Age?[1]

He illustrates his conception by the example of the Biblical ordinance forbidding the wearing of clothes made of wool mixed with linen. In Hebrew this mixture is termed *sha'atnez*.

The Torah says (Deut. 22 : 11): 'Thou shalt not wear *sha'atnez*,'— this could not have been written before Adam himself had clad himself in this coarse, material stuff which in mystical language is known as 'skin of the serpent.' Thus the Torah could not have contained such a prohibition, for what bearing could this *sha'atnez* have had on the soul of man, which was originally clothed in a purely spiritual garment? And indeed the original combination of letters in the Torah before the fall was not *sha'atnez tsemer u-fishtim* (*sha'atnez* of wool and linen), but the same consonants in another combination, namely *satan-'az metsar u-tofsim*, a warning to Adam not to exchange his original garment of light for the garment of serpent's skin, symbolizing the demonic power named *satan-'az*, 'insolent Satan.' Further, the words embodied a warning to the effect that these powers would assuredly bring fear and affliction, *metsar*, upon man and attempt to gain possession of him,

[1] Cordovero, *Shi'ur Komah*, Warsaw, 1883, 63b.

u-tofsim, and thereby bring him down to Hell. But what brought about this change in the combination of letters, so that we now read *sha'atnez tsemer u-fishtim*? It came about because when Adam put on the skin of the serpent his nature became material, so necessitating a Torah that gave material commandments. This called for a new reading of the letters to convey the meaning of a commandment. And so it is with all other commandments based on the corporeal and material nature of man.'[1]

The same source deals also with the eschatological aspect of the question.

In regard to the new interpretations of the Torah that God will reveal in the Messianic Age, we may say that the Torah remains eternally the same, but that in the beginning it assumed the form of material combinations of letters which were adapted to the material world. But some day men will cast off this material body; they will be transfigured and recover the mystical body that was Adam's before the fall. Then they will understand the mystery of the Torah, its hidden aspects will be made manifest. And later, when at the end of the sixth millennium [that is, after the true Messianic redemption and the beginning of the new aeon] man becomes a still higher spiritual being, he will penetrate still deeper into the hidden mystery of the Torah. Then everyone will be able to understand the miraculous content of the Torah and the secret combinations and will thereby learn much concerning the secret essence of the world . . . For the fundamental idea of the present disquisition is that the Torah, like man himself, put on a material garment. And when man rises up from his material garment [that is, his corporeal condition] to a more subtle, spiritual one, so also will the material manifestation of the Torah be transformed, and its spiritual essence will be apprehended in ever-rising degrees. The veiled faces of the Torah will become radiant, and the righteous will study them. And yet in all these stages the Torah will be the same as it was in the beginning; its essence will never change.'[2]

The same idea was taken up by Isaac Luria and developed in a similar direction. 'The literal meaning of the commandments in Paradise was different and far more spiritual than now, and what pious men now enact in material performance of the command-

[1] Abraham Azulai, *Hesed le-Abraham*, Sulzbach, 1685, II, 27. This author made extensive use of a manuscript of Cordovero's chief work *Elima Rabbathi*, from which he took many interesting ideas.

[2] *Ibid.*, II, 11, undoubtedly taken from the same source. Similar passages may also be found in Cordovero's published works, e.g., *Shi 'ur Komah*, 85d.

ment, they will then, in the paradisiacal garment of the soul, so enact as God intended when He created man.'[1]

These ideas represent a most illuminating combination of the *absolute* and the *relative*. In line with orthodox belief, the Torah remains an essentially unchanging and absolute entity. But at the same time, seen in historical perspective, it takes on specific meaning only in relation to the changing state of man in the universe, so that the meaning itself is subject to change. The later Kabbalists spoke of four worlds which constitute such a spiritual hierarchy, the world of divine emanation, *'atsiluth*, the world of creation, *beri'ah*, the world of formation, *yetsirah*, and the world of activation, *'asiyah*. These worlds are not successive but exist simultaneously and form the different stages by which the creative power of God materializes. The revelation of the Torah as the organ of Creation must necessarily have come to all these worlds in some form, and indeed we learn certain things about its structure in these stages. Texts originating in the school of Israel Saruk (c. 1600) develop the following idea: in the highest world, the world of *'atsiluth*, the Torah was merely a sequence of all the combinations of consonants that can be derived from the Hebrew alphabet. This was the original garment which sprang from the inner linguistic movement of *en-sof*, which was spun as it were from the immanent 'beatitude' pervading *en-sof*, the infinite transcendent Godhead, both in its hidden essence and when it first thought of revealing its infinite power. In their original order, these innermost elements of the Torah contained the germs of all the possibilities included in this linguistic movement. It is only in the second world that the Torah is manifested as a sequence of holy names of God, which were formed by certain combinations of elements that were present in the world of *'atsiluth*. In the third world the Torah appears as a sequence of angelic names and powers, in accordance with the law of this world that is inhabited by angelic beings. Only in the fourth and last world could the Torah appear as it does to us.[2] The laws that determine the inner

---

[1] Cf. the long passage in *Sha'ar Ma'amare Rezal*, Jerusalem, 1898, 16c, which Vital cites under Luria's name.

[2] Naphtali Bacharach, *'Emek ha-Melekh*, 4a. Similar theories are developed at length in many works of the Lurianic school in both authentic and apocryphal expositions of the Lurianic doctrine. By far the most important passage of this kind is the long quotation from a manuscript of Joseph ibn

structure of each of these worlds are disclosed by the particular
form in which the Torah appears in it. If it is asked why we do
not perceive the Torah directly in this function, the answer is
precisely that this aspect of the Torah as a representation of the
cosmic laws governing the different worlds was hidden by the
changes undergone by its outward form after the fall of man.

Nowhere, I believe, has this mystical 'relativization' of the
Torah been expressed in more outspoken terms than in a fragment from a book of Rabbi Eliyahu Kohen Ittamari of Smyrna
(d. 1729), the manuscript of which was available to Hayim Joseph
David Azulai, who quoted from it. This Rabbi Eliyahu was a
celebrated preacher and Kabbalist, known for his asceticism and
piety, although his theology is strangely shot through with ideas
that originated in the heretical Kabbalism of the followers of
Sabbatai Zevi, the false Messiah. In this fragment an attempt is
made to explain why, according to Rabbinic law, the scroll of the
Torah used in the synagogue must be written without vowels and
punctuation. This, says the author,

is a reference to the state of the Torah as it existed in the sight of God,
before it was transmitted to the lower spheres. *For He had before Him
numerous letters that were not joined into words as is the case today, because the
actual arrangement of the words would depend on the way in which this lower
world conducted itself.* Because of Adam's sin, God arranged the letters
before Him into the words describing death and other earthly things,
such as levirate marriage. Without sin there would have been no death.
The same letters would have been joined into words telling a different
story. That is why the scroll of the Torah contains no vowels, no punctuation, and no accents, as an allusion to the *Torah which originally
formed a heap of unarranged letters.*[1] The divine purpose will be revealed
in the Torah at the coming of the Messiah, who will engulf death forever, so that there will be no room in the Torah for anything related

[1] In Hebrew: *tel shel 'othiyoth bilti mesuddaroth.*

Tabul, a disciple of Isaac Luria, preserved in the beginning of Abraham
Hazkuni, *Shtei Yadoth*, Amsterdam, 1726, 3a. Here we read, among other
radical statements, that the Torah was originally meant to be composed of
six books (as the oral Law, the Mishnah, still is). The sixth book, however,
which was to be the *Torah de-'atsiluth*, has become invisible to our eyes and
has been removed from the beginning of our Torah. It is now revealed only
to the adepts and the initiate, but in the Messianic Age it will become part
of the visible Torah.

to death, uncleanness, and the like. For then God will annul the present combination of letters that form the words of our present Torah and will compose the letters into other words, which will form new sentences speaking of other things. This is the meaning of the words of Isaiah [51 : 4]: 'A Torah will proceed from me,' which was already interpreted by the ancient rabbis to mean: 'A new Torah will proceed from me.'[1] Does this mean that the Torah is not eternally valid? No, it means that the scroll of the Torah will be as it is now, but that God will teach us to read it in accordance with another arrangement of the letters, and enlighten us as to the division and combination of the words.'[2]

It would be hard to conceive of a more daring formulation of the principle involved in this theory. It will scarcely come as a surprise that Azulai, pious rabbi that he was, should have protested in horror against so radical a thesis. Yet in his protest, curiously enough, he invokes Nahmanides' doctrine of the original character of the Torah in opposition to the doctrine of Eliyahu Kohen, which, he said, was without foundation in authentic Rabbinical tradition and hence without validity. Clearly he was unable to discern the unbroken line of development leading from Nahmanides to the doctrine of Eliyahu Kohen, who merely drew the ultimate logical consequence of Nahmanides' position. In any case it strikes me as highly significant that a celebrated rabbi, enjoying great prestige and high moral authority,[3] should have been able to accept so radical a thesis and that a radically spiritualist and utopian conception of the Torah in the Messianic Age could be built up upon a general principle widely accepted in Kabbalistic circles. It is also interesting to note that the same Azulai who was so indignant over the mystical extremism of Eliyahu Kohen should himself in one of his books have formulated a thesis that is scarcely less radical. There is an ancient midrash to the effect that anyone who spends the whole day reading the verse (Gen. 36 : 22): 'And Lotan's sister was

[1] *Leviticus Rabbah*, XIII, 3, ed. Margulies, p. 278. Cf the discussion of the passage in W. D. Davies, *The Torah in the Messianic Age*, Philadelphia, 1952, pp. 59–61.

[2] Azulai, *Devash le-Fi*, Livorno, 1801, 50a. The authenticity of the quotation is confirmed also by a parallel in Eliyahu Kohen's *Midrash Talpiyoth* s.v. *'amen*, in which this idea is also developed, ed. Czernowitz, 1860, 49d.

[3] Eliyahu Kohen is the author of one of the most popular ethical treatises of the late Kabbalah, *Shevet Musar*.

Timna,' which strikes the reader of the Torah as particularly meaningless and irrelevant, will attain eternal beatitude. Azulai offers the following explanation of this aphorism:

When a man utters words of the Torah, he never ceases to create spiritual potencies and new lights, which issue like medicines from ever new combinations of the elements and consonants. If therefore he spends the whole day reading just this one verse, he attains eternal beatitude, for at all times, indeed, in every moment, the composition [of the inner linguistic elements] changes in accordance with the condition and rank of this moment, and in accordance with the names that flare up within him at this moment.[1]

Here again the unlimited mystical plasticity of the divine word is taken as a principle, illustrated in the present case by what would seem to be about the most insignificant words of the Torah. All in all, this is perhaps the only way in which the idea of a revealed word of God can be taken seriously.

What strikes me as still more remarkable is that a formulation of this principle, very similar to that of Eliyahu Kohen, should be attributed to Israel Baal-Shem, founder of the Hasidic movement in Poland and Russia. In a work from the early period of Hasidism, emanating from the circle of his younger contemporary and friend, Pinhas of Koretz, we read:

Indeed it is true that the holy Torah was originally created as an *incoherent jumble of letters*.[2] In other words, all the letters of the Torah, from the beginning of Genesis to the end of Deuteronomy, were not yet combined to form the words we now read, such as 'In the beginning God created' or 'Go from thy land,' and so on. These words, on the contrary, were not yet present, for the events of Creation that they record had not yet taken place. Thus all the letters of the Torah were indeed jumbled, and only when a certain event occurred in the world did the letters combine to form the words in which the event is related. When, for example, the Creation of the world or the events in the life of Adam and Eve took place, the letters formed the words that relate these events. Or when someone died, the combination 'And so-and-so died' came into being. So it was with all other matters. As soon as something happened, the corresponding combinations of letters came into being. *If another event had occurred in its place, other combinations of*

---

[1] H. J. D. Azulai, *Devarim 'Ahadim*, Livorno, 1788, 52c–d.
[2] In Hebrew, *be-tha'aroboth 'othiyoth*.

letters would have arisen, for know that the holy Torah is God's infinite wisdom.'[1]

In a way this very naturalistic view of the original nature of the Torah seems reminiscent of Democritus' theory of the atoms. The Greek word *stoicheion* has the meanings: letter and element, or atom. According to Democritus, the diverse attributes of things are explained by the diverse movements of the same atoms. This concordance between letters as the elements of the world of language and atoms as the elements of reality was already noted by certain of the Greek philosophers. Aristotle's succinct formulation: 'Tragedy and comedy come from the same letters,'[2] not only amplified Democritus' idea but stated a principle which recurs in the Kabbalistic theory of the Torah; namely, that the same letters in different combinations reproduce the different aspects of the world.

VI

We have spoken of the principle of relativization according to which the manifestations of the absolute Torah vary with the historical period, and we have observed the different readings corresponding to the different states of man, in Paradise, in the world of sin and exile, and in the age of Messianic redemption and transfiguration. This same principle found a different and still wider application in another Kabbalistic doctrine. I have in mind the doctrine of the cosmic cycles or *shemittoth*,[3] which, though the authors of the *Zohar* did not adopt it and have nothing to say of it, played an important rôle in the older Kabbalah and exerted a considerable influence on certain later developments in Jewish mysticism. This doctrine is set forth in an extremely difficult work, which has not yet been adequately investigated. Its title, *Sefer*

---

[1] This thesis was first put forward in the Hasidic collection *Ge'ullat Yisrael*, published under the name of Israel Baal-Shem, Ostrog, 1821, 1d–2a. Very similar ideas are also discussed in early Hasidic collections, as, for example, under the name of two other prominent Hasidim of the eighteenth century in the collection *'Imre Zaddikim* (a Hasidic manuscript written c. 1800), Zhitomir, 1900, pp. 31–2.

[2] Aristotle, *De generatione et corruptione*, 315B, as an addition to his summary of the doctrine of Democritus.

[3] Cf. my remarks, *Major Trends*, pp. 178–80.

ha-Temunah, can mean both 'Book of Configuration,' namely, the configuration of the Hebrew letters, or 'Book of the Image,' namely, the image of God. For the letters, which are products of God's creative power, also form the mystical image of God, as it appears in the world of the *sefiroth.*

This book appeared about 1250 in Catalonia; the identity of its author is still unknown.[1] It deals, among other topics, with the different aspects of the Torah, not within the history of a single creation such as that recorded in the Bible, but through a series of creations, each of them governed by one of the seven lower *sefiroth.* For God's creative power is exerted in every *sefirah* and in a cosmic cycle, or *shemittah,* which is essentially the product of that *sefirah.* Each *shemittah* is governed by a different one of God's attributes, and only in the complete series of seven *shemittoth,* constituting a Great Jubilee, is the totality of God's creative powers manifested. These speculations are based on the Biblical ordinance concerning the sabbatical year and the jubilee, formulated in the fifteenth chapter of Deuteronomy. Each of these cycles endures for seven thousand years; then, in the fiftieth millennium the whole of Creation returns to the womb of the third *sefirah,* named 'return' or 'penitence,' or even, in the opinion of some of the later Kabbalists, to nothingness.

What concerns us here is the author's view of the nature of the Torah in the various *shemittoth.* For him too the Torah is in essence the primordial Torah, contained in, or sprung from, God's wisdom. The letters of this primordial Torah are hidden deep within the divine widsom; their form and order are utterly beyond our knowledge. For us they have neither form nor limit. But with every *shemittah* this hidden, perfect Torah enters into a state determined by the dominant attribute of God, and in this state the Torah becomes the revelation pertaining to this *shemittah.* Thus in every *shemittah* the absolute essence of the Torah is relativized. Within the organic unity of each aeon or cycle of Creation this Torah is a legitimate form, the only form in which the Torah can be apprehended, and hence irrevocably valid for the duration of this aeon. In other words: in every *shemittah* men will read something entirely different in the Torah, because in each one the divine wisdom of the primordial Torah appears under a different aspect. For in these cycles the nature of the

[1] The best edition of the book is that of Lwów, 1892.

creatures themselves is not at all the same, but is subject to great changes, and what in our present world can be said only of the angels will in another world be true of man and his works. In each cycle the letters not only appear in different forms, but also enter into different combinations. In each cycle their arrangement into words and hence their specific meaning will be different. The relation between these ideas and those discussed in the previous section is clear. But the difference between them is also evident. For in the present view the Torah cannot be manifested in different ways in the course of a single aeon, but only through the passage from one aeon to another.

The author of the *Book Temunah* was interested chiefly in the three first *shemittoth*, governed by the attributes of grace, of severity or judgment, and of mercy. The second *shemittah* is the Creation in which we live. The preceding one was ruled by the law of grace, the infinite stream of divine love, which knew no restrictions or negations. And so also were its creatures and the Torah under which they lived. Read differently than now, it contained no prohibitions, but only affirmations of the beatific bond between the creature and his Creator. Since there was no evil desire and no serpent, the Torah made no mention of these things. It is clear that this conception very largely, though in a different form, anticipated the idea conceived fifty years later by the author of the *Ra'ya Mehemna* concerning the rule of the Torah in its Tree-of-Life aspect. There is likewise a parallel between the Torah in the second aeon of the *Book Temunah* and the Torah as Tree of Knowledge in the *Ra'ya Mehemna*. For the Creation of this world of ours, characterized by divine severity, by restriction and judgment, knows evil desires and temptation. Its history could hardly have been otherwise, and so its Torah, too, inevitably assumed the form under which we know it today. Hence it contains prohibitions and commandments and its whole content is the conflict between good and evil. Indeed, the author goes so far as to say that the letters of the Torah had originally refused to enter into this particular combination and to submit to use—or abuse—by the creatures that would inhabit this aeon. And along the same lines, he stresses the utopian element, representing a return to the purer forms of the preceding *shemittah*, that will prevail in the third and next cycle. The Torah will once again deal only with the pure and holy, the sacrifices prescribed in it will be of a purely spiritual nature, betokening thankful recognition of God's rule, and love of the Creator. There will no longer be any exile, hence no further migration of the soul as in the present aeon. Transformed and transfigured, the evil desire in man will no longer conflict, but will harmonize, with his desire for good.

Thus this work combines the strict traditionalist view that not one letter of the Torah as given on Mount Sinai may be changed, with the conception that in other aeons this same Torah, without modifying its essence, will show another face. The author does not sidestep the consequences of a utopian antinomianism which the author of the *Ra'ya Mehemna* did not dare to formulate so sharply. If, as the *Book Temunah* states, 'what is forbidden here below is permitted on high,'[1] it follows logically that things which are forbidden in the present aeon according to the present manner of reading the Torah may well be permitted or even ordained in another aeon governed by another attribute of God, namely, mercy and compassion instead of severe judgment. Indeed, one can hardly overlook the potential antinomianism of certain views concerning the manifestation of the Torah in the various aeons, expressed in the *Book Temunah* and other works of the same school.

In this connection there are two strange ideas that deserve special attention. Not infrequently the Kabbalists of this school express the belief that in our *shemittah*, or cosmic cycle, a letter of the Torah is missing. This statement was interpreted in two ways. In one view, which seems to have been shared by the author of the *Book Temunah*, a certain letter of the alphabet is in its present form incomplete and faulty, whereas it was perfect in the preceding *shemittah* and will again be so in the next. Since every letter represents a concentration of divine energy, it may be inferred from the deficiency of its present visible form that the power of severe judgment, which sets its stamp on our world, impedes the activity of the hidden lights and forces and prevents them from being fully manifested. The limitations of our life under the rule of the visible Torah show that something is missing in it which will be made good only in another state of being. In the view of these Kabbalists the faulty letter of the Torah is the consonant *shin*, which we write with three prongs, ש, but which in its complete form should have four. They found an indication of this in the

[1] *Sefer ha-Temunah,* 62a.

Talmudic prescription that both forms of the letter *shin* should be engraved in the leather capsule that is fastened to the head in the ritual of putting on the phylacteries, or *tefillin*. In the other view, which is far more radical, a letter is actually lacking in our alphabet; in our aeon this letter is not manifested and hence does not occur in our Torah. The implications of this view are obvious. The original divine alphabet and hence the complete Torah contained 23 letters, one of which has become invisible to us and will again be made manifest only in the next *shemittah*.[1] It is only because this letter is missing that we now read positive and negative ordinances in the Torah.[2] Every negative aspect is connected with this missing letter of the original alphabet.

The second idea is based on a passage in the Talmud[3] to the effect that the complete Torah contained seven books. The Kabbalists related each of the books to one of the seven *sefiroth* which govern the seven cycles or aeons. Only in the present *shemittah* did this Heptateuch become a Pentateuch (in this calculation the fourth book of Moses, Numbers, is held to consist of three books). The second of these three books has shrunk to two verses (Num. 10 : 35, 36) which are the only sign of its existence. Joshua ibn Shu'eib, a well-known Spanish rabbi and Kabbalist of the fourteenth century, was able to reconcile this thesis with his otherwise orthodox views. According to him, the power inherent in the Torah will expand in a future aeon and we shall perceive seven books.[4] The author of the *Book Temunah* says expressly that one book has disappeared from sight, 'for the Torah which contained it, and its light which shone formerly, have already vanished.'[5] He also says that the first chapter of Genesis, the third verse of which contains a reference to a *shemittah* that consisted wholly of light without darkness, is a vestige of a more complete Torah which was revealed to the *shemittah* of grace but denied to ours.

This notion of invisible parts of the Torah which will one day be made manifest endured for centuries in a number of variants and was taken into the Hasidic tradition. Rabbi Levi Isaac of

[1] This theory is quoted by David ibn Zimra, *Magen David*, Amsterdam, 1713, 47b, from a work stemming from the same group of Kabbalists as the *Book Temunah*.

[2] In another text from the same group, MS Vatican, Hebr. 223, Fol. 197a.

[3] Shabbath 116a.

[4] Joshua ibn Shu'eib, *Derashoth*, Cracow, 1573, 63a.

[5] *Temunah*, 31a.

Berdichev, one of the most celebrated mystics of this movement, gives a particularly daring and impressive formulation of
this idea. He starts by feigning surprise at the Midrashic interpretation of Isaiah 51 : 4: 'A Torah will go forth from me,'
taking it to mean: 'A new Torah will go forth from me.' How is
this possible when it is an article of Jewish faith that there is no
other Torah beside the one given to Moses, which cannot be
exchanged for any other? Why, it is even forbidden to change so
much as a single letter. 'But the truth is that also the white, the
spaces in the scroll of the Torah, consist of letters, only that we
are not able to read them as we read the black letters. But in the
Messianic Age God will also reveal to us the white of the Torah,
whose letters have become invisible to us, and that is what is
meant by the statement about the "new Torah".'[1]

Unquestionably this doctrine left room for all manner of heretical variants and developments. Once it was supposed that a
revelation of new letters or books could change the whole outward manifestation of the Torah without touching its true
essence, almost anything was possible![2] Nevertheless, these Kabbalists stressed the absolute authority of the Torah, as we read it
in this present *shemittah*, and did not envisage the possibility that
such a change might occur without a cosmic cataclysm that
would usher in a new *shemittah*. Thus the antinomian utopia was
relegated to a sphere of history entirely outside of our own. The
one step that could lend actuality to such virtual antinomianism
would be taken when the passage from one *sefirah* or one *shemittah* to the next would be situated within historical time instead of
being postponed to the ensuing aeon. It is curious to note that
such a step was seriously considered by a Kabbalist of strictly
conservative bent. In the view of Rabbi Mordecai Yaffe of Lublin,

---

[1] *'Imre Zaddikim*, Zhitomir, 1900, p. 10, in the notes of a student on the
teachings of the Rabbi of Berdichev. (This is the source of M. Buber's
adaptation in *Tales of the Hasidim: The Early Masters*, New York, 1947, p.
232.) Cf. also the speculations on the black and white in the Torah, discussed
above (cf. Note 1, p 50).

[2] I have found an interesting parallel to these inferences in the article of
Elisa von der Recke, reprinted in Friedrich von Oppeln-Bronikowski,
Der Schwarzkünstler Cagliostro nach zeitgenössischen Berichten, Dresden, undated,
p. 98. In a lecture delivered in Mitau in 1779, Cagliostro declared that 'three
chapters in the Bible are missing and exist only in the hands of the magicians,' on whom the possession of these chapters confers enormous powers.

who wrote at the end of the sixteenth century, the present *shemittah* actually began at the time of the revelation on Mount Sinai, and the generations which lived before this event belonged to the preceding *shemittah* of grace.[1] No new creation of heaven and earth was necessary to bring about this change of aeon. If this view could be put forward in the sixteenth century without giving offence to anyone, we need not be surprised that similar ideas of a more radical, in fact of a definitely revolutionary character, should have made their appearance in the course of the great Messianic outburst in the seventeenth century. Sabbatai Zevi, the pseudo-Messiah, and his followers also thought it possible that a new *shemittah* might set in with the redemption, that the Torah which would govern this new aeon might indeed be revealed by the Messiah, and that this Torah would be a radical departure from the old law.

In this connection we must consider once again the notion of the *torah de-'atsiluth*, the Torah in the supreme state of revelation. Toward 1300, certain forms of this conception were known in circles influenced by the *Book Temunah*. They did not, however, relate it directly to the doctrine of the different aspects of the Torah in the *shemittoth*. They believed, for example, that the angels had received their understanding of the Torah from the *torah de-'atsiluth* and had transmitted it to Moses with all its secret implications when he went up to heaven to receive the Torah.[2] Here then the *torah de-'atsiluth* is the Torah in its pure essence, or the Torah in its mystical aspects, but not the Torah of a particular aeon or of a particular *shemittah*.

The beliefs held by the radical wing of the Sabbatian movement—that great outburst of spiritualist Messianism—disclose striking parallels to the development which the teachings of Joachim of Floris underwent in the middle of the thirteenth century at the hands of the radical 'spirituals' of the Franciscan Order. What Joachim meant by the 'Eternal Gospel' is essentially the same as what the Kabbalists meant by *torah de-'atsiluth*. Joachim believed that in this Evangelium Aeternum the mystical meaning of the Book would be revealed in a new spiritual age and would take the place of the literal meaning. That is exactly what

[1] Mordecai Yaffe, *Levush 'Or Yekaroth*, Lemberg, 1881, II, 8d.
[2] Cf. *Sod 'Ilan ha-'Atsiluth*, ed. Scholem, in *Kobets 'al Yad* of the Mekitse Nirdamim Society, V, Jerusalem, 1950, p. 94.

mutatis mutandis, the *torah de-'atsiluth* meant to the Kabbalists before the Sabbatian movement. But some of the Franciscan followers of Joachim identified their master's writings with the 'Eternal Gospel,' which they regarded as a new revelation of the Holy Ghost. This is very much what happened to the *torah de-'atsiluth* among the Sabbatians. The teachings of the antinomians, who took their clue from Sabbatai Zevi and certain of his prophets in Salonica, were themselves taken as the new spiritual Torah—Sabbatai Zevi, it was believed, had brought this new Torah into the world to abrogate the old *torah de-beri'ah*, which they identified with the Torah of the pre-Messianic period. The mystical content of the Torah was freed from its bond with the traditional meaning of the text; it became independent and in this new state could no longer be expressed in the symbols of traditional Jewish life. In fact, it came into conflict with them: the fulfilment of the new spiritual Torah implied the abrogation of the *torah de-beri'ah*, which was taken to represent a lower state of being and identified purely and simply with Rabbinical Judaism. Antinomianism led to a mystical nihilism which preached the transvaluation of all hitherto existing values and adopted the slogan: *bittulah shel torah zehu kiyumah*, 'the annulment of the Torah is its fulfilment.'[1]

This identification of the *torah de-'atsiluth* with the Torah of the new aeon is perhaps formulated most clearly in *Sha‘are Gan Eden*, 'The Gates of Paradise,' a book written early in the eighteenth century by the Volhynian Kabbalist Jacob Koppel Lifschitz. The author of this posthumously published work formulated and recommended nearly all the theses of Sabbatianism, but managed to avoid giving offence by prefacing his book with a violent, but patently insincere, denunciation of the sectarians and their secret doctrines, which in reality he himself espoused.

In this book we read:

In the *shemittah* in which we live, the commandments of the Torah are a divine necessity. . . . This Torah is called *torah de-beri'ah* and not *torah de-'atsiluth*. For in this *shemittah* all Creation, *beri'ah*, stems from a sphere, from which they [its works] develop and combine in a manner appropriate to the law of this *shemittah*. Consequently, we speak of a Torah of Creation, *torah de-beri'ah*. But in the preceding *shemittah*,

---

[1] On this thesis see my article on Sabbatianism in Poland in *Revue de l'histoire des religions*, CXLIII, pp. 209–32.

which was one of grace and in which there was consequently neither evil desire nor reward nor punishment, a different cosmic law [*han-hagah*] necessarily prevailed. The words of the Torah were so inter-woven as to meet the requirements of this specific cosmic law, and the actions that brought the preceding *shemittah* into being came from a higher sphere, namely that of wisdom. And so, accordingly, its Torah is called *torah de-'atsiluth*, for the meaning of *'atsiluth* is the secret of divine wisdom ... At the end of the sixth millennium the light which precedes the cosmic sabbath will spread its rays, swallowing death and driving the unclean spirit from the world. Then many commandments will be abrogated, for example, those relating to clean and unclean. Then a new cosmic law will prevail, in keeping with the end of this *shemittah*, as it is written in the *Book Temunah*. That is the meaning of the ancient words: 'A new Torah will go forth.'[1] This does not mean that the Torah will be replaced by another, for that would be contrary to one of the thirteen fundamental dogmas of Judaism [formulated by Maimonides]. Instead, the letters of the Torah will combine in a differ-ent way, according to the requirements of this period, but not a single letter will be added or taken away. Thanks to this new combination, the words will take on a new meaning. Then men's knowledge will increase, and all, great and small, will know God by virtue of the light that will flare up from the mystery of the divine thought on the eve of the cosmic sabbath. It is not necessary to speak at length of this, for all these matters are fully explained in the *Book Temunah*, where they may be found.[2]

Tishby, who in his analysis of this work was first to recognize the ambiguous nature of this theory, rightly pointed out[3] that though the *Book Temunah* speaks of processes which will set in at the end of the present *shemittah*, processes connected with the extinction of mankind and nature, it contains no trace of the doc-trine here attributed to it. We have examined its actual doctrines above. Only the Messianic beliefs of the eighteenth-century author led him to read the idea of a specific law for the final period of our *shemittah* into the. *Book Temunah*, with a view to explaining how the passage from the old to the new Torah, which is the *torah de-'atsiluth*, can take place in our own aeon. Of course the heretical Kabbalists among the Sabbatians might justifiably have cited the authority of Cordovero and other authors who, as

---

[1] Cf. the literature mentioned in Note 1, p. 34.
[2] *Sha'are Gan 'Eden*, Cracow, 1880, 12c.
[3] J. Tishby, *Kenesseth*, IX, Jerusalem, 1945, pp. 252–4.

we have seen above, actually spoke of such an eschatological change in man's way of reading the Torah. We may indeed say that Kabbalistic speculation paved the way, and laid the conceptual groundwork for such a conception, even if the Kabbalists may have been unaware of the potential antinomianism inherent in their theories.

In following the development of certain of the Kabbalists' central ideas concerning the mystical essence of the Torah, we have seen how lasting an influence these ideas exerted on the mystical theologies of Judaism. One is amazed at the energy and consistency with which these conceptions were formulated and developed. Quite a few of the ideas, which have here been traced back to their origins and their most precise and classical formulations, recur in one form or another in literally thousands of works of subsequent Hebrew literature. Sometimes the sharp edges, that were not lacking in the Kabbalistic formulations, were smoothed off and the tone somewhat muffled. But there can be no doubt as to the fundamental significance of these ideas for an understanding of many aspects of Jewish literature.

3. Kabbalah and Myth

BY way of introduction I should like to tell a short but true story. In 1924, clad in the modest cloak of modern philology and history, a young friend of mine went to Jerusalem, wishing to make contact with the group of Kabbalists who for the last two hundred years have there been carrying on the esoteric tradition of the Oriental Jews. Finally he found a Kabbalist, who said to him: I am willing to teach you Kabbalah. But there is one condition, and I doubt whether you can meet it. The condition, as some of my readers may not guess, was that he ask no questions. A body of thought that cannot be constructed from question and answer—that is indeed a strange phenomenon among Jews, the most passionate questioners in the world, who are famous for answering questions with questions. Here perhaps we have a first oblique reference to the special character, preserved even in its latest forms, of this thinking which expounds but has ceased to inquire, a thinking which might, as Schelling put it, be termed a 'narrative philosophy.' To the great philosopher of mythology, it may be remembered, such a narrative philosophy was an ideal.

I

In order to clarify the problem involved in a discussion of Kabbalah and myth, it will be well to consider the traditional view, shared in recent generations by Jews and non-Jews alike, in regard to the function of Judaism in the history of religions. Such an approach will help to elucidate the specific paradox which makes the thinking of the Jewish Kabbalists so attractive, but at the same time so disturbing to the thoughtful observer.

The original religious impulse in Judaism, which found its valid expression in the ethical monotheism of the Prophets of Israel and its conceptual formulation in the Jewish philosophy of religion of the Middle Ages, has always been characterized as a reaction to mythology. In opposition to the pantheistic unity of God, cosmos, and man in myth, in opposition to the nature myths of the Near-Eastern religions, Judaism aimed at a radical separation of the three realms; and, above all, the gulf between the Creator and His creature was regarded as fundamentally unbridgeable. Jewish worship implied a renunciation, indeed a polemical rejection, of the images and symbols in which the mythical world finds its expression. Judaism strove to open up a region, that of monotheistic revelation, from which mythology would be excluded. Those vestiges of myth that were preserved here and there were shorn of their original symbolic power and taken in a purely metaphorical sense. Here there is no need to expatiate on a matter that has been amply discussed by students of Biblical literature, theologians, and anthropologists. In any case, the tendency of the classical Jewish tradition to liquidate myth as a central spiritual power is not diminished by such quasi-mythical vestiges transformed into metaphors.

This tendency was very much accentuated by the rationalistic thinking of medieval Rabbinical Judaism; its unbroken development from Saadya to Maimonides gave rise to a problem closely related to the subject that will concern us here. The philosophers and theologians were concerned first and foremost with the *purity* of the concept of God and determined to divest it of all mythical and anthropomorphic elements. But this determination to defend the transcendent God against all admixture with myth, to reinterpret the recklessly anthropomorphic statements of the Biblical text and the popular forms of religious expression in terms of a purified theology, tended to empty the concept of God. For once the fear of sullying God's sublimity with earthly images becomes a paramount concern, less and less can be said of God. The price of God's purity is the loss of His living reality. For the living God can never be subsumed under a pure concept. What makes Him a living God in the mind of a believer is precisely what involves Him in some part of the human world, what makes it possible for man to see Him face to face in a great religious symbol. Reformulated in rational terms, all this vanishes.

To preserve the purity of the concept of God without loss of His living reality—that is the never-ending task of theology.

The history of Judaism, perhaps to a greater degree than of any other religion, is the history of the tension between these two factors—purity and living reality—a tension which has necessarily been heightened by the special character of Jewish monotheism. For in Judaism everything depended on preserving and expounding the pure unity of this God, on safeguarding the idea of God against all admixture with elements of pluralism. But to preserve God's living reality at the same time—that called for a state of perfect balance between the two factors, and this balance has always been precarious. The more the philosophers and theologians strove to formulate a unity which negates and eliminates all symbols, the greater became the danger of a counterattack in favor of the *living* God, who, like all living forces, speaks in symbols. Inevitably, men of intense religious feeling were drawn to the full, rich life of the Creator, as opposed to the emptiness, however sublime, of a pure and logically flawless theological formula. And it is this counterattack, this 'reaction,' which has given so much dramatic tension to the history of Judaism in the last 2,000 years. For not only the popular religion responding to the simple Jew's undiminished need of expression, but also the great impulses of Jewish mysticism are to be understood in this light. And this brings us to the special problem of the Kabbalah.

In the esoteric tradition of the Kabbalah, the highly ramified mystical tendencies in Judaism developed and left their historical record. The Kabbalah was not, as is still sometimes supposed, a unified system of mystical and specifically theosophical thinking. There is no such thing as '*the* doctrine of the Kabbalists.' Actually, we encounter widely diversified and often contradictory motivations, crystallized in very different systems or quasi-systems. Fed by subterranean currents probably emanating from the Orient, Kabbalism first came to light in those parts of southern France, where among non-Jews the Catharist, or Neo-Manichaean, movement was at its height. In thirteenth-century Spain it quickly attained its fullest development, culminating in the pseudo-epigraphic *Zohar* of Rabbi Moses de Leon, which became a kind of Bible to the Kabbalists and for centuries enjoyed an unquestioned position as a sacred and authoritative text. In sixteenth-century Palestine, Kabbalism knew a second flowering, in the course of which it became a central historical and spiritual current in Judaism; for it supplied an answer to the question of the meaning of exile, a question which had taken on a new urgency with the catastrophe of the expulsion of the Jews from Spain in 1492. Fired with Messianic fervor in the seventeenth century, Kabbalism became an explosive force in the great Messianic movement centering round Sabbatai Zevi, which even in its collapse provoked a mystical heresy, a heretical Kabbalah, whose impulses and developments, paradoxically enough, played a significant part—long overlooked and becoming clear to us only today—in the rise of a modern Judaism.

II

Toward 1180 the earliest Kabbalist document, the *Book Bahir*, assuredly one of the most astonishing, not to say incredible, books in the Hebrew literature of the Middle Ages, made its appearance in southern France. No one knows exactly where it came from. It is a wretchedly written and poorly organized collection of theosophical sayings in the form of Bible commentaries, for the most part imputed to imaginary authorities supposedly living in the Talmudic period. It is a very small book, consisting of only thirty to forty pages, but these few pages bear witness to a new force in Judaism. It is this new force that will concern us here. The gulf separating the religious world of this text from the Rabbinical tradition amid which it made its appearance may best be shown by a brief quotation from the circular letter of a southern French rabbi, Meir ben Simeon of Narbonne, who in the first half of the thirteenth century expressed his indignation at the blasphemous character of the *Bahir*. This pious man of the old school wrote of the Kabbalists—I shall try to render his vigorous prose as faithfully as possible:

They boast in mendacious speeches and statements of having found confirmation and encouragement [for their ideas] in countries inhabited by scholars and knowers of the Torah. But God save us from inclining to such heretical words, concerning which it would be best to keep silence in Israel. And we have heard that a book has already been written for them, which they call *Bahir*, that is, luminous, but no light shines through it. This book has come to our knowledge, and we found out that they attribute it to Rabbi Nehunia ben Hakanah [a celebrated early Talmudist]. God forbid! Pure invention. That saint didn't have a thing to do with it, and is not to be counted among the wicked. The language of the book and its whole content show that its author is a man who is without feeling for language or style.

What was it that so aroused the indignation of this pious reader? It was the reappearance, in the midst of medieval Judaism, of a frankly mythical statement, presented, moreover, without the slightest apology for its boldness, as though it were the most natural thing in the world. A few passages from the book will give the reader an idea of the nature of this 'theology.' In a passage about the creation of the angels we read:[1]

And all admit that they were not created until the second day, lest anyone might say: Michael spread out [the universe] in the south of the vault, Gabriel in the north, and the Holy One, blessed be He, measured in the middle; rather [as it is written in Isa. 44 : 24]: 'I am the Lord that maketh all things; that stretcheth forth the heavens alone; that spreadeth abroad the earth by myself (*me'itti*)—who would be with me' (*mi'itti*), says the text.

So far the text is largely taken from an ancient Jewish book, a midrash on Genesis. But the continuation in the *Bahir* (§ 14) is new and unexpected:

It is I who have planted this 'tree,' that all the world may delight in it, and with it I have spanned the All and called it 'All'; for on it depends the All, and from it emanates the All, all things need it, and look upon it, and yearn for it, and from it all souls go forth. I was alone when I made it, and no angel can raise himself over it and say: I was there before thee; for when I spanned my earth, when I planted and rooted this tree and caused them to take delight in each other and [myself] delighted in them—who could have been with me to whom I might have confided this secret?

This tree of God, which is the tree of the world but at the same time the tree of souls, is spoken of in other fragments of the *Bahir*. In some passages, however, it is not represented as something planted by God, but as the mythical structure of God's creative powers:

And what is [this] 'tree,' of which you have spoken? He said to him: All powers of God are [disposed] in layers and they are like a tree: just

[1] I quote the *Book Bahir* according to the paragraphing of my German translation, Leipzig, 1923. The translation itself has been corrected here and there.

as the tree produces its fruit through water, so God through water increases the powers of the 'tree.' And what is God's water? It is *hokhmah* [wisdom], and that [i.e., the fruit of the tree] is the soul of the righteous men who fly from the 'source' to the 'great channel,' and it rises up and clings to the tree. And by virtue of what does it flower? By virtue of Israel: when they [the children of Israel] are good and righteous, the *Shekhinah* dwells among them, and by their works they dwell in the bosom of God, and He lets them be fruitful and multiply (§ 85).

None of the notions that occur in this passage is explained in the book; all are taken to be self-evident. There is no explanation of what the 'tree,' the 'source,' or the 'great channel' are. In another passage (§ 67) we read that 'holy Israel' occupies the crown and the heart of the tree. The symbolism of the tree of the world and of God runs through the whole book, but no attempt is made to relate it to the traditional concepts of Jewish theology and its doctrine of divine attributes.

Or let us consider certain statements about evil, which were bound to arouse indignation. Concerning Satan we read in one fragment (§ 109):

It teaches that there is in God a principle that is called 'Evil,' and it lies in the north of God, for it is written [Jer. 1 : 14]: 'Out of the north the evil shall break forth upon all the inhabitants of the land, that is to say, all evil that comes upon all the inhabitants of the land breaks forth out of the north. And what principle is this? It is the form of the hand [one of the seven holy forms which represent God as the original man], and it has many messengers, and all are named 'Evil,' 'Evil' . . . And it is they that fling the world into guilt, for the *tohu* is in the north, and *tohu* means precisely the evil that confuses men until they sin, and it is the source of all man's evil impulses.

No less astonishing than this assertion that evil is a principle or quality within God himself is the following exegesis (§ 26):

Rabbi Amora sat and lectured: What is the meaning of the verse [Ps. 87 : 2]: 'The Lord loveth the gates of Zion more than all the dwellings of Jacob'? The 'gates of Zion'—these are the 'gates of the the world'; for gate means an opening, as it is written [Ps. 118 : 19]: 'Open to me the gates of righteousness.' Thus God said: I love the gates of Zion when they are open. Why? Because they are on the side of evil; but if Israel does good in the sight of God and is worthy that [the gates] be opened, He loves it more than all the "dwellings of Jacob," where there is always peace.'

This much is certain: the last thing we should expect to find in a work of Jewish piety is the notion that the 'gates of Zion,' through which, to the Jewish mind, the creative energy of Israel is communicated and in which it is concentrated are 'on the side' of Evil. The fundamental views of Kabbalistic theosophy are set forth in a form that is often paradoxical, usually unintelligible to us, and always surprising. It is a difficult text, full of puzzling theses, many of which are 'explained' by similes and parables that are even more baffling than what they are supposed to clarify and sometimes express far more radically than the theses themselves the mythical nature of the ideas which are not so much developed in this book as flung down in it. But here I shall break off; for it is not my purpose to embark on an analysis of the rich mythical content of the *Bahir*. I have done so in my book *The Origin of the Kabbalah*. The few quotations I have given may serve to show that in the *Bahir* we are no longer dealing with mythical vestiges employed poetically or allegorically, but with the reappearance of a stratum of myth within Judaism itself.

How enormously the *Bahir* differs from all previous Jewish literature dealing with cosmogony and cosmology is shown by a book that appeared only fifty years earlier, in southern France or northern Spain. I have in mind Judah ben Barzilai's compendious commentary on the *Book of Creation*, the earliest monument of speculative Jewish thinking. Not only the Kabbalists but also many of the rationalistic philosophers of the Middle Ages cited it as an authority; strictly speaking, it was not a Kabbalistic work, but there is no doubt that it provided Jewish mysticism with several of its basic concepts and ideas. Many of the old passages on cosmology are charged with mythical content. In his commentary Judah ben Barzilai discusses these passages in detail.[1] But though he is obviously given to esoteric speculation, his whole emphasis is on allegory. Behind the myths he finds the philosophical ideas of his time, especially those of Saadya. All the more astonishing is the re-emergence, two generations later, of a very different tradition in the *Bahir*.

For the Kabbalists were no longer concerned with the allegorical expression of a cosmology that might have been communicated in other ways. Their creations were symbols in the strict sense.

---

[1] *Commentar zum Sepher Jezira*, ed. S. J. Halberstamm, Berlin, 1885.

They looked upon the world of Judaism as a symbolic transparency, through which the secret of the cosmos could be discerned. From the first the Kabbalah was characterized by a revival of myth; many observers, especially, it goes without saying, among the opponents of Kabbalism, have been struck by the mythical implications of its images and symbols. In a book with the promising title *Heidentum und Kabbala* (Paganism and Kabbalah) (1893), showing an abundance of source material but little insight, Solomon Rubin, a Jewish rationalist of the last century, goes so far as to expose the Kabbalists as polytheists.

The reappearance of myth in the Kabbalah can be envisaged most clearly from two different standpoints, which are precisely the two poles of Jewish religious thinking: the idea of God and the idea of the Law. For it is evident that the mystical transformation of a religion sets in at the points that are most essential to the content of that religion, and so preserves its character as a specific historical phenomenon within a concrete religion.

I have spoken of the problem arising from the radical character of Jewish monotheism and of the danger that the concept of the one God cease to be a meaningful reflection of what is revealed in the fulness of man's inwardness, and become a mere formal abstraction. But to the Kabbalist the unity of God is manifested from the first as a living, dynamic unity, rich in content. What to the Jewish theologians were mere attributes of God, are to the Kabbalist potencies, hypostases, stages in an intradivine life-process, and it is not for nothing that the images with which he describes God are first and foremost images pertaining to the organism. The tree that was originally planted by God becomes an image of God. It is by way of this tree that God's energies flow into the process of Creation. I shall have occasion to discuss some of the more striking mythical motifs involved in this symbolism of the so-called tree of the ten *sefiroth*.

Equally pronounced and significant for the history of Judaism was the restoration of the mythical character of the Torah. For what, in Rabbinical Judaism, separated the Law from myth? The answer is clear: the dissociation of the Law from cosmic events. In Rabbinical Judaism, the Law is only in part, if at all, grounded in the memory of historical happenings—but it is no longer in any sense regarded as the representation of a mythical event in cult. The exodus from Egypt, which plays so important a role in the Torah, had ceased for Jewish consciousness to be a mythical event. And nothing perhaps characterizes this separation of an almost self-subsisting Law from its emotional roots than a little Talmudic anecdote that is frequently cited in Rabbinical literature. A heathen came to a famous rabbi of the first century A.D. and asked him to explain the regulations concerning the red heifer, one of the most obscure rituals in the Torah. The rabbi gave him a rather feeble answer, clearly evading the question. When the heathen had gone, the rabbi's students said to him: you have disposed of him with a blade of straw, but what have you to say to us? And the rabbi only said, *hok hakakti, gezerah gazarti*, I have [says God] ordained a law, I have decreed an ordinance.[1] This answer to a question which in connection with one ordinance or another was bound to arise time and time again is typical and reveals a profound break with all myth. Let speculative philosophy concern itself with the reasons for laws; to the Rabbinical mind the question was irrelevant or at most took on a certain significance in eschatological perspectives. And this divorce of the Law from its emotional roots is one of the great and fundamental, but also dangerous and ambivalent, achievements of the *Halakhah*, of normative Rabbinical Judaism.

But here we encounter a new paradox: the Kabbalists lived in this world of the Law, of the *Halakhah*, and were passionately devoted to it, but in their hands the demythicized Law became the vehicle of a new mythical consciousness, which often gives the impression of being old as the hills. For the question of the reasons for the commandments could not be downed.

Religious feeling rebelled against the rationalistic answer, namely, Maimonides' doctrine of the pedagogical and polemical meaning of the commandments. And in the Kabbalah, accompanied as it is by a consciousness of the absolute dignity and authority of the Law, the Torah is transformed into a *Corpus mysticum*.

Thus at the heart of the Kabbalah we have a myth of the one God as a conjunction of all the primordial powers of being and a myth of the Torah as an infinite symbol, in which all images and all names point to a process in which God communicates Himself.

[1] *Pesikta*, ed. S. Buber, 40b.

III

This reappearance of myth in the Kabbalah brings up several closely related problems, which it will be well to discuss at least briefly.

The first point to be mentioned in this connection is the conflict between conceptual thinking and symbolic thinking, which gives the literature and history of the Kabbalah their unique character. Beginning with its earliest literary documents, the Kabbalah expressed itself essentially in images, often distinctly mythical in content. This is equally true in the *Bahir*, in the writings of the thirteenth-century Castilian gnostics, in the *Zohar*, and in the work of Isaac Luria in Safed. But also, and almost always concurrently, we find a tendency toward speculative justification and conceptual interpretation of these symbols. The symbols, of course, are the primary and dominant phenomenon. For they cannot be fully and truly expressed in terms of the concepts which the speculative or philosophical Kabbalists often try desperately to substitute for them. Conceptions such as the *Shekhinah*, the *tsimtsum*, the breaking of the vessels, to mention only a few examples which will be discussed at least briefly in the following, can be truly understood only as symbols. The discursive thinking of the Kabbalists is a kind of asymptotic process: the conceptual formulations are an attempt to provide an approximate philosophical interpretation of inexhaustible symbolic images, to interpret these images as abbreviations for conceptual series. The obvious failure of such attempts shows that images and symbols are nothing of the sort. And it also shows something else. The Kabbalists created images and symbols; perhaps they revived an age-old heritage. But they seldom had the courage to commit themselves without reservation to these images that impressed themselves so distinctly on their minds. Usually they sought a compromise: the bolder the image, the more certain we may be that the author employing it will append a restrictive and apologetic 'If it is permissible to speak in such a way . . .' or something of the sort. But we must not forget that it is not always the same Kabbalists who create the mythical images and who timidly restrict their import or try to explain them as daring abbreviations for more or less inoffensive, though sometimes far-reaching, trains of thought. The great classical documents of the Kabbalah, the *Bahir*, the *Zohar*, and the Lurianic books, show little restraint in their production and use of images which, from a theological point of view, are questionable if not definitely scandalous. They do not exercise restraint; it would be more accurate to say that they delight in images and carry them as far as possible. Other important Kabbalists, in whom the purely mystical impulse is stronger, sometimes avoid mythical conceptions and try to transform the philosophical concepts of the Platonic tradition into mystical symbols —this is the case particularly with Azriel of Gerona, Abraham Abulafia of Saragossa, and Moses Cordovero of the Safed school. The tension which with all their affinity never ceased to exist between gnosis and Platonism may thus be said to have been repeated in the heart of Judaism.

But this leads us to another point. Are these images, with which the Kabbalists describe the secret world and hidden life of the Godhead, indigenously Jewish, or do they spring from an older heritage? Here the situation is highly complex. Some of these symbols show a definite affinity to older material, but it is difficult to say for sure how much was actually borrowed. For between the world of myth and the Kabbalistic images we discern the bridge of gnosticism, whose metaphysical and historical relations to the Kabbalah both represent a serious problem. Here I cannot take up the problem of the historical filiation of the Kabbalah and its possible connection with gnostic traditions; I have elsewhere dealt with these matters at length.[1] Suffice it to say that tenuous as the threads connecting the oldest Kabbalistic tradition with gnostic tradition may be, I am convinced that they existed. On the other hand, certain arguments might be adduced to account for the presence of gnostic themes in Kabbalism, not so much by historical contact as by a parallelism of psychological and structural development, which would seem more plausible in the twelfth and thirteenth centuries than direct historical influence. For even the Catharist heretics were relatively free from the gnostic elements in Manichaeism and largely unfamiliar with them. In the light of prolonged investigations on the subject, I feel justified in saying that apart from certain basic features whose importance I do not wish to minimize the gnosis of the Kabbalah developed independently from within. There is no need to choose

[1] In my book, *Reshith ha-Kabbalah*, Jerusalem-Tel Aviv, 1948, an English translation of which is to appear shortly.

between a historical and a psychological explanation of the origin of the Kabbalah; both elements played a part. Precisely those Kabbalistic systems that are most gnostic in character, those for example of the *Zohar* and of Isaac Luria, can be fully explained as developing from within, on Jewish foundations.

This observation, however, carries us still deeper into the problem of the Kabbalah; for gnosticism itself, or at least certain of its basic impulses, was a revolt, partly perhaps of Jewish origin, against anti-mythical Judaism, a late eruption of subterranean forces, which were all the more pregnant with myth for being cloaked in philosophy. In the second century of our era, classical Rabbinical Judaism banished this form of heresy, seemingly for good; but in the Kabbalah this gnostic view of the world not only re-emerged as a theosophical interpretation of Jewish monotheism—and this at the height of the medieval Jewish rationalism—but was able to assert itself at the center of Judaism as its most secret mystery. In the *Zohar* and in Isaac Luria gnostic and quasi-gnostic symbols became for pious orthodox Kabbalists the profoundest expression of their Jewish faith. In its first and crucial impulse the Kabbalah was a mythical reaction in realms which monotheistic thinking had with the utmost difficulty wrested from myth. Or in other words: the lives and actions of the Kabbalists were a revolt against a world which consciously they never wearied of affirming. And this of course led to deep-seated ambiguities.[1]

The world from which they came, the strict monotheism of the Law, of the *Halakhah*, the ancient Judaism in which they knew themselves to be rooted, could not readily accept this eruption of myth at its very center. Foreign mythical worlds are at work in the great archetypal images of the Kabbalists, even though they sprang from the depths of an authentic and productive Jewish religious feeling. Without this mythical contribution, the impulses of the Kabbalists would not have taken form, certainly not the form we know, and this is what gives them their ambiguous and seemingly contradictory character. Gnosis, one of the last great manifestations of myth in religious thinking, conceived at least in part as a reaction against the Jewish conquerors of myth, gave the Jewish mystics their language. The importance of this paradox cannot be over-emphasized. Once again the language of

[1] Here I have made some use of formulations from *Major Trends*, pp. 34–5.

the gnostics had to be transformed; for the intention behind those ancient mythical images, which the gnostics bequeathed to the authors of the *Bahir* and to the entire Kabbalah, was, ultimately, to destroy a law that had broken the mythical order. In large parts of the Kabbalah the vengeance of myth against its conquerors is perfectly evident, and this is the source of the countless inner contradictions in its symbols. Like certain of the earlier gnostic systems, Kabbalistic speculation derives a peculiar note from its endeavor to construct and describe a mythical world by means of a thinking that excluded myth. Here, in the realm of mysticism and mystical experience, a new world of myth arose out of the theosophical contemplation of God's secret life considered as the central religious reality. Perhaps there is no other more significant example of this same dialectic than the religion of Jacob Boehme, whose affinity with the world of Kabbalism was noted by his earliest adversaries but, strange to say, has been forgotten by the more recent writers on Boehme.

From the start this resurgence of mythical conceptions in the thinking of the Jewish mystics provided a bond with certain impulses in the popular faith, fundamental impulses springing from the simple man's fear of life and death, to which Jewish philosophy had no satisfactory response. Jewish philosophy paid a heavy price for its disdain of the primitive levels of human life. It ignored the terrors from which myths are made, as though denying the very existence of the problem. Nothing so sharply distinguishes philosophers and Kabbalists as their attitude toward the problem of evil and the demonic. By and large, the Jewish philosophers dismissed it as a pseudo-problem, while to the Kabbalists it became one of the chief motives of their thinking. Their feeling for the reality of evil and the horror of the demonic, which they did not evade like the philosophers but tried to confront, related their endeavors in a central point with the popular faith and with all those aspects of Jewish life in which these fears found their expression. Unlike the philosophical allegorists who looked for metaphysical ideas in the ritual, the Kabbalists, indeed, in their interpretations of the old rites often reconstituted their original meaning, or at least the meaning they had in the minds of the common people. The demonization of life was assuredly one of the most effective and at the same time most dangerous factors in the development of the Kabbalah, but this again demonstrates its kinship with the religious preoccupation of the Jewish masses. Thus it is less paradoxical than it may seem at first sight that a largely aristocratic group of mystics should have enjoyed so enormous an influence among the common people. It would be hard to find many religious customs and rituals that owed their existence or development to philosophical ideas. But the number of rites owing their origin, or at least the concrete form in which they imposed themselves, to Kabbalistic consideration is legion. In this descent from the heights of theosophical speculation to the depths of popular thought and action, the ideas of the Kabbalists undoubtedly lost much of their radiance. In their concrete embodiment, they often became crude. The dangers with which myth and magic threaten the religious mind are exemplified in the history of Judaism by the development of the Kabbalah, and anyone who concerns himself seriously with the thinking of the great Kabbalists will be torn between feelings of admiration and revulsion.

IV

The mythical character of Kabbalistic 'theology' is most clearly manifested in the doctrine of the ten *sefiroth*, the potencies and modes of action of the living God.[1] The Kabbalistic doctrine of the dynamic unity of God, as it appears in the Spanish Kabbalists, describes a theogonic process in which God emerges from His hiddenness and ineffable being, to stand before us as the Creator. The stages of this process can be followed in an infinite abundance of images and symbols, each relating to a particular aspect of God. But these images in which God is manifested are nothing other than the primordial images of all being. What constitutes the special mythical structure of the Kabbalistic complex of symbols is the restriction of the infinitely many aspects under which God can be known to ten fundamental categories, or whatever we may wish to call the conception underlying the notion of the *sefiroth*. In the *Book of Creation*, where the term originates, it means the ten archetypal numbers (from *safar*=to count), taken

[1] It may be worth mentioning that as far as I know the first author to have called the Kabbalah the 'mythical theology of the Jews' is the Protestant theologian J. B. Carpzow, who employs this phrase on p. 39 of his *Introductio in Theologiam Judaicam*, 1687, printed at the beginning of his edition of Raimundus Martini's *Pugio Fidei*.

as the fundamental powers of all being, though in this early work each *sefirah* is not yet correlated with a vast number of symbols relating it to other archetypal images to form a special structure. This step was first taken by the *Bahir* and the medieval theosophy of the Kabbalah, reviving gnostic exegeses concerning the world of the aeons and going far beyond them.

The totality of these potencies, united in the primordial *dekas*, forms the world of the *sefiroth*, of the unfolding divine unity which embraces the archetypes of all being. This world, it cannot be over-emphasized, is a world of divine being, but it overflows without interruption or new beginning into the secret and visible worlds of Creation, all of which in their structure recapitulate and reflect the intradivine structure. In the Kabbalistic view, this process, which turns outward in Creation, is nothing other than the exoteric aspect of a process which takes place in God himself and whose separate stages, by the particular ways in which they combine the motifs here at work, determine the peculiar mythical form of this doctrine of the *sefiroth*. On a new plane of mystical experience and contemplation, the mythical structures reappear, no longer in the persons of the old gods, but concentrated in a new and often unique way in the one world—or the world seen as one—of the tree of the *sefiroth*. An analysis of all the mythical images, at once old and new, that appear so superabundantly in this Kabbalistic symbolism, is one of the most fascinating tasks confronting the student of the Kabbalah. For this symbolism is central to the writings of the early Kabbalists, especially those of the Spanish period. And in this respect few books are more fascinating to the student of the age-old heritage represented in mystical symbols than the gnostic homilies of the *Zohar* or the grandiose attempt at a systematic development of this symbolism, embodied in the *Gates of Light* (*Sha'are 'Orah*) by Joseph Gikatila.

Two or three examples will show that we have indeed to do with a reappearance of the myth so mercilessly 'liquidated' by Jewish theology.

The paradoxical way in which the Kabbalah did away with the idea of a *creatio ex nihilo* by restoring it to the realm of myth strikes me as typical of the whole process with which we are dealing. It was through this conception of a creation out of nothing over against the conquest of chaos by the Creator-God, that the so-called rational theology of late Rabbinism, going still further than the

Biblical position on Creation, tried to break definitively with all vestiges of myth. The substitution of nothingness for chaos seemed to provide a guarantee of the Creator-God's freedom as opposed to all mythical determination by fate. His Creation thus ceases to be a struggle and a crisis and becomes a free act of love. None of this is retained in the Kabbalah, except for the naked formula itself, which is proclaimed with the utmost passion and displayed as a banner. But its meaning has been reversed. As can be gathered from my previous remarks about the meaning of the *sefiroth* and the tree of the *sefiroth*, there is no room in this world for the *nihil* of the theological conception. Emerging from His hiddenness, God appears in His potencies, in the trunk and branches of the theogonic and cosmogonic 'tree,' extending his energy to wider and wider spheres. Everywhere the changes are continuous. If there were a breach, a nothing, in the earliest beginning, it could only be in the very essence of God. And this is the very conclusion at which the Jewish mystics arrived, while retaining the old formula. The chaos that had been eliminated in the theology of the 'creation out of nothing' reappeared in a new form. This nothing had always been present in God, it was not outside Him, and not called forth by Him. It is this abyss within God, coexisting with His infinite fulness, that was overcome in the Creation, and the Kabbalistic doctrine of the God who dwells 'in the depths of nothingness,' current since the thirteenth century, expresses this feeling in an image which is all the more remarkable in that it developed from so abstract a concept. We may speak of a productive misunderstanding, by which mythical images were re-discovered at the very heart of philosophical concepts. Characteristic of such misunderstanding is the interpretation, which makes its first appearance in Azriel of Gerona, of the Aristotelian *steresis* as the mystical nothing which, after form and matter, is the third principle of all being.

To be sure, this nothing, which is a transcendent being situated in God himself, is not always mentioned by name in Kabbalistic writings. Let us take for example the first lines of a famous passage in which the *Zohar* describes the beginning of Creation within God himself:

In the beginning, when the King's will began to take effect, He engraved signs into the heavenly sphere. A dark flame issued from within the most hidden recess, from the mystery of the Infinite, like a mist forming in the unformed, enclosed in the ring of that sphere, neither white nor black, neither red nor green, of no color whatever. Only when the flame began to assume size and dimension, did it produce radiant colors. For from the innermost center of the flame sprang forth a well out of which colors issued and spread upon everything beneath, hidden in the mysterious hiddenness of the Infinite. The well broke through and yet did not break through the ether [of the sphere]. It could not be recognized at all until a hidden, supernal point shone forth under the impact of the final breaking through. Beyond this point nothing is knowable, and that is why it is called *reshith*, beginning, the first of those creative words by which the universe was created. (I, 15a.)

Nowhere in this cosmogonic myth, which is continued at length, is there any further mention of a nothing. It is replaced, under an entirely different aspect, by the aura of light, which surrounds *en-sof*, the infinite, beginningless and uncreated. When, as it does in other passages, the *Zohar* speaks expressly of such a nothing, it is always taken as God's innermost mode of being, which becomes creative in the emanation of the *sefiroth*. 'Nothing' is itself the first and highest of the *sefiroth*. It is the 'root of all roots,' from which the tree draws nourishment. It should not be supposed that this root resulted from a free act of Creation. Such an act of Creation was introduced only by the later Kabbalists, particularly Moses Cordovero, and in another form by Isaac Luria.

The primordial point mentioned in the passage just quoted was taken to be the second *sefirah* or first departure from the divine nothing implied by the image of the point. It is the world seed, the supreme formative and male-paternal potency, which is sown in the primordial womb of the 'supernal mother', who is the product but also the counterpart of the original point. Fertilized in this womb, the world seed through her emanates the other seven potencies, which the Kabbalists interpret as the archetypes of all Creation, but also as the seven 'first days' of the first chapter of Genesis, or in other words as the original stages of intradivine development. The special nature of each of these seven potencies is described in images drawn both from elemental nature and from human life.

These symbols are enormously rich in mythical implications. But nowhere, I believe, is the mythical content more evident than in the symbolism which identifies this God of the *sefiroth* with man in his purest form, *Adam Kadmon*, Primordial Man. Here the God who can be apprehended by man is himself the First Man. The great name of God in His creative unfolding is Adam, as the Kabbalists declared on the strength of a *gematria*, or numerical equation (isopsephism), which is indeed startling.[1] The *Bahir* had spoken of the 'seven holy forms of God,' each corresponding to a part of the human body. From here it was only a short step to *Adam Kadmon*, a conception from which the anthropomorphic and mythical view of God never ceased to draw new justification and new nourishment. The esoteric thinking of the *Zohar*—as the book repeatedly points out—is wholly concerned with the primordial world of man, as creature and as the increate *Adam Kadmon*. For this secret world of the Godhead manifested in the symbol of man is both at once; it is the world of the 'inner' man, but also the realm which opens up only to the contemplation of the believer and which the *Zohar* terms the 'secret of faith,' *raza de-mehemanutha*.

The mythical nature of these conceptions is most clearly exemplified by the distinction between the masculine and feminine, begetting and receiving potencies in God. This mythical element recurs, with rising intensity, in several pairs of *sefiroth*, and is expressed most forcefully in the symbolism of the last two. The ninth *sefirah*, *yesod*, is the male potency, described with clearly phallic symbolism, the 'foundation' of all life, which guarantees and consummates the *hieros gamos*, the holy union of male and female powers.

This notion of feminine potencies in God, which attain their fullest expression in the tenth and last *sefirah*, represents of course a repristination of myth that seems utterly incongruous in Jewish thinking. Consequently it seems necessary to say a few words about this idea, that is, about the Kabbalistic conception of *Shekhinah*, which is a radical departure from the old Rabbinical conception. Here I shall limit myself to a few central motifs essential to an understanding of this fundamental idea, but it should not be overlooked that entirely different motifs, which we cannot discuss at present, are also associated with it in Kabbalistic literature.

In Talmudic literature and non-Kabbalistic Rabbinical Judaism,

[1] *Yod he vav he* (the four letters of the name of God) have in Hebrew the numerical value 45, as does the word Adam.

the *Shekhinah*—literally in-dwelling, namely of God in the world—is taken to mean simply God himself in His omnipresence and activity in the world and especially in Israel. God's presence, what in the Bible is called His 'face,' is in Rabbinical usage His *Shekhinah*. Nowhere in the older literature is a distinction made between God himself and His *Shekhinah*; the *Shekhinah* is not a special hypostasis distinguished from God as a whole. It is very different in the usage of the Kabbalah, beginning with the *Bahir*, which already contains most of the essential Kabbalistic ideas on the subject. Here the *Shekhinah* becomes an aspect of God, a quasi-independent feminine element within Him. Such an independence, as we have seen above, is realized in a sense in the third *sefirah*, which is the upper mother or upper *Shekhinah*, but also, strange to say, the demiurgic potency. Of the seven potencies that emanate from it, the first six are symbolized as parts of the Primordial Man's body and epitomized in the phallic 'foundation,' which, oddly enough, is the symbolic representation of the Righteous One (*Zaddik*), as the God who maintains the powers of generation within their legitimate bounds. God is the Righteous One insofar as He provides all living things with the vital energy which holds them to their own law. And so likewise the man who maintains his generative powers within their rightful limits and measures, and hence by extension the man who gives each thing its due, who puts each thing in its proper place, is the Righteous Man to whom the Kabbalists relate the verse from Proverbs (10 : 25): 'The righteous is the foundation of the world.'

The tenth *sefirah*, however, no longer represents a particular part of man, but, as complement to the universally human and masculine principle, the feminine, seen at once as mother, as wife, and as daughter, though manifested in different ways in these different aspects. This discovery of a feminine element in God, which the Kabbalists tried to justify by gnostic exegesis, is of course one of the most significant steps they took. Often regarded with the utmost misgiving by strictly Rabbinical, non-Kabbalistic Jews, often distorted into inoffensiveness by embarrassed Kabbalistic apologists, this mythical conception of the feminine principle of the *Shekhinah* as a providential guide of Creation achieved enormous popularity among the masses of the Jewish people, so showing that here the Kabbalists had uncovered one of the primordial religious impulses still latent in Judaism.

Two other symbolic representations among many are of particular importance for an understanding of the Kabbalistic
Shekhinah: its identification on the one hand with the mystical
Ecclesia of Israel and on the other hand with the soul (*neshamah*).
Both these ideas make their appearance in the *Bahir*. In the Talmud and Midrash we find the concept of the 'Community of
Israel' (from which the Christian concept of the Ecclesia is
derived), but only in the sense of a personification of the real, historical Israel and as such definitely differentiated from God. Since
time immemorial the allegorical interpretation of the Song of
Songs as referring to the relationship between God and the
Jewish Ecclesia had enjoyed general acceptance in Judaism; but
there was nothing in this interpretation to suggest the elevation of
the Ecclesia to the rank of a divine potency or hypostasis. Nowhere does the Talmudic literature identify the *Shekhinah* with
the Ecclesia. In the Kabbalah, however, it is precisely this identification that introduces the symbolism of the feminine into the
sphere of the divine. Through this identification, everything that
is said in the Talmudic interpretations of the Song of Songs about
the Community of Israel as daughter and bride was transferred to
the *Shekhinah*. It is impossible, I believe, to say which was the
primary factor: the revival by the earliest Kabbalists of the idea of
a feminine element in God, or the exegetic identification of the
previously distinct concepts of the Ecclesia and the *Shekhinah*, the
specifically Jewish metamorphosis in which so much of the gnostic
substance entered into Jewish tradition. Here I cannot distinguish
between the psychological and the historical process, the peculiar
unity of which constitutes the decisive step taken by Kabbalistic
theosophy. But, as we have seen, there is also a third element: the
symbolism of the *Shekhinah* as the soul in the *Bahir* and the *Zohar*.
The sphere of the *Shekhinah* as the dwelling place of the soul—
this is an entirely new conception. The highest abode of the soul
known to older Jewish systems was in or under God's throne.
The notion that the soul had its origin in the feminine precinct
within God himself was of far-reaching importance for the psychology of the Kabbalah. But if we are fully to appreciate the mythical character of the *Shekhinah*, we must look into two further
conceptions that are inseparable from it, namely, its ambivalence
and its exile.

Both as woman and as soul, the *Shekhinah* has its terrible aspect.

Insofar as all the preceding *sefiroth* are encompassed in it and can exert a downward influence only through its mediation, the powers of mercy and of stern judgment are alternately preponderant in the *Shekhinah*, which as such is purely receptive and 'has nothing of its own.' But the power of stern judgment in God is the source of evil as a metaphysical reality, that is to say, evil is brought about by a hypertrophy of this power. But there are states of the world, in which the *Shekhinah* is dominated by the powers of stern judgment, some of which have issued from the *sefirah* of judgment, made themselves independent and invaded the *Shekhinah* from without. As the *Zohar* puts it: 'At times the *Shekhinah* tastes the other, bitter side, and then her face is dark.' It is no accident that an age-old moon symbolism should have risen to the surface in this connection. Seen under this aspect, the *Shekhinah* is the 'Tree of Death,' demonically cut off from the Tree of Life. While in most other contexts she is the merciful mother of Israel, she becomes at this stage the vehicle of the power of punishment and stern judgment. But here it must be stressed that these almost demonic aspects of the *Shekhinah* as 'lower mother' do not yet appear in the 'upper mother,' the third *sefirah*, which, to be sure, is a demiurge (*yotser bereshith*), but in a positive sense, free from the pejorative shading attaching to the term in the old gnostic systems. Strange and contradictory motifs are woven into a unique whole in this symbolism of the third *sefirah*, which as primordial mother of all being is particularly 'charged' with myth. Its structure is exceedingly complex, and here I cannot go into it more deeply.

However, this conception of the 'ambivalence,' the alternating phases of the *Shekhinah*, is related to that of its exile (*galuth*). The exile of the *Shekhinah* goes back to the Talmud. 'In every exile into which the children of Israel went, the *Shekhinah* was with them.'[1] In the Talmud this means only that God's presence was always with Israel in its exiles. In the Kabbalah, however, it is taken to mean that *a part of God Himself is exiled from God.* These two ideas, the exile of the Ecclesia of Israel in the Midrash and the exile of the soul from its original home—a conception found in many religions and not only among gnostics—fused in the Kabbalist myth of the exile of the *Shekhinah.* This exile is sometimes represented as the banishment of the queen or of the king's

[1] Megillah 29a.

daughter by her husband or father. Sometimes the *Shekhinah* is represented as overpowered by the demonic powers of the 'other side,' which break into her realm, subjugate her, and make her subservient to their activities of stern judgment.

In the earlier Kabbalah, for the most part, this exile is not described as originating in the first beginning of Creation. This development took place only with the Safed Kabbalah of the sixteenth century. The exile of the *Shekhinah*, or in other words, the separation of the masculine and feminine principles in God, is usually imputed to the destructive action and magical influence of human sin. Adam's sin is perpetually repeated in every other sin. Instead of penetrating the vast unity and totality of the *sefiroth* in his contemplation, Adam, when faced with the choice, took the easier course of contemplating only the last *sefirah* (since it seemed to represent everything else) separately from the other *sefiroth*, and of mistaking it for the whole of the Godhead. Instead of preserving the unity of God's action in all the worlds, which were still pervaded and governed by the secret life of the Godhead, instead of consolidating this unity by his own action, he shattered it. Since then there has been, somewhere deep within, a cleavage between the upper and the lower, the masculine and feminine. This cleavage is described in many symbols. It is the separation of the Tree of Life from the Tree of Knowledge, or of life from death; it is the tearing of the fruit from the tree to which it should cling, it is the pressing of the juices and power of judgment from the sacred fruit of the *Shekhinah*. In the context of the symbolism of the *Shekhinah* all these images are subject to profound interpretations. But the cleavage is also expressed in cosmic symbols, such as the lessening of the moon, degraded to the status of a lightless receiver of light. For the religious feeling of the early Kabbalists the exile of the *Shekhinah* was a symbol of our own guilt, and the aim of religious action must be to end this exile or at least to work in this direction. The reunion of God and His *Shekhinah* constitutes the meaning of redemption. In this state, again seen in purely mythical terms, the masculine and feminine are carried back to their original unity, and in this uninterrupted union of the two the powers of generation will once again flow unimpeded through all the worlds. The Kabbalists held that every religious act should be accompanied by the formula: this is done 'for the sake of the reunion of God and His *Shekhinah*.' And indeed, under Kabbalistic influence, this formula was employed in all subsequent liturgical texts and books of later Judaism, down to the nineteenth century, when rationalistic Jews, horrified at a conception they no longer understood, deleted it from the prayer books destined for the use of Westernized minds. In concluding my discussion of this point, I should simply like to mention the fact that symbolical representations of this myth of the *Shekhinah* and its exile, so important for the history of the Kabbalah, were discovered in innumerable old rites and a still greater number of new ones. From beginning to end, the ritual of the Kabbalists is colored by this profoundly mythical idea. We shall have more to say of it in the next chapter.

V

In the foregoing we have discussed a few Kabbalistic symbols, which, it seems to me, excellently illustrate the nature of the problem of Kabbalah and myth. But in the systems of the early Kabbalists, and particularly of the *Zohar*, we find not only a revival of isolated mythical motifs, but also a dense texture of mythical ideas often constituting fully developed myths. Many of the Kabbalists, as we have seen, busied themselves with the speculative and theological reinterpretation of such mythical thinking. But interesting as such reinterpretation may be from the standpoint of the history of ideas, it cannot blind us to the psychic substance underlying the myths. In many cases, I am almost inclined to think, the speculative reformulation of myths was quite secondary even in the minds of those who engaged in it and served merely as an exoteric disguise for the mythical content which they looked upon as a holy mystery.

Apart from the *Zohar*, myth is exemplified most strikingly and magnificently in the most important system of the late Kabbalah, the system of Isaac Luria (1534–72) of Safed, and later in the heretical *theologoumena* of the Sabbatians, whose Kabbalistic Messianism was in part inspired by Luria. Both the orthodox Kabbalah of Luria and the heretical Kabbalah of Nathan of Gaza (1644–80), prophet and theologian of Sabbatai Zevi, the Kabbalistic Messiah, provide amazingly complete examples of gnostic myth formation within or on the fringe of Rabbinical Judaism. The one is a strictly orthodox form of such gnosis, the other a heretical, antinomian deviation. Both forms of Kabbalistic myth are closely related to the historical experience of the Jewish people, and this no doubt accounts in large part for the fascination which both, but especially the Lurianic Kabbalah, have undoubtedly exerted on large sections of the Jewish people, namely, those whose keen religious sensibility prepared them to play a leading role in the religious development. Here I cannot enter into the heretical mythology of the Sabbatians; but I should like to describe, at least in its broad outlines, the structure of Lurianic myth as an unparalleled example of the contexts with which we are here concerned. It may seem presumptuous to attempt such a summary of a body of thought which in its canonical literary form fills several thick volumes,[1] especially as much of it can be fathomed only in the practice of mystical meditation and, as far as I can see, defies theoretical formulation. And yet the under-lying structure, Luria's fundamental myth, is so amazingly clear that even a brief analysis of it should prove fruitful.

From a historical point of view, Luria's myth constitutes a response to the expulsion of the Jews from Spain, an event which more than any other in Jewish history down to the catastrophe of our time gave urgency to the question: why the exile of the Jews and what is their vocation in the world? This question, the question of the meaning of the Jews' historical experience in exile, is here dealt with even more deeply and fundamentally than in the *Zohar*; it lies indeed at the heart of the new conceptions which are the essence of Luria's system.

Luria's new myth is concentrated in three great symbols, the *tsimtsum*, or self-limitation, of God, the *shevirah*, or breaking of the vessels, and the *tikkun*, or harmonious correction and mending of the flaw which came into the world through the *shevirah*.

The *tsimtsum* does not occur in the *Zohar*. It originates in other old treatises, but became truly significant only with Luria. It is an amazing conception. The *tsimtsum* ushers in the cosmic drama. But this drama is no longer, as in older systems, an emanation or projection, in which God steps out of Himself, communicates or reveals Himself. On the contrary, it is a withdrawal into Himself. Instead of turning outward, He contracts His essence, which becomes more and more hidden. Without the *tsimtsum* there

[1] Cf. the sources quoted in the chapter on Luria in my *Major Trends*, pp. 411–15.

would be no cosmic process, for it is God's withdrawal into Himself that first creates a pneumatic, primordial space—which the Kabbalists called *tehiru*—and makes possible the existence of something other than God and His pure essence. The Kabbalists do not say so directly, but it is implicit in their symbolism that this withdrawal of the divine essence into itself is a primordial exile, or self-banishment. In the *tsimtsum* the powers of judgment, which in God's essence were united in infinite harmony with the 'roots' of all other potencies, are gathered and concentrated in a single point, namely, the primordial space, or pleroma, from which God withdraws. But the powers of stern judgment ultimately include evil. Thus the whole ensuing process, in which these powers of judgment are eliminated from, or 'smelted out' of, God, is a gradual purification of the divine organism from the elements of evil. This doctrine, which definitely conflicts with other themes in Luria's own system and is more than questionable from a theological point of view, is consistently attenuated or disregarded in most expositions of the Lurianic system. In the *Tree of Life*, the great work of Luria's disciple Hayim Vital, the *tsimtsum* becomes, not a necessary and fundamental crisis in God Himself, but a free act of love, which however, paradoxically enough, first unleashes the powers of stern judgment.

In the primordial space, or pleroma, the 'roots of judgment' discharged in the *tsimtsum* are mixed with the residue of God's infinite light, which has withdrawn from it. The nature of the forms that come into being in the pleroma is determined by the co-operation and conflict between these two elements and by the workings of a third element, a ray from God's essence, which subsequently breaks through and falls back into the primordial space. For Luria, the events that take place in the pleroma are intradivine. It is these manifestations of the infinite in the pleroma which for Luria constitute the one living God. He tries to describe the genesis of these manifestations. For the part of God which has not entered into the process of *tsimtsum* and the following stages, His infinite essence, that remains hidden, is often of little importance to man here below. The conflict between the personal character of God even before the *tsimtsum* and His true impersonal essence, which takes on personality only with the process begun in the *tsimtsum*, remains unresolved in the classical forms of the Lurianic myth.

In the pleroma arise the archetypes of all being, the forms, determined by the structure of the *sefiroth*, of *Adam Kadmon*, of the creator God who takes a hand in Creation. But the precarious co-existence of the different kinds of divine light produces new crises. Everything that comes into being after the ray of the light from *en-sof* has been sent out into the pleroma is affected by the twofold movement of the perpetually renewed *tsimtsum* and of the out-ward flowing emanation. Every stage of being is grounded in this tension. From the ears, the mouth, and the nose of the Primordial Man burst forth lights which produce deeply hidden configura-tions, states of being and inner worlds beyond the penetration of the human mind, even in meditation. But the central plan of Creation originates in the lights which shine in strange refraction from the eyes of *Adam Kadmon*. For the vessels which, themselves consisting of lower mixtures of light, were designed to receive this mighty light of the *sefiroth* from his eyes and so to serve as vessels and instruments of Creation, shattered under its impact. This is the decisive crisis of all divine and created being, the 'breaking of the vessels,' which Luria identifies with the Zoharic image of the 'dying of the primordial kings.' For the *Zohar* inter-prets the list of the kings of Edom in Genesis 36, who reigned and died 'before there were kings in Israel,' as an allusion to the pre-existence of worlds of stern judgment, which were destroyed by the excess of this element within them. In Luria the death of the kings from lack of harmony between the masculine and feminine elements, described in the *Zohar*, is transformed into the 'breaking of the vessels,' also a crisis of the powers of judgment, the most unassimilable parts of which are projected downward in this cata-clysm to lead an existence of their own as demonic powers. Two hundred and eighty-eight sparks from the fire of 'judgment,' the hardest and the heaviest, fall, mingling with the fragments of the broken vessels. For after the crisis nothing remains as it was. All the lights from the eyes of *Adam Kadmon* return upward, rebounding from the vessels, or break through downward. Luria describes the laws governing this event in detail. Nothing remains in its proper place. Everything is somewhere else. But a being that is not in its proper place is in exile. Thus, since that prim-ordial act, all being has been a being in exile, in need of being led back and redeemed. The breaking of the vessels continues into all the further stages of emanation and Creation; everything is in some way broken, everything has a flaw, everything is unfinished.

But what was the reason for this cleavage in God? This question was bound to arise in the Lurianic Kabbalah, though a definitive solution was never arrived at. The esoteric answer, which puts it down as a purification of God himself, a necessary crisis, whose purpose it was to eliminate evil from God, undoubtedly reflects Luria's own opinion but, as we have seen, it was seldom stated openly—an exception is Joseph ibn Tabul, Luria's second important disciple. Others content themselves with the time-honoured allusion to the law of the organism, to the image of the seed that bursts and dies in order to become wheat. The powers of judgment are likened to seeds of grain which are sowed in the field of the *tehiru* and sprout in Creation, but only in the metamorphosis they undergo through the breaking of the vessels and the death of the primordial kings.

Thus the original crisis, which in gnostic thinking is fundamental to an understanding of the drama and secret of the cosmos, becomes an element in the experience of exile. As an experience affecting God Himself, or at least in the manifestation of His essence, exile takes on the enormous dimensions which it had obviously assumed for the Jews of those generations. It was the very boldness of this gnostic paradox—exile as an element in God Himself—that accounted in large part for the enormous influence of these ideas among the Jews. Before the judgment seat of rationalist theology such an idea may not have much to say for itself. But for the human experience of the Jews it was the most powerful and seductively appropriate of symbols.

And so the vessels of the *sefiroth*, which were to receive the world emanating from *Adam Kadmon*, are broken. In order to mend this breach or restore the edifice which, now that the demonized powers of pure judgment have been eliminated, would seem to be capable of taking on a harmonious and definitive form, healing, constructive lights have issued from the forehead of *Adam Kadmon*. Their influence ushers in the third stage in the symbolic process, which the Kabbalists called *tikkun*, restoration. For Luria this process takes place partly in God, but partly in man as the crown of all created being. It is an intricate process, for though the powers of evil were cast out in the breaking of the vessels, they were not wholly eliminated. The process of elimination must continue, for the configurations of the *sefiroth* that now arise still contain vestiges of the pure power of judgment, and these must either be eliminated or transformed into constructive powers of love and mercy. In five figures, or configurations, which Luria calls *partsufim*, 'faces' of God or of *Adam Kadmon*, Primordial Man is reconstructed in the world of *tikkun*. These five faces are *'arikh*, 'Long-suffering'; the Father; the Mother; the *ze'ir 'anpin*, 'Impatient'; and his feminine complement, the *Shekhinah*, who in turn is manifested in two configurations, Rachel and Leah. Everything that the *Zohar* had to say about the *conjunctio* of the masculine and feminine in God is now set forth with infinite precision and transferred to the formation of the last two *partsufim* and the relation between them. By and large, *ze'ir* corresponds to the God of revelation in traditional Judaism. He is the masculine principle, which through the breaking of the vessels has departed from its original unity with the feminine and must now be restored on a new plane and under new aspects. The Lurianic gnosis is concerned chiefly with the interrelation of all those figures, their influence and reflection in everything that takes place below, in the worlds of Creation, Formation, and 'Making,' which come into being below the sphere of the *Shekhinah*, the last stage of the 'world of emanation.' Everything that happens in the world of the *partsufim* is repeated with increasing intensity in all the lower worlds. These worlds form in an unbroken flow from the lights which grow steadily dimmer—Luria seems to have held that the tenth *sefirah* of every world, that is, the *Shekhinah*, functions at once as a mirror and filter, which throws back the substance of the lights pouring into it and lets through, or transmits, only their residue and reflection. But, in the present state of things, the world of Making is mixed with the world of demonic powers, or 'shells,' *kelippoth*, which accounts for the crudely material character of its physical manifestation. In essence —and here we have a pure Neoplatonic conception—the world of nature is purely spiritual. Only the breaking of the vessels, in which everything fell from its proper place, caused it to mingle with the demonic world. Thus to separate them once more is one of the central aims of all striving for the *tikkun*.

The crucial stages of this mission have been entrusted to man. For, though much of the process of restitution has already been carried out in God Himself by the setting up of the *partsufim*, it remains to be completed, according to the plan of Creation, by the last reflection of *Adam Kadmon*, who makes his appearance in the lowest form of 'Making' (*'asiyah*) as Adam, the first man of Genesis. For Adam was by nature a purely spiritual figure, a 'great soul,' whose very body was a spiritual substance, an ethereal body, or body of light. The upper potencies still flow into him, though refracted and dimmed in their descent. Thus he was a microcosm reflecting the life of all the worlds. And it was up to him, through the concentrated power of his meditation and spiritual action, to remove from himself all the 'fallen sparks' that were still in exile, and to put them in their proper place. If Adam had fulfilled this mission, the cosmic process would have been completed on the first Sabbath, and the *Shekhinah* would have been redeemed from exile, from her separation from the masculine, from *ze'ir*. But Adam failed. His failure is described with the help of various symbols, such as the premature consummation of the union between masculine and feminine, or, in the symbolism of the early Kabbalists, the trampling of the young plants in Paradise and the tearing of the fruit from the tree.

Adam's fall corresponds on the anthropological plane to the breaking of the vessels on the theosophical plane. Everything is thrown into worse confusion than before and it is only then that the mixture of the paradisiacal world of nature with the material world of evil takes on its full significance. Complete redemption was within Adam's grasp—all the more drastic is his fall into the depths of material, demonized nature. Thus in the symbolism of Adam's banishment from Paradise, human history begins with exile. Again the sparks of the *Shekhinah* are everywhere, scattered among all the spheres of metaphysical and physical existence. But that is not all. Adam's 'great soul,' in which the entire soul substance of mankind was concentrated, has also shattered. The first man, with his vast cosmic structure, shrinks to his present dimensions. The sparks of Adam's soul and the sparks of the *Shekhinah* disperse, fall, and go into exile where they will be dominated by the 'shells,' the *kelippoth*. The world of nature and of human existence is the scene of the soul's exile. Each sin repeats the primordial event in part, just as each good deed contributes to the homecoming of the banished souls. Luria draws on Biblical history as an illustration of this process. Everything that happens reflects observance or nonobservance of the secret law of the *tikkun.* At every stage Biblical history offers an opportunity for redemption, but at the decisive point man always fails to take advantage of it. At the highest point in his striving, the exodus of Israel from Egypt and the Revelation on Mount Sinai, man is brought down again by his worship of the golden calf. But the essential function of the Law, both of the Noahide law binding on all men and of the Torah imposed specially upon Israel, is to serve as an instrument of the *tikkun.* Every man who acts in accordance with this Law brings home the fallen sparks of the *Shekhinah* and of his own soul as well. He restores the pristine perfection of his own spiritual body. Seen from this vantage point, the existence and destiny of Israel, with all their terrible reality, with all their intricate drama of ever renewed calling and ever renewed guilt, are fundamentally a symbol of the true state of all being, including—though this was seldom said without reservations—divine being. Precisely because the real existence of Israel is so completely an experience of exile, it is at the same time symbolic and transparent. Thus in its mythical aspect the exile of Israel ceases to be only a punishment for error or a test of faith. It becomes something greater and deeper, a symbolic mission. In the course of its exile Israel must go everywhere, to every corner of the world, for everywhere a spark of the *Shekhinah* is waiting to be found, gathered, and restored by a religious act. And so, surprisingly enough, still meaningfully anchored in the center of a profoundly Jewish gnosis, the idea of exile as a mission makes its appearance. Disintegrating Kabbalism was to bequeath this idea to the rationalistic Judaism of the nineteenth and twentieth centuries. It had lost its deeper meaning, but even then it preserved a vestige of its enormous resonance.

But the exile of the body in outward history has its parallel in the exile of the soul in its migrations from embodiment to embodiment, from one form of being to another. The doctrine of metempsychosis as the exile of the soul acquired unprecedented popularity among the Jewish masses of the generations following the Lurianic period.

In submitting to the guidance of the Law, Israel works toward the restitution of all things. But to bring about the *tikkun* and the corresponding state of the cosmos is precisely the aim of redemption. In redemption everything is restored to its place by the secret magic of human acts, things are freed from their mixture and consequently, in the realms both of man and of nature, from their servitude to the demonic powers, which, once the light is removed from them, are reduced to deathly passivity. In a sense the *tikkun* is not so much a restoration of Creation—which though planned was never fully carried out—as its first complete fulfillment.

Thus fundamentally every man and especially every Jew participates in the process of the *tikkun*. This enables us to understand why in Kabbalistic myth the Messiah becomes a mere symbol, a pledge of the Messianic redemption of all things from their exile. For it is not the act of the Messiah as executor of the *tikkun*, as a person entrusted with the specific function of redemption, that brings Redemption, but your action and mine. Thus for all its setbacks the history of mankind in its exile is looked upon as a steady progress toward the Messianic end. Redemption is no longer looked upon as a catastrophe, in which history itself comes to an end, but as the logical consequence of a process in which we are all participants. To Luria the coming of the Messiah means no more than a signature under a document that we ourselves write; he merely confirms the inception of a condition that he himself has not brought about.

Thus the Lurianic Kabbalah is a great 'myth of exile and redemption.' And it is precisely this bond with the experience of the Jewish people that gave it its enormous power and its enormous influence on the following generations of Jews.

We have come to the end of this brief exposition. We have seen how the Jews built their historical experience into their cosmogony. Kabbalistic myth had 'meaning,' because it sprang from a fully conscious relation to a reality which, experienced symbolically even in its horror, was able to project mighty symbols of Jewish life as an extreme case of human life pure and simple. We can no longer fully perceive, I might say, 'live,' the symbols of the Kabbalah without a considerable effort, if at all. We confront the old questions in a new way. But if symbols spring from a reality that is pregnant with feeling and illumined by the colorless light of intuition, and if, as has been said,[1] all *fulfilled* time is mythical, then surely we may say this: what greater opportunity has the Jewish people ever had than in the horror of defeat, in the struggle and victory of these last years, in its utopian withdrawal into its own history, to fulfil its encounter with its own genius, its true and 'perfect nature'?

[1] Gerardus van der Leeuw, *Eranos-Jahrbuch*, XVII (1949), pp. 27-8.

4. Tradition and New Creation in the Ritual of the Kabbalists

I

IT lies in the very nature of mysticism as a specific phenomenon within historical systems of religion that two conflicting tendencies should converge in it. Since historical mysticism does not hover in space, but is a mystical view of a specific reality; since it subjects the positive contents of a concrete phenomenon such as Judaism, Christianity, or Islam to a new, mystical interpretation without wishing to come into conflict with the living reality and traditions of these religions, mystical movements face a characteristic contradiction. On the one hand, the new view of God and often enough of the world cloaks itself in the deliberately conservative attitude of men who are far from wishing to infringe on, let alone, overthrow tradition, but wish rather to strengthen it with the help of their new vision. Yet, on the other hand, despite this attitude of piety toward tradition, the element of novelty in the impulses that are here at work is often enough reflected in a bold, if not sacrilegious, transformation of the traditional religious contents. This tension between conservative and innovationist or even revolutionary tendencies runs through the whole history of mysticism. Where it becomes conscious, it colors the personal behavior of the great mystics. But even when in full lucidity they choose to take a conservative attitude toward their tradition, they always walk the steep and narrow path bordering on heresy.

This general observation applies fully to the Kabbalistic movement in Judaism. With the exception of the Messianic and heretical forms of Sabbatianism in the seventeenth and eighteenth centuries, its systems were all conceived as conservative ideologies within the frame of Rabbinical Judaism. Yet, nearly all these systems are so revolutionary in implication that their conservative character was time and again called into question. In the Kabbalah, moreover, and perhaps in many analogous movements in other religions, an additional tension makes its appearance within the new progressive forces. The mystical trend which changes the face of historical tradition while striving to preserve it unchanged, which extends the limits of religious experience while trying to consolidate them, is ambivalent in character; on the one hand it strives forward, while on the other, in delving for new layers of religious experience, it unearths age-old, archaic elements. The rejuvenation of religion repeatedly finds its expression in a return to ancient images and symbols, even when these are 'spiritualized' and transformed into speculative constructions. It is assuredly not the spiritualized, speculative interpretations that have had the most lasting influence. If I may be permitted a rather bold figure: the old God whom Kabbalistic gnosis opposed to the God of the philosophers proves, when experienced in all His living richness, to be an even older and archaic one.

I have dealt in the preceding chapter with this problem of the re-emergence of myth in a monotheistic religion. My present purpose, in a manner of speaking, is to examine the practical implications of this central phenomenon. For the truth is that the Kabbalistic conceptions which exerted an influence on ritual were exclusively those in which contact was renewed with a mythical stratum, whether disguised in allegory or directly communicated in symbols. The speculative interpretations, however sublime, that are frequently enough intertwined with mythical images in the Kabbalah produced no new rites, and it is interesting to note that many of those Kabbalists who made a conscious effort to bar mythical images from their thinking showed extreme reserve toward such new rites as those which the Kabbalah brought forth with lavish abundance in Safed. But such scruples did not prevent the Kabbalah from achieving its widest popularity precisely by providing new rites, and in the following we shall note several striking examples of this intimate connection between the ritual and myths of the Kabbalists.

But I am getting ahead of myself. Before we can enter into the specific problem of ritual among the Kabbalists, we shall do well to consider the question of Jewish ritual in general, particularly in its classical Rabbinical form. Was it possible, in a religion that is generally known as a classical and radical form of ritualism, to develop new rites and endow the old ones with new meaning? This question leads us to the special problem of ritual in Rabbinical Judaism, which can perhaps be formulated as follows: on the one hand, we have here a way of life based entirely on the performance of ritual, a tendency to absorb life itself into a continuous stream of ritual, and not merely to extract ritual acts from its flow at particular climaxes and turning points. But in this Judaism, on the other hand, the performance of sacred actions, of ritual, is largely divorced from the substrate that has always been the mother of ritual, that is, from the myths that are represented in the mime or drama of ritual.

The Jewish rites developed in the Talmud still reveal an intimate bond with the life of man in nature. The first of the six parts of the Mishnah, the first codification of Jewish religious law and ritual, relates almost entirely to the life of a largely agrarian population. It is an attempt to develop and order the prescriptions of the Torah in a manner applicable to agrarian life (regulations on harvesting and gleaning; on first fruits and the sabbatical year; on the sowing of plants belonging to the same genus but to different species, which is regarded as an unwarranted mixing of things, etc.). But in the Diaspora of the early Middle Ages this contact with the earth was gradually lost. The rites based on it became obsolete, because the corresponding ordinances of the Torah were held to be 'dependent on the Land,' that is, applicable in Palestine and without validity elsewhere. Thus the ritual of the Jews in the Diaspora took on its characteristic paradoxical form, in which the natural year is replaced by history. On the one hand we find a hypertrophy of ritual, which becomes all-pervading, a state of affairs that finds its clearest expression in a passage in the Talmud: The Ecclesia of Israel says to God: 'Lord of the world, far more ordinances than Thou hast imposed on me have I imposed on myself, and I have kept them.'[1] On the other hand this same ritual is cut off from its roots in, and ties with, the natural world. A nature ritual is transformed into a historical ritual that no longer reflects the cycle of the natural year, but replaces it by historical

[1] Erubin 21b.

reminiscence, which became the principal basis of the liturgical year. The primordial past of Israel is recapitulated in the holiday ritual, which henceforth has its emotional roots in history rather than in the life and death of nature.

In the Bible the historical memories which form the basis of the three great pilgrimage festivals are still related to the harvest seasons. But only the feeblest vestiges of this connection remained alive for the Jews in exile. Moreover, the primordial history that is here recollected was no longer regarded by the celebrants as a mythical history, enacted in another dimension of time, but as the real history of the Jewish people. Thus this history-saturated ritual was accompanied by no magical action. The rites of remembrance produce no *effect*, they create no immediate bond between the Jew and his natural environment, and what they 'conjure up' without the slightest gesture of conjuration is the memory, the community of generations, and the identification of the pious with the experience of the founding generation which received the Revelation. The ritual of Rabbinical Judaism makes nothing happen and *transforms* nothing. Though not devoid of feeling, remembrance lacks the passion of conjuration, and indeed there is something strangely sober and dry about the rites of remembrance with which the Jew calls to mind his unique historical identity. Thus this ritualism par excellence of Rabbinical Judaism is lacking precisely in the ecstatic, orgiastic element that is always somewhere present in mythical rituals. The astonishing part of it is that a ritual which so consciously and emphatically rejected all cosmic implications should have asserted itself for many generations with undiminished force, and even continued to develop. A penetrating phenomenology of Rabbinical Judaism would be needed to determine the nature of the powers of remembrance that made this possible and to decide whether other secret factors may not after all have contributed to this vitality. For our present purposes it suffices to have described the situation. It should also be borne in mind that all those rites which in traditional Judaism are devoted not to *remembrance*, to historical recollection, but to the *sanctification* of man in the face of God are also completely divorced from the solemnity of action on a mythical plane. They appeal to something in man and undertake to repress something which strikes a historical observer as very close to myth. But nowhere does the Jewish literature of the Middle

Ages bare the mythical character of these rites—except among the Kabbalists.

II

In none of their systems did the Kabbalists fail to stress the inter-relation of all worlds and levels of being. Everything is connected with everything else, and this interpenetration of all things is governed by exact though unfathomable laws. Nothing is without its infinite depths, and from every point this infinite depth can be contemplated.

The two images employed in the Kabbalistic ontologies—the endless chain with its interrelated links and the concentric layers of the nut—seem to contradict one another. But to the Kabbalist there was no contradiction between the reality of the spiritual world and its connection with the natural world, which is what these images are intended to suggest—the two symbols are used by the author of the *Zohar*.[1] In the chain of being, everything is magically contained in everything else. It is in this sense that we must understand the statement often made by later Kabbalists (e.g., Cordovero) to the effect that a man's ascent to higher worlds and to the borders of nothingness involves no motion on his part, for 'where you stand, there stand all the worlds.' Thus the world of the Godhead, which the Kabbalists conceive as the dynamic world of the *sefiroth*, containing the infinite unity of divine being, not only in its hidden essence but also in its creative unfolding, must not be interpreted as a world of pure transcend-ence. Frequently it is that too, but the Kabbalists are essentially interested in showing how the world of the *sefiroth* is related to the world outside of God. All being in the lower realm of nature, but also in the upper worlds of the angels and pure forms, of the 'Throne' of God, has in it something, a sefirotic index as it were, which connects it with one of the creative aspects of divine being, or, in other words, with a *sefirah*, or a configuration of *sefiroth*. It is the transcendence that shines into created nature and the symbolic relationship between the two that give the world of the Kabbalists its meaning. 'What is below is above and what is inside is outside.' But this formula defines only one aspect, an essential one to be sure, of the Kabbalistic world. The symbolic

[1] Moses de Leon, *Sefer ha-Rimmon*, MS British Museum, Add. Or. 26,920, Fol. 47b, and *Zohar*, I, 19b.

aspect must be completed by the magical aspect, for in the Kab-balistic view everything not only *is in* everything else but also *acts upon* everything else. The two aspects of the Kabbalah are essential to its attitude toward ritual. For it is the question: what are the dimensions of human action, to what depth does it pene-trate, what realm of being does it represent?—that gave the Kab-balistic conception of ritual its significance and its influence in the religious history of the Jews. Sacred action, the enactment of the law, but also of every pious usage, is related to a world and effective in a world that we have recognized to be mythical.

In this connection I should like to cite a few passages from the early Kabbalists, who formulated this idea with the utmost clarity. These passages deal for the most part with the significance of the commandments (*mitsvoth*) of the Torah, among which must be included the ritual contained in, or developed from, these same commandments. Isaac the Blind, one of the earliest Provençal Kabbalists (c. 1200) writes:[1] 'Although Thy commandment seems finite at first, it expands *ad infinitum*, and while all perishable things are finite, man can never look upon the meaning of Thy com-mandment as finite.' Thus though the performance of a concrete, determinate rite seems to be a finite act, it opens up a view of the infinite, and Azriel of Gerona, one of Isaac's disciples, drawing the logical consequence from this view, attributed to God's com-mandments an element of divine being,[2] a belief which, largely through the *Zohar*, was taken up by the Kabbalah as a whole. The action of a man performing a rite is the finite embodiment of something which is present in mystical substantiality in the pleroma of the *sefiroth*. Menahem Recanati, who at the turn of the thirteenth century wrote a widely disseminated work about the Kabbalistic interpretation of the commandments, says in his introduction:

On the basis of the lower world we understand the secret of the law according to which the upper world is governed, as well as the things that have been called the ten *sefiroth*, whose 'end is in their beginning just as the flame is attached to the coal'[3] . . . and when these ten

[1] In his (still unprinted) commentary on the *Book Yetsirah*, I, 6.

[2] 'The commandments themselves are *kabod*,' i.e., essentially a component of the divine pleroma; cf. Azriel's commentary on the Aggadoth of the Talmud, ed. Tishby, 1943, p. 39.

[3] A quotation from the first chapter of the *Book Yetsirah*.

sefiroth were made manifest, something corresponding to that supreme form became visible in every other creature, as it is written: [Job 8 : 9]: 'Our days upon earth are a shadow'—meaning: our days are a mere shadow of the transcendence of the 'primordial days'—and all created being, earthly man and all other creatures in this world, exist according to the archetype [*dugma*] of the ten *sefiroth*.[1]

In the language of the Kabbalists this world of the archetypes is often called the *merkabah*, the chariot of God, and Recanati goes on to say that every detail in the ritual of the Torah is connected with a particular part of the *merkabah*. These 'parts,' to be sure, form a mysterious organism. 'Every commandment has a high principle and a secret foundation, which can be derived from no commandment other than this particular one, which alone contains these mysteries; but just as God is one, so all the commandments together form *one* power'—that of infinite divine life.

The Torah as the totality of these commandments is rooted in this divine world, the pleroma of the *sefiroth*. 'God,' says Recanati, 'is accordingly not something trascending the Torah, the Torah is not outside of God and He is not outside of the Torah, and that is why the sages of the Kabbalah were justified in saying that the Holy One, blessed be He, is Himself the Torah.' These words of Recanati mean that the ritual takes God into human action, which derives its mystical dignity from this relationship to the dynamic world of the *sefiroth*. But this mystical dignity, which Recanati imputes to ritual, is at the same time mythical. For here ritual action is related to the realm of divine action, and intradivine happening, the richly diversified life of His unity, achieves its symbolic expression in ritual. But here we encounter the second aspect of the Kabbalistic world, which I have termed magical. For ritual action not only *represents*, but also *calls forth* this divine life manifested in concrete symbols. This fundamental duality has at all times been characteristic of the Kabbalistic attitude toward ritual. Those who carry out the *mitsvah* always do two things. They *represent* in a concrete symbol its transcendent essence, through which it is rooted in, and partakes of, the ineffable. But at the same time they transmit to this transcendent essence (which the later Kabbalists call the 'upper root' of ritual action) an influx of energy. Recanati goes so far as to say that although this influx of

[1] Recanati, *Ta'ame ha-Mitsvoth*, Basel, 1581, 3a.

energy is provoked by human action, it springs from the 'nothing-ness of the divine idea' (that is, the source of the upper *sefiroth* in the divine Nihil). And it would be hard to find a better illustra-tion of the intimate relationship between mysticism and myth in Kabbalistic thinking than the words with which Recanati con-cludes this discussion. Those who perform the ritual, he declares, 'lend stability, as it were, to a part of God Himself, if it is per-missible to speak in this way.' The two restrictives, the 'as it were' and the 'if it is permissible to speak in this way,' in a single sentence, whose boldly mythical character they do not diminish, fully disclose the dilemma facing the Kabbalists in their striving to transform Judaism into a mystery religion. No end of similar utterances may be found in the same author[1] and in many other Kabbalists.

Thus the Kabbalah in its conservative function was able to take over almost unchanged the rites of medieval Judaism, those recognized in principle as well as those actually practiced. The bond with an infinitely fruitful stratum, from which feeling draws nourishment, was restored, though at the price of a theological paradox. The principle, repeatedly stressed in the *Zohar*, that all 'upper happening'—a term of far-reaching implications, as we have seen—required 'stimulation' by a 'lower happening' shows clearly to what extent ritual had come once again to be regarded as an action of cosmic import.

Here, to be sure, two different lines of development can be distinguished. In one case, the old rites, hallowed by tradition, were interpreted in accordance with the new (or if you will, age-old) conceptions; in the other, new rites were devised, and these new rites, springing precisely from the mythical element in Kabbalistic thinking, lent it a new expression, directly reflecting Kabbalistic feeling and requiring no reinterpretations or exegeses.

---

[1] There is a very similar formulation in Recanati's commentary on the Torah: 'Both in parts and structure the human form is wholly modeled on the form of the divine man. But since the human members are formed in accordance with the purpose of creation [i.e., according to the cosmic order], they should be a replica and throne for the heavenly members, and in them he should increase power and emanation from the primordial *nihil* [*afisath ha-'ayin*]; otherwise [in case of misuse] he brings about the exact opposite. And this is the secret meaning of the verse (Lev. 24 : 20): 'as he hath caused a blemish in a man [namely, in his sublime, primordial form], so shall it be done to him again.'

The existing ritual was not changed. It was taken over more or less intact. The Kabbalists justified it in this form as a bond between man and his metaphysical origins. The traditional ritual was thus transformed by means of a mystical instrument, which operates in a cosmic area and penetrates through world upon world to the depths of the Godhead—the Kabbalists found such an instrument in what they called *kavvanah*, that is, the mystical 'intention' or meditation which accompanies the ritual act. The rite itself, says a Lurianic source, is the body, mystical *kavvanah* is its soul, 'and if anyone performs the sacred action without the right intention, it is like a body without a soul.'[1] *Kavvanah* singles out the precise aspect of the Godhead to which each concrete step prescribed by the ritual applies, and the sum of the steps that make up a given rite circumscribes its symbolic movement. Thus in the medium of meditation, an outward action is transformed into a mystical movement of the human will, which strives to adapt itself to the divine will. Both in theory and in the technique of its practice, *kavvanah* was accordingly a mystical instrument in the fullest sense of the word, by means of which every ritual action was transformed into a mystery rite performed by the initiate. Such rituals, the whole liturgy of prayer, for example, which were worked out in great detail, often included a complete set of instructions governing the ascent of *kavvanah* from the lowest realms to the highest. These elaborate rituals are not always restricted to concentration on the various *sefiroth* and their workings; in its ascent, which in some ways suggests the journey of the soul to heaven, *kavvanah* must also pass through the realms intermediate between the sensible world and the *sefiroth*. These 'upper' realms, whose character varies from one Kabbalistic cosmology to another, are also areas of human action in its mythical dimension. The Kabbalists did not always distinguish very precisely between them and the other 'upper' realm of the Godhead itself, though the specialized treatises on *kavvanah* show a very definite awareness of the very different modes of being represented in each of these worlds and stages.

Highly characteristic in this connection is an important passage in the *Zohar*,[2] the introduction to a detailed interpretation of the morning prayer. Here the four stages of community prayer are described as four successive functions. Each of these functions is

---

[1] *Shulhan 'Arukh of R. Isaac Luria*, 1681, 31d.   [2] *Zohar*, II, 215b.

designated as a *tikkun*, which in Hebrew means at once a perfecting, a betterment, and a correction, though in other contexts it may simply mean an institution or arrangement. What then, according to the *Zohar*, is perfected or repaired in these four stages of prayer? First, man himself, who purifies and perfects himself in the sacred action; secondly, the natural world of Creation, which if it were endowed with speech would join man in hymns of praise; thirdly, the 'upper' world of the angelic orders; while, fourthly, the *tikkun* of prayer is none other than that of the 'Holy Name' itself, the name of God, in which the sefirotic world is encompassed. Thus one who prays rises from the depths to the world of the Godhead, and in every world he accomplishes something with his words of praise and veneration. He not only acknowledges the greatness of Creation and the Creator; he also puts order in Creation and brings about something which is necessary to its perfect unity and which without his act would remain latent.

The unity between above and below, the achievement of which the *Zohar* designates over and over again as the purpose of ritual, must accordingly be understood under several aspects. The creation of unity is a mystical action in the depths of the Godhead, because, as we have explained above, it stimulates the creative power; but at the same time it is in every sense a mythical action, because it unites heaven and earth, the heights and depths of the cosmos. But finally, it is not only creation but also, and increasingly so as the history of the Kabbalah advanced, restitution, since the original unity, as is made plain above all in the *Zohar* and the early Kabbalah, was not only shaken but actually destroyed by man. According to the Lurianic Kabbalah, it is true, the breach did not originate with man, but was inherent in the structure of divine being (and hence to an immeasurably greater degree in the structure of created being), but this had little effect on the aspect of ritual with which we are now concerned. The essential is that in this perspective ritual always has an eschatological implication. For a *tikkun* that is regarded as a restoration of unity from multiplicity is necessarily related in some way to redemption. The Safed Kabbalah expressed this eschatological tension in the life of the Jews with incomparable power.

But even if we disregard eschatology, we may say that, in the minds of the early Kabbalists, the primary function of ritual was to establish a connection between man as a microcosm and the great world or 'Great Man,' that is, *Adam Kadmon*. Undoubtedly the idea of the microcosm, and especially its implications for human conduct, played an enormous part in the conceptions of the Kabbalists. Long before the Kabbalah the Talmudists played with the idea of a correspondence between the commandments of the Torah and the structure of man. Here the 248 positive commandments correspond to the 248 members of man and the 365 prohibitions to the 365 days of the year (or the 365 blood vessels in the body.) Thus each member of man's body was made to fulfil one of the commandments, and each day of the year to sanctify man through his self-restriction to the realm of the permissible. The Kabbalists took up this conception and developed it. The Ten Commandments became for them the roots of a mystical structure expressed in the 613 commandments of the Torah; but this structure is identical with that of the mystical figure formed by the ten *sefiroth* in the body of *Adam Kadmon*. Thus man's action restores the structure of *Adam Kadmon*, which is at the same time the mystical structure of God as He reveals Himself. Just as the idea of the microcosm meant that because the world is wholly contained and reflected in man, he acts upon the world with direct magic, so the Kabbalistic conception implies the idea of a magical nexus which, however sublimated and spiritualized, is brought about magically by ritual. The old Jewish gnostics of the second or third century had spoken, to the horror of the medieval philosophers, of a 'body of the Godhead' (*sh'iur komah*), whose parts they even claimed they could measure.[1] The Kabbalists took up this conception and identified it with *Adam Kadmon*. The Kabbalistic books of ritual repeatedly stress the connection between the commandments and this body of the Godhead.[2]

Finally, I should like to mention still another perspective that is of the utmost importance for the Kabbalistic attitude toward ritual. In addition to its positive aspect, the *tikkun*, the restoration of the right order, the true unity of things, has a corresponding negative aspect, which in the Lurianic Kabbalah is

---

[1] On these conceptions, cf. my *Major Trends*, pp. 63–7, and *Jewish Gnosticism*, pp. 36–42.

[2] There are special books which develop the commandments of the Torah as members of the *shi'ur komah*.

termed *berur*. *Berur* (literally 'selection') is the elimination of the negative factors that disturb the right order, that is, the elimination of the powers of the demonic and Satanic, of the 'other side' (*sitra ahra*) as the Kabbalists called it. Particularly the Lurianic theory of ritual implies that the Torah aims at a progressive repression and elimination of the 'other side,' which is at present mixed with all things and threatens to destroy them from within. This elimination is the purpose of many rites, and it is of interest to note that we possess, from the hand of Joseph Karo of Safed, the greatest Rabbinical authority of the sixteenth century, not only what remained for a long time the most authoritative codification of the Jewish religious law, but also a visionary Kabbalistic journal, in which the personified spirit of the Mishnah, speaking from within the author, made revelations concerning the secrets of the Torah.[1] And one of these revelations is that the purpose of all the ordinances and rites of the Torah is to eliminate the 'shells' from the holy.[2] And this in the mouth of the author of the *Shulhan 'Arukh*.

Of course the 'other side' cannot be wholly defeated except in an eschatological perspective, and in the world as it is such a total defeat is not even desirable. This explains why, in interpreting some of the more obscure rites of the Torah, as early a work as the *Zohar* declares that the 'other side' has its legitimate place in them, that these rites serve to contain it within the proper limits but not to destroy it, for this is possible only in the Messianic Age. It is in this sense that the *Zohar* interprets the ritual of the scapegoat that is sent out into the wilderness on the Day of Atonement (Lev. 16), the sin offering of a kid at the new moon (Num. 28 : 15), the leper's offering of a bird (Lev. 14), and the rites connected with the red heifer (Num. 19), as well as certain rites introduced only by late Rabbinical Judaism. Needless to say, the struggle between God and the demonic power which He Himself has called forth opens the way to radically mythical views of ritual. The considerable vogue enjoyed, particularly in the nineteen-thirties, by Oskar Goldberg's book, *Die Wirklichkeit der Hebräer, Einleitung in das System des Pentateuch* (The Reality

[1] R. Zwi Werblowsky, *Joseph Karo, Lawyer and Mystic*, Oxford, 1962.
[2] Joseph Karo, *Maggid Mesharim*, Vilna, 1879, 34d, in which the scapegoat ritual on the Day of Atonement is interpreted at length as a progressive separation between the two sides, the 'holy' and the 'unclean'.

of the Hebrews, an Introduction to the System of the Penta-teuch),[1] shows what fascination is still (or once again) exerted by interpretations of ritual, featuring Kabbalistic conceptions and delighting, above all, in their demonic aspects. Although Gold-berg, whose ideas about the *Kabbalah* are naïve and rather grotesque, consistently attacks it in developing his own ideas about the Torah and its ritual, and although he substitutes a modern biologico-political jargon for the old Kabbalistic ter-minology, the truth of the matter is that what he represents as the exact literal meaning of the Torah chapters he deals with is an essentially Kabbalistic interpretation.

III

The attitude of the Kabbalah toward ritual is governed by certain fundamental conceptions which recur in innumerable variants. In its role of representation and excitation, ritual is expected, above all, to accomplish the following:

1. Harmony between the rigid powers of judgment and the flowing powers of mercy.
2. The sacred marriage, or *conjunctio* of the masculine and feminine.
3. Redemption of the *Shekhinah* from its entanglement in the 'other side.'
4. Defense against, or mastery over, the powers of the 'other side.'

Over and over again we meet with these conceptions emphasiz-ing different elements in the doctrine of the *sefiroth*, sometimes singly and sometimes in combination. The blowing of the *shofar* on New Year's Day, for example, is explicitly associated with the first and fourth purposes. The rituals of the great festivals and particularly of the Sabbath are related to the sacred marriage. Often a single ritual represents the whole sefirotic world in all its aspects. But this interpretation of the rites, not only as symbols of mysteries but also as vehicles of the divine potencies, involves a

[1] Berlin, 1925. Erich Unger, in *Wirklichkeit, Mythos, Erkenntnis*, Munich, 1930, attempted a philosophical justification of Goldberg's Kabbalistic metaphysics.

danger which is present in any body of mysticism employing traditional forms. The abundance of ritual forms threatens to stifle the spirit, try as the spirit may to bend them to its purposes and transfigure them with its contemplation. This contradiction is inseparable from the development of all such mystical rituals, as the adversaries of mysticism have seldom failed to point out.

The lengths to which the Kabbalists went as early as the thirteenth century, in transforming all human action and expresssion into a sacral ritual, may be shown by two examples which define opposite poles. Needless to say, the *Shema Yisrael*, the formula from Deuteronomy 6 : 4, which plays a central role in most liturgies and which in Rabbinical Judaism serves to express the quintessence of monotheistic faith, exerted a special fascination on the Kabbalists. 'Hear, O Israel, the Lord, our God, the Lord is one' —unquestionably, but what kind of unity is meant? A unity removed from all human knowledge, or a unity that reveals itself in the living movement of the divine emanation? From the outset the Kabbalists made every effort to prove that this formula, so all-important in the liturgy, refers to nothing other than to the process in which the ten *sefiroth* are manifested as the living and effective unity of God. This they tried to demonstrate by speculations about the three words *YHWH*, *Elohenu*, *YHWH*, and about the letters of the *ehad*, the Hebrew word for 'one.' According to the manuals of even the oldest schools of the Kabbalah, the mystical meditation, which seeks to penetrate the words in their Kabbalistic sense, passes through the entire world of the *sefiroth*, 'from bottom to top and top to bottom.'[1] Not any single aspect, however important, of this world, but the whole of it, is said to be concentrated in this formula. Three centuries later, Kabbalistic thinking had so increased in complexity that the Sabbatian prophet Heshel Tsoref (1633–1700), silversmith in Vilna, was able to devote more than 3,000 pages to the theosophical and eschatological mysteries of this one verse.

Here we have a mystical view of a sacred formula, which to this day has retained its sacred character for all religious Jews. A very different matter is the transformation of essentially profane acts into ritual. Perhaps eating and sexual intercourse may be considered as only bordering on this category, for in mythical

[1] Isaac the Blind, quoted in Me'ir ibn Sahula, *Be'ur* to the Torah commentary of Nahmanides, Warsaw, 1875, 32d; *Zohar*, I, 233a and II, 216b.

thinking if not in Rabbinical Judaism these acts are closely bound up with the sacral sphere. Thus one will scarcely be surprised at the importance that the Lurianic Kabbalah and in its wake Hasidism (which in this respect was far from being as original as is sometimes claimed) attached to the sacral character of these activities (particularly of eating). A highly characteristic example, it seems to me, is the following remark about the patriarch Enoch, cited also by Martin Buber,[1] though it might be pointed out that the tale did not originate with Polish eighteenth-century Hasidism, but among the German Hasidim of the thirteenth century.[2] The patriarch Enoch, who according to an old tradition was taken from the earth by God and transformed into the angel Metatron, is said to have been a cobbler. At every stitch of his awl he not only joined the upper leather with the sole, but all upper things with all lower things. In other words, he had accompanied his work at every step with meditations which drew the stream of emanation down from the upper to the lower (so transforming profane action into ritual action), until he himself was transfigured from the earthly Enoch into the transcendent Metatron, who had been the object of his meditations. This tendency toward the sacral transformation of the purely profane forms the opposite pole in the Kabbalistic conception of human action as cosmic action. It is interesting to note that a very similar legend is to be found in a Tibetan tantric text, the 'Tales of the Eighty-four Magicians.'[3] Here another such mythical Jacob Boehme, the *guru* Camara (which means shoemaker) receives instruction from a yogi concerning the leather, the awl, the thread, and the shoe considered as the 'self-created fruit.' For twelve years he meditates day and night over his shoemaking, until he attains perfect enlightenment and is borne aloft.

In line with the general principles here set forth, the Kabbalists strove from the very first to *anchor the ritual of Rabbinical*

---

[1] Cf. Martin Buber, *The Origin and Meaning of Hasidism*, New York, 1960, p. 126. Oddly enough, Buber draws from this tale an inference diametrically opposed to that drawn by the sources in which it is quoted.

[2] The source used in the following is demonstrably the oldest. It was handed down to the Kabbalist Isaac of Acco (1300) by his teacher Yehudah ha-Darshan Ashkenazi (*Me'irath 'Enayim*, MS Leiden, Warner 93, Fol. 158a). Moses Cordovero took it over from Isaac of Acco (without indicating his source) and gave it wide currency.

[3] Translated by A. Grünwedel, in *Bässler-Archiv*, V (1916), p. 159.

Judaism in myth by means of a mystical practice. The first attempts applied primarily to the liturgy and everything connected with it. The ecstatic rites, by which the early Jewish *merkabah* mystics of Talmudic times effected the ascent of the soul to God, were replaced, through the medium of *kavvanah*, by the ritual of prayer, which soon revealed dangers and abysses unsuspected by the naïve worshipper. In the Lurianic exercise of *kavvanah*, the conclusion of the morning prayer, in which the devotee originally threw himself on the ground, involved a mortal peril. Once the devotee has risen to the highest height and knows himself to be encompassed in the divine name, which he has 'unified,' he is supposed to leap into the abyss of the 'other side,' in order, like a diver, to bring up sparks of holiness, there held in exile. 'But only a perfect *Zaddik* can accomplish this meditation, for he alone is worthy to descend and make a selection from among the *kelippoth*, the realms of the "other side," even against their will. If anyone else sends his soul down among the *kelippoth*, he may well prove unable to raise up the other fallen souls, or even to save his own, which will remain in those realms.'[1]

The holiday and Sabbath rites were also subjected to such a transformation. The early Kabbalists were especially given to speculation concerning the so-called *hukkim*, obscure rites mentioned in the Torah. Undoubtedly these rites, for which we can find no rational explanation, had their origin in myth, and it was to the mythical sphere that the Kabbalists once again related them. They were no less attracted to the ordinances applicable only to Palestine, which, for that reason, could no longer be carried out concretely (e.g., those concerning the heave-offering or the jubilee-year). The sacrificial cult, to be sure, was expressly looked upon as a concrete, physical rite which, projected outward, represents exactly the same thing as prayer in the medium of the pure word. According to this doctrine, prayer is nothing other than a sacrifice in which a man offers up himself.[2]

[1] H. Vital, *Sha'ar ha-Kavvanoth*, Jerusalem, 1873, 47a. This radical practice was developed from a *Zohar* passage (III, 120b), in which it is said that at this point of supreme ecstasy the *Zaddik* 'surrenders himself to the Tree of Death' and must be prepared to die.

[2] Cf. my article, 'Der Begriff der Kawwana in der alten Kabbala,' *Monatsschrift für Geschichte und Wissenschaft des Judentums*, LXXVIII (1934), pp. 517-18.

The attempts—such as we find in the *Zohar* and several other fourteenth-century works—to prove that the entire ritual of Judaism was originally Kabbalistic in nature were long of only limited influence. The situation changed in the sixteenth century, when the Safed Kabbalah embarked on the triumphal march that was to make it a dominant force in Judaism. I have discussed its principal ideas in the preceding chapter. The implications drawn from these ideas were eminently practical. This new, Messianist Kabbalah strove to reach the masses of the people. But in this it was aided far less by the obscure gnostic explanations of the old rites, which the people practiced regardless of how they interpreted them, than by the propagation of new rites which met with immediate understanding because they expressed those mythical aspects of the Kabbalah that appealed most strongly to the popular mind. The Safed Kabbalists took some of their ideas from the *Zohar*, and rites which its author had only dreamed of and projected back into a remote archaic past came to be practiced by thousands of people. Many of these new rites recommended by the *Zohar*, which attributed them to Simeon ben Yohai and his circle, were practiced for the first time in Safed. Pious associations were founded to propagate such rites, first in Palestine, later in Italy and Poland; often their members concentrated on a single rite, but performed this one rite with the utmost precision and perseverance.

Under the influence chiefly of the Lurianic Kabbalah, works came to light in which the old and the new ideal were combined. The *Shulhan 'Arukh* of Joseph Karo, a codification of Rabbinical ritual containing little reference to Kabbalistic ideas, was succeeded in the seventeenth century by the *Shulhan 'Arukh of Isaac Luria*[1] and by many similar works highly informative for the student of ritual. Not illogically, the *Tree of Life*, in which Hayim Vital had expounded the Lurianic myth, was followed by the *Fruit of the Tree of Life*, in which this same myth was applied to Kabbalistic ritual. But the most significant account of the life of a pious practitioner of Kabbalistic ritual is to be found in the compendious *Hemdath Yamim*, 'The Adornment of Days,' one of the most remarkable and controversial works of Kabbalistic litera-

---

[1] A revised version of an excerpt made by Jacob Zemach in Damascus in 1637 from those parts of Hayim Vital's works that dealt with ritual.

ture.[1] Here the old mingles with the new, and the anonymous author's unmistakable sympathy for the Messianic aspirations of Sabbatai Zevi is fused with the mystical asceticism of the Lurianic school to form an organic whole. Small wonder that this magnificent and in part delightfully written account of Kabbalistic ritual should have made a profound impression among the Jews of the Orient, among whom it was written, and that its influence should have survived until the beginning of the present century. What the *Hemdath Yamim* meant for the *life* of the Jews according to the Kabbalah, another book of the Lurianic Kabbalah undertook to describe with regard to their *death*. This was the *Ma'abar Yabbok*, 'The Crossing of the River Yabbok' (that is, the passage from life to death), by the Italian Kabbalist Aaron Berakhiah Modena (c. 1620). A comparison between works such as these and the accounts of the life and death of the Jews written before the appearance of the Kabbalah shows how effectively and enduringly the new movement changed the face of Judaism in all its aspects, theoretical as well as practical.

I should now like to illustrate this development of specifically Kabbalistic rites by a few striking examples.

IV

Many of the Kabbalistic rites, needless to say, were strictly esoteric in character and could only be performed by groups of initiates. Some of these were very old, going back to the mystics who were the precursors of the thirteenth-century Kabbalists. In the oldest literature we find descriptions of rites bearing the character of special initiations. Largely theurgic in nature, they were not, like the Kabbalistic rites we shall discuss below, accompanied by display that would also be understood by, and appeal to, the unlearned public.

A rite of initiation in the strictest sense is that concerned with the transmission of the name of God from master to pupil. Evidently a much older oral tradition concerning the utterance of such names was still alive in Germany and France in the twelfth

---

[1] This book, printed six times between 1731 and 1763, was written in Jerusalem at the end of the seventeenth or, as new investigations by Tishby suggest, at the beginning of the eighteenth century.

century. Eleazar of Worms (c. 1200) describes this initiation as follows:[1]

The name is transmitted only to the reserved—this word can also be translated as 'the initiate'—who are not prone to anger, who are humble and God-fearing, and carry out the commandments of their Creator. And it is transmitted only over water. Before the master teaches it to his pupil, they must both immerse themselves and bathe in forty measures of flowing water, then put on white garments and fast on the day of instruction. Then both must stand up to their ankles in the water, and the master must say a prayer ending with the words: 'The voice of God is over the waters! Praised be Thou, O Lord, who revealest Thy secret to those who fear Thee, He who knoweth the mysteries.' Then both must turn their eyes toward the water and recite verses from the Psalms, praising God over the waters.

At this time the master evidently transmits the one among the secret names of God that the adept is permitted to hear, whereupon they return together to the synagogue or schoolhouse, where they recite a prayer of thanksgiving over a vessel full of water.

A theurgic ritual that has come down to us from the same school gives instructions for 'putting on the Name'—a purely magical procedure. We possess numerous manuscripts of a 'Book of the Putting on and Fashioning of the Mantle of Righteousness,'[2] in which the ancient Jewish conception that names can be 'put on'[3] is taken very concretely.[4] A piece of pure deerskin parchment is selected. From it are cut a sleeveless garment, modeled after the high priest's ephod, covering shoulders and chest down to the navel and falling along the sides to the loins,

---

[1] The text is unprinted. I have used MS Warner 24 in Leiden, in which it appears as an introduction to Eleazar's *Sefer ha-Shem* (Fol. 237). Bahya ben Asher seems to be referring to it when in 1291, in his Torah commentary (ed. Venice, 1544, 147c) he says on Leviticus 16 : 30: 'It is a tradition of the mystics to transmit the name of God only over water.'

[2] *Sefer ha-Malbush ve-Tikkun me'il ha-Tsedakah*, e.g., MS British Museum, Margoliouth 752, Fol. 92–3.

[3] Cf. the apocryphal *Odes of Solomon*, 39 : 7, which shows Paul's usage in Rom. 13 : 14, and Gal. 3 : 27 to be Jewish; cf. also G. Quispel, *Gnosis als Weltreligion*, Zürich, 1951, pp. 55–6.

[4] A parallel to the baptismal ritual of certain gnostic sects, in which the baptizee 'puts on' the mystical name of Jesus; cf. Quispel in *Eranos-Jahrbuch*, XXI (1952), p. 126.

and a hat connected with the garment. On this magic garment the secret names of God are inscribed. Then the adept must fast for seven days, touch nothing unclean, eat nothing of animal origin, neither eggs nor fish, but only peas, beans and the like. At the end of seven days he must go at night to the water and call out the Name—evidently the name written on the garment—over the water. If he perceives a green form in the air above the water, it is a sign that there is still something unclean in the adept and that the same preparations must be repeated for another seven days, accompanied by alms and acts of charity. 'And pray to your Creator that you will not be shamed once again. And if you see the form in bright red over the water, know that you are inwardly clean and fit to put on the Name. Then go into the water up to your loins and put on the venerable and terrible Name in the water.' This ritual is thought to give the adept irresistible strength. He is advised, while 'putting on the Name,' to invoke the angels associated with it. They appear before him, but all he sees is a moving wisp of smoke. This magic significance of water as the only appropriate medium for such initiation—a conception widespread among non-Jews, e.g., baptism—does not occur in Talmudic literature or in any other Jewish traditions.[1] I doubt whether this initiation in water was practiced after the fourteenth century.

It seems to me that the oldest instructions for making a golem must be regarded as a theurgic ritual, in which the adept becomes aware of wielding a certain creative power. These instructions are contained in the writings of the same Kabbalist to whom we owe the preservation of the above-mentioned rites. The problem of the golem is exceedingly complicated, and I have treated it separately in Chapter 5. In the present context I should merely like to point out that these specifications for the making of a golem are not so much an element of legend as a description of a precise ritual, calculated to induce a very definite *vision*, namely a vision of the creative animation of the golem. It was from this rite as described in authentic sources that the popular mind developed a legend.

Let us now turn to those Kabbalistic rites developed on the basis of older conceptions, which were observed for centuries by large sections of the Jewish people and in some cases are still practiced today. Perhaps it will be best to begin with a few rites

[1] Cf. M. Ninck, *Die Bedeutung des Wassers im Kult und Leben der Alten*, 1921.

based on the sacred marriage, an idea that plays a central role in the *Zohar* and among all subsequent Kabbalists. What took place in this *hieros gamos* (*zivvuga kadisha*, as the *Zohar* calls it) was primarily the union of the two *sefiroth*, *tif'ereth* and *malkhuth*, the male and female aspects of God, the king and his consort, who is nothing other than the *Shekhinah* and the mystical Ecclesia of Israel. The wide range of meaning contained in the symbol of the *Shekhinah* thus enabled the masses of the people to identify this sacred marriage with the marriage between God and Israel, which for the Kabbalists was merely the outward aspect of a process that takes place within the secret inwardness of God himself.

No holiday could more appropriately be interpreted as a sacred marriage feast in this sense than the Feast of Weeks on the fiftieth day after Passover. This festival, commemorating the Revelation on Mount Sinai, which according to the Torah took place fifty days after the exodus from Egypt, is the festival of the covenant between God and Israel. From covenant to marriage was only a short step for the Kabbalists. The *Zohar* relates[1] that Simeon ben Yohai and his associates attached a special mystical significance to the night preceding this festival. For in this night the bride makes ready for marriage with the bridegroom, and it was thought fitting that all those 'belonging to the palace of the bride' (i.e., the mystics and students of the Torah) should keep her company and partake, through a festive ritual, in the preparations for her marriage. It is the mystics who clothe the *Shekhinah* in the proper ornaments, with which on the following morning she will take her place beneath the bridal canopy. The complete bridal ornament, as the Talmudists had inferred from Isaiah 3, consisted of twenty-four items. But according to the *Zohar*, these twenty-four items are the twenty-four books of the Bible. Consequently, anyone who in this night recites selections from all twenty-four books and adds mystical interpretations of their secrets adorns the bride in the right way and rejoices with her all through the night. In this night the adept becomes the 'best man of the *Shekhinah*,' and when next morning the bridegroom asks after those who have so splendidly adorned the bride, she points him out and calls him to her presence.

[1] *Zohar*, I, 8a and III, 98a. There is a very interesting parallel to these passages in the Hebrew writings of Moses de Leon; cf. *Sod Hag Shavuoth*, MS Schocken Kabb. 14, Fol. 87a.

From the beginning of the sixteenth century a set ritual took form on the basis of this passage in the *Zohar*. The whole night before the mystical marriage was spent in vigil, songs were sung, and a specific selection from all the books of the Bible, from all the treatises of the Mishnah, and from the parts of the *Zohar* dealing with the festival, was recited. This rite became exceedingly popular and is widely practiced to this day. Indeed, the conception of a marriage was carried so far that on the following morning, at the lifting up of the Torah in the synagogue and before the reading of the Ten Commandments, certain Kabbalists were in the habit of reading a formal contract, stating the terms of marriage between 'Bridegroom God' and the 'Virgin Israel.'[1] Israel Najara, the poet of the Safed circle, wrote a poetic marriage contract, probably the first of its kind—a lyrical, mystical paraphrase of the marriage document prescribed by Jewish law.[2] This and similar 'documents,' announcing the consummation of the sacred marriage, achieved wide popularity. Here we have a mixture of allegory and the purest symbolism; for whereas the story of the marriage of Israel with God on the day of the Revelation is after all only an allegory, though a profoundly meaningful one, the conception of the *Shekhinah*'s marriage with her Lord is a mystical symbol expressing something that transcends all images.

But it is the ritual of the Sabbath, and especially of the eve of the Sabbath, that underwent the most noteworthy transformation in connection with this idea of the sacred marriage. It would be no exaggeration to call the Sabbath *the* day of the Kabbalah. On the Sabbath the light of the upper world bursts into the profane world in which man lives during the six days of the week. The light of the Sabbath endures into the ensuing week, growing gradually dimmer, to be relieved in the middle of the week by the rising light of the next Sabbath. It is the day on which a special pneuma, the 'Sabbath soul,' enters into the believer, enabling him to participate in the right way in this day which shares more than any other day in the secrets of the pneumatic world. Consequently it was also regarded as a day specially consecrated to the study of the Kabbalah.

The Kabbalists cited three separate passages in the Talmud,

---

[1] I have heard such reading in recent years in Sefardic synagogues in Jerusalem.

[2] Najara, *Zemiroth Yisrael*, Venice, 1599, 114a ff.

which were brought together and presented in a new light by this conception of the Sabbath as a sacred marriage. The first tells us that on the eve of the Sabbath certain rabbis used to wrap themselves in their cloaks and cry out: Come let us go to meet Queen Sabbath. Others cried: Come, O Bride, come, O Bride. The second passage relates that on Friday evening Simeon ben Yohai and his son saw an old man hurrying through the dusk with two bundles of myrtle. They asked him, what are you doing with those bundles? He replied: I will honor the Sabbath with them.[1] The third passage tells us that Torah scholars used to perform marital intercourse precisely on Friday night.[2] These disparate reports are interpreted in the Kabbalistic books of ritual as indications that the Sabbath is indeed a marriage festival. The earthly union between man and woman, referred to in the third passage, was taken as a symbolic reference to the heavenly marriage.[3] These themes were combined with the mystical symbolism identifying Bride, Sabbath, and *Shekhinah*. Still another mystical notion that played a part in the Kabbalistic Sabbath ritual, was the 'field of holy apple trees,'[4] as the *Shekhinah* is frequently called in the *Zohar*. In this metaphor the 'field' is the feminine principle of the cosmos, while the apple trees define the *Shekhinah* as the expression of all the other *sefiroth* or holy orchards, which flow into her and exert their influence through her. During the night before the Sabbath the King is joined with the Sabbath-Bride; the holy field is fertilized, and from their sacred union the souls of the righteous are produced.

On the basis of these conceptions, which are set forth at length in the *Zohar*, the Safed Kabbalists, beginning in the middle of the sixteenth century, developed a solemn and highly impressive ritual which is not mentioned in earlier sources. Its dominant theme is the mystical marriage. A strange twilight atmosphere made possible an almost complete identification of the *Shekhinah*,

[1] Cf. Moritz Zobel, *Der Sabbath*, Berlin, 1935, pp. 59, 64.   [2] Kethuboth 62b.

[3] This symbolism contradicts the thought of Simeon ben Yohai in the early Midrash, who termed the Sabbath and the community of Israel bride and groom and interpreted the sanctification of the Sabbath in the Ten Commandments as a marriage concluded through the 'hallowing' of the Bride-Sabbath. Cf. Zobel, *Der Sabbath*, p. 49.

[4] On the strength of a Talmudic phrase (Ta'anith 29a)—'like an apple orchard'—which in the Talmud however merely characterizes a particularly pleasant odor.

not only with the Queen of the Sabbath, but also with every Jewish housewife who celebrates the Sabbath. This is what gave this ritual its enormous popularity. To this day the Sabbath ritual is pervaded by memories of the old Kabbalistic rite, and certain of its features have been preserved intact.

I shall try to describe this ritual in its original and meaningful form.[1] On Friday afternoon, some time before the onset of the Sabbath, the Kabbalists of Safed and Jerusalem, usually clad in white—in any case neither in black nor red, which would have evoked the powers of stern judgment and limitation—went out of the city into an open field, which the advent of the *Shekhinah* transformed into the 'holy apple orchard.' They 'went to meet the Bride.' In the course of the procession the people sang special hymns to the Bride and psalms of joyful anticipation (such as Psalm 29 or Psalms 95–9). The most famous of these hymns was composed by Solomon Alkabez, a member of Moses Cordovero's group in Safed. It begins:

> Go, my beloved, to meet the Bride,
> Let us receive the face of the Sabbath . . .

In this hymn, which is still sung in the synagogue, mystical symbolism is explicitly combined with Messianic hopes for the redemption of the *Shekhinah* from exile. When the actual procession into the fields was dropped, the congregation 'met the Bride' in the court of the synagogue, and when this observance in turn fell into disuse, it became customary, as it is to this day, to turn westward at the last verse of the hymn and bow to the approaching Bride. It is recorded that Luria, standing on a hill near Safed, beheld in a vision the throngs of Sabbath-souls coming with the Sabbath-Bride. A number of our sources tell us that the Sabbath Psalms were sung with closed eyes, for as the Kabbalists explained, the *Shekhinah* is designated in the *Zohar* as 'the beautiful virgin who has no eyes,' that is to say, who has lost her eyes from weeping in exile.[2] On Friday afternoon the Song

[1] In the following I use chiefly the descriptions of the ritual given in the *Shulhan 'Arukh of Isaac Luria* and in *Hemdath Yamim*, Vol. I. This is not the place for analyses of the development of the different parts of the ritual, such as are sadly lacking in the literature of Jewish studies.

[2] In *Zohar*, II, 95a, this virgin is the Torah—cf. above Chapter II, p. 55— and the literal meaning of the metaphor applied to a virgin 'upon whom no eyes are directed' (whom no one sees).

of Songs, traditionally identified with the indissoluble bond between 'the Holy One, blessed be He, and the Ecclesia of Israel,' but here taken also as an epithalamion for the *Shekhinah*, was also intoned. Only after the meeting-of-the-Bride were the traditional Sabbath prayers spoken.

After the prayer the mystical ritual was resumed at home. According to Isaac Luria, it was highly commendable and 'rich in mystical significance' to kiss one's mother's hands on entering the house. Then the family marched solemnly around the table, from which they took in silence the two bundles of myrtle for the Bride and Bridegroom, and sang a greeting to the angels of the Sabbath, that is, the two angels who according to the Talmud[1] accompany each man to his home at the onset of the Sabbath. The four stanzas of the hymn to the angels, 'Peace be with you, you angels of peace,' are followed by recitation of the thirty-first chapter of Proverbs, which seems to sing the praises of the noble housewife and her activities, but which the Kabbalists interpreted line by line as a hymn to the *Shekhinah*. Strange to say, it was through the mystical reinterpretation of the Kabbalists that this praise of the Jewish housewife found its way into the Sabbath ritual. This 'hymn to the matron' is to be sung in a melodious voice by the seated company. Then, before the meal, as the *Zohar* prescribes, the master of the house 'explicitly utters the mystery of the meal,' that is, he introduces the sacred action in words which describes its secret meaning and at the same time conjure the *Shekhinah* to partake of the meal with her Bridegroom ('Small-faced,' or better 'Impatient') and the 'Holy Old One.' This solemn Aramaic invocation runs:

> Prepare the meal of perfect faith
> To rejoice the heart of the holy King,
> Prepare the meal of the King.
> This is the meal of the field of holy apples,
> And the Impatient and the Holy Old One—
> Behold, they come to partake of the meal with her.

What happens in this sacred action is described in Isaac Luria's great hymn, one of the few authentic works that have come down to us from the hand of this greatest of the Safed Kabbalists. Luria wrote hymns of this kind for each of the Sabbath meals. In the

[1] Shabbath 119a.

solemn drapery of their Zoharic Aramaic, they suggest the grandiloquent gesture of a magician, conjuring up a marvellous pageant for all to see. They read like the hymns of a mystery religion. Here I should like to quote the hymn for the Friday evening meal.

I sing in hymns
to enter the gates,
of the field of apples
of holy ones.

A new table
we lay for her,
a beautiful candelabrum
sheds its light upon us.

Between right and left
the Bride approaches
in holy jewels
and festive garments.

Her husband embraces her
in her foundation,[1]
gives her fulfilment,
squeezes out his strength.

Torment and cries
are past.
Now there are new faces
and souls and spirits.

He gives her joy
in twofold measure.
Lights shine
and streams of blessing.

Bridesmen, go forth
and prepare the bride,
victuals of many kinds
and all manner of fish.[2]

[1] The ninth *sefirah, yesod*, 'the foundation,' is correlated with the male and female sex organs.

[2] The fish is a symbol of fertility. The widespread custom of eating fish on Friday is connected with the custom of consummating marriages on Friday night.

To beget souls
and new spirits
on the thirty-two paths
and three branches.[1]

She has seventy crowns
but above her the King,
that all may be crowned
in the Holy of Holies.

All worlds are formed
and sealed within her,
but all shine forth
from the 'Old of Days.'

To southward I set
the mystical candelabrum,
I make room in the north
for the table with the loaves.

With wine in beakers
and boughs of myrtle
to fortify the Betrothed,
for they are feeble.

We plait them wreaths
of precious words
for the coronation of the seventy
in fifty gates.

Let the *Shekhinah* be surrounded
by six Sabbath loaves
connected on every side
with the Heavenly Sanctuary.

Weakened and cast out
the impure powers,
the menacing demons
are now in fetters.

---

[1] Souls issue from 'Wisdom' by 32 paths. The two branches are grace, judgment, and appeasing love, the three 'pillars' of the world of the *sefiroth*, from which come the souls. The seventy crowns of the bride in the following line are mentioned in *Zohar*, II, 205a.

In the eyes of the Kabbalists, this hymn was in a class apart. Unlike other table songs for the eve of the Sabbath, which could be sung or not, as one pleased, it was an indispensable part of the ritual. In Luria's hymn new meaning was not injected into an old prayer by means of mystical exegesis or *kavvanah*; rather, an esoteric conception creates its own liturgical language and form. The culmination of the hymn, the chaining of the demons on the Sabbath, when they must flee 'into the maw of the great abyss,' recurs in Luria's hymns for the other two meals. The last song, sung at the dusk that ends the Sabbath day, strongly emphasizes this exorcism of the 'insolent dogs,' the powers of the other side —it is not a mere description of an exorcism, it *is* an exorcism:

> The insolent dogs must remain outside and cannot come in,
> I summon the 'Old of Days' at evening until they are dispersed,
> Until his will destroys the 'shells.'
> He hurls them back into their abysses, they must hide deep in their
>   caverns.
> And all this now, in the evening, at the festival of *ze'ir anpin*.[1]

I shall not go into all the other Sabbath rites of the Kabbalists. But there is still one point I should like to bring up in this connection. Just as the 'reception of the Bride' marks a beginning of the holy day even before the onset of the actual Sabbath, so some Kabbalists attached great importance to a fourth Sabbath meal (mentioned very briefly in the Talmud as the custom of a single individual) which takes place after the *havdalah*, the prayer of division between Sabbath and weekday, and extends far into the night. This meal (at which among some of the Kabbalists nothing was eaten) escorts the Bride out of our domain, just as the ritual described above led her into it. Some Kabbalists attached the utmost importance to this mythical meal to 'accompany the Queen.' Whereas the three official Sabbath meals were associated with the patriarchs, Abraham, Isaac, and Jacob, this one was identified with David, the Lord's anointed, the Messiah. But according to the *Zohar*, these forefathers are the 'feet of the divine throne,' or *merkabah*. Small wonder that Nathan of Gaza, the prophet and spokesman of the Kabbalistic messiah. Sabbatai

---

[1] *Ze'ir anpin* means in the *Zohar* the 'Impatient One' in contrast to the 'Patient One' as an aspect of God. In Luria it is taken literally as 'he with the little face.' He is the Godhead in its endless development and growth, as Lord of the *Shekhinah*.

Zevi, prolonged this fourth meal until midnight. 'He used to say: This is the meal of the King Messiah, and made a great principle of it.'[1]

V

Kabbalistic rites of a very different type are those in which the exile of the *Shekhinah* is dramatized and lamented. The markedly ascetic note and apocalyptic mood which entered into Kabbalism after the expulsion of the Jews from Spain were reflected in such rituals. The historical experience of the Jewish people merged indistinguishably with the mystical vision of a world in which the holy was locked in desperate struggle with the satanic. Everywhere and at every hour the simple and yet so infinitely profound fact of exile provided ground enough for lamentation, atonement, and asceticism. From this living experience there sprang a great wealth of rites. In the following I shall try to illustrate, by two striking examples, the emergence of these new rites that gave concrete expression to the myth of exile. Both were widely performed for centuries, and not a few learned Talmudists complained that simple believers, unversed in Rabbinical lore, devoted greater fervor and care to the performance of such rites that appealed directly to their feeling, than to fulfilling the commandments of the Torah.

The first of these rites is the midnight lamentation, *tikkun hatsoth*. A Talmudist of the third century said: 'The night is divided into three watches, and in each watch sits the Holy One, blessed be He, and roars like a lion: Woe unto me who have destroyed my house and burned my temple and sent my children into exile among the Gentiles.'[2] Strange to say, almost a thousand years passed before this passage came to be reflected in ritual. Not until the eleventh century did Hai Gaon, head of a Talmudic academy in Babylonia, declare that pious men, vying with God, lament the destruction of the Temple in all three night watches.[3]

---

[1] *'Inyane Shabbetai Zevi*, ed. A. Freimann, 1913, p. 94. It is in this light that we must understand the prescriptions of the *Hemdath Yamim* and the significance of this meal in the Hasidic movement.

[2] Berakhoth 3a.

[3] Hai's statement may be related to a similar recommendation in the *Seder Eliyahu Rabbah*, ed. Friedmann, p. 96. But it should also be borne in mind that meanwhile the midnight vigil, introduced in the fifth century, had become customary among Christian monks.

His father, Sherira Gaon, calls it a pious usage to rise at midnight and sing hymns and songs.[1] Strange to say, he does not speak of lamentation. It was among the Kabbalists in Gerona, roughly in the year 1260 (if, as I presume, the text to which we owe our information[2] originated in Spain at this time), that a rite combining these two themes first came into existence. 'The Hasidim of the highest rank rise at night to sing hymns at every vigil; amid prayer and supplication they fling themselves on the ground, lie sobbing in the dust, shed floods of tears, acknowledge their transgression, and confess their sins.'

Related to very different mythologems, the midnight vigil makes its appearance in numerous passages of the *Zohar*, and is described as a Kabbalistic exercise. At midnight God enters Paradise to rejoice with the righteous. All the trees in Paradise burst into hymns. A wind rises from the north, a spark flies from the power of the north, the fire in God, which is the fire of the power of judgment, and strikes the Archangel Gabriel (who himself sprang from this power in God) under his wings.[3] His cry awakens all the cocks at midnight. In other versions a north wind blowing from Paradise carries the spark to earth, where it strikes a cock directly under his wings, so causing cocks to crow at midnight.[4] Then it is time for the pious to arise, as King David did in his time, and study the Torah until dawn, or, according to others,[5] intone songs to the *Shekhinah*. For from midnight on the power of

---

[1] Cf. the references in A. Freimann's edition of the *Responsa* of Maimonides, No. XXV, p. 21.

[2] The anonymous *Sefer ha-Yashar*, a book of moral exhortation, which has been attributed to various authorities. The passage occurs in Chapter III, ed. Cracow, 1586, 8a.

[3] *Midrash ha-Ne'elam* to Ruth, in *Zohar Hadash*, Warsaw, 1884, 87d, and in *Zohar*, III, 23a, 171b, etc. Here there is a play on the etymological connection between Gabriel ('power of God'), *gever* ('cock'), and *gevurah* ('power', in the *Zohar* always the power of stern judgment). In III, 172a, it is said that the Angel Gabriel notes the deeds of men during the day and reads them at midnight after his heavenly 'cock's crow.' If he were not paralyzed by his misshapen toes—a motif I have never encountered elsewhere—he 'would burn the world with his flame in this hour.'

[4] I, 10b, 77b; III, 22b. Dr. Zwi Werblowsky has informed me that Abeghian (*Armenischer Volksglaube*, Leipzig, 1898, p. 38) mentions this same conception of a heavenly cock crow which, before the earthly cock crow, awakens the choirs of angels to the praise of God. Indeed a remarkable parallel worthy of further investigation.

[5] III, 302a (= *Zohar Hadash*, 53b).

stern judgment, which governs the world in the evening, is broken, and this in the opinion of the Kabbalists explains why the spirits and demons are powerless after the first cock crow.[1]

In the *Zohar* these themes are already brought into relation with the exile of the *Shekhinah*.[2] At midnight God remembers 'the hind that lies in the dust'[3] and sheds two tears 'which burn more than all the fire in the world' and fall into the great sea.[4] At this hour He breaks out in lamentations which shake all 390 worlds. That in why in the middle watch of the night the angels sing hymns of praise for only two hours and then fall silent. For these angels are named *Avele Zion*, those who lament for Zion[5]—a highly remarkable transference of the name of a group of Jewish ascetics in the early Middle Ages to a class of angels. According to certain passages, all this seems to happen before the north wind rises in Paradise. At midnight the *Shekhinah*, who is in exile, sings songs and hymns to her spouse,[6] and according to others a dialogue or even a *hieros gamos* is enacted between God and the *Shekhinah*.[7]

From all these rich conceptions, however, the *Zohar* does not develop a true rite of lamentation. It demands only that the mystics should keep vigil and join the throng of 'companions of the *Shekhinah*' through study and meditation on the mysteries of the Torah. There is still no mention of a ritual of lamentation over the exile. And though among the generations following the *Zohar* (1285–90) we sometimes hear of pious vigils in remembrance of the destruction of the Temple,[8] we still learn nothing of a set ritual relating specifically to the midnight hour.

---

[1] Menahem Recanati (c. 1300) already gave this correct interpretation of this passage (*Zohar*, III, 284a) in his Torah commentary (Venice, 1545, 179b).

[2] Especially in the two important passages *Zohar Hadash* to Ruth, 87d, and *Zohar*, II, 195b–196b.

[3] I, 4a, Cf. also in *Zohar Hadash*, 47d.

[4] III, 172b. The motif of the two tears comes from a Talmud passage, Berakhoth 59a.

[5] All this according to *Zohar*, II, 195b.   [6] *Zohar*, III, 284a.

[7] In *Midrash ha-Ne'elam* to Ruth, *Zohar Hadash*, 87d (the dialogue) and in the *Zohar* itself, II, 205a (the union).

[8] In Solomon ben Adreth in Barcelona (c. 1300) and in Asher ben Yehiel in Toledo (c. 1320). A reference in F. Baer, *Die Juden im christlichen Spanien*, I, Berlin, 1929, p. 474, has been mistakenly interpreted by some writers to mean that an organization for the performance of this ritual was founded in Saragossa in 1378.

In Safed the picture changes. The memory of a half-forgotten observance combined with the Zoharic conceptions of midnight and of the exiled *Shekhinah* to create a new rite symbolizing the experience of the Jews of that generation. The strange part of it is that these 'rites of exile' should have arisen in Palestine and not in the countries of the Diaspora. The Kabbalists who in the middle of the sixteenth century came to Safed from all over the world, in the intention of founding a 'community of holy men,' carried with them this acute consciousness of exile and gave it perfect ritual expression in the very place where they expected the process of Messianic redemption to begin.

Concerning Abraham Halevi Berukhim, one of the most active members of this group, we read that 'always at the midnight hour he ran through the streets of Safed, weeping and crying out: Arise in God's name, for the *Shekhinah* is in exile, the house of our sanctuary is burned, and Israel is in great distress. He wailed outside the windows of the learned and did not desist until he saw that they had arisen from their sleep.'[1] It might be added that this mystic, who at the wailing wall in Jerusalem beheld a vision of the *Shekhinah*, clad in black and weeping and lamenting, was looked upon by his companions in Safed as an incarnation of the Prophet Jeremiah, or at least as a spark from his soul. In Isaac Luria's group this observance was given set forms.[2] The Lurianic midnight rite has two parts, the 'rite for Rachel' and the 'rite for Leah.' For according to this Kabbalah, Rachel and Leah are two aspects of the *Shekhinah*, the one exiled from God and lamenting, the other in her perpetually repeated reunion with her Lord. Consequently the *tikkun Rachel*, or 'rite for Rachel,' was the true rite of lamentation. In observing it, men 'participate in the suffering of the *Shekhinah*' and bewail not their own afflictions, but the one affliction that really counts in the world, namely, the exile of the *Shekhinah*.

The mystic, then, should rise and dress at midnight; he should go to the door and stand near the doorpost, remove his shoes and

[1] Letters from Safed, ed. S. Assaf, *Kobetz 'al Yad*, III (Jerusalem, 1940), p. 122.

[2] The classical form of this rite, which later became widespread in Europe, is that described in Nathan Hannover's often reprinted *Sha'are Zion*, Prague, 1662. Cf. also Jacob Zemach, *Nagid u-Metsavveh* (1712), 5b (the following quotations are from both sources), and Vital's *Pri 'Ets Hayyim*, XVII.

veil his head. Weeping, he should then take ashes from the hearth and lay them on his forehead, on the spot where in the morning the *tefillin*, the phylacteries, are applied. Then he should bow his head and rub his eyes in the dust on the ground, just as the *Shekhinah* herself, the 'Beautiful One without eyes,' lies in the dust. Then he recites a set liturgy composed of Psalm 137: '(By the rivers of Babylon, there we sat down, yea, we wept'), Psalm 79 ('O God, the heathen are come into thine inheritance; thy holy temple have they defiled'), the last chapter of Lamentations, and certain special laments written in Safed and Jerusalem. Five of these songs became an almost invariable feature of this ritual.

Then the 'rite for Leah' is performed; here the emphasis is no longer on exile but on the promise of redemption. Messianic Psalms are recited and a long hymn, in the form of a dialogue between God and the mystical Community of Israel, is sung. In this hymn, written by Hayim Kohen of Aleppo, a student of Vital, the *Shekhinah* complains about her exile, and God paints the prospect of redemption in glowing colors. To each stanza of promise, the *Shekhinah* replies with a stanza of lamentation. Even the unlearned, the Kabbalists held, should perform this rite, for the 'time from midnight to morning is a time of grace, and a ray of this grace falls upon him even in the daytime.' After these two parts of the ritual a third was recommended, the 'rite for the soul,' *tikkun ha-nefesh*, in which the adept concentrated on the idea of uniting God and the *Shekhinah* with every single organ of his body, 'so that thy body may become a chariot for the *Shekhinah*.'

After the great Messianic outbursts of 1665–6 this rite became a subject of dispute between the Sabbatians and their adversaries. The Sabbatians declared, though with varying degrees of radicalism, that the rite for Rachel had become obsolete now that the *Shekhinah* was on her way home from exile. To mourn for her now was like mourning on the Sabbath day.[1] Accordingly they performed only the second part of the ritual, the rite for Leah, expressive of Messianic hopes. Certain pious men, who had grave reservations about the Sabbatian movement and could not accept the omission of the lament, performed this rite, but remained standing or seated in their customary place inside the room, instead of sitting by the door. Orthodox Kabbalists continued to insist on careful observance of the ritual of lamentation.

[1] Cf. my remarks on the subject in *Zion*, XIV (1949), pp. 50, 59–60.

Our second example of this ritual dramatizing the exile of the *Shekhinah* is the ritual of *yom kippur katan*, or Lesser Day of Atonement, as the Kabbalists called the day before the new moon, that was to be devoted to fasting and repentance. This special day came to be widely celebrated; the name *yom kippur katan* was first used in Safed.[1] According to an old and deep-rooted tradition, the actual day of the new moon, when the moon is reborn, is a day of rejoicing on which fasting is expressly prohibited; otherwise the Kabbalists would doubtless have chosen the new moon itself as a day of fasting and atonement, devoted to recollection of the cosmic event of exile. For the main reasons for the choice of this day had to do with the new moon. But how was the joy that originally accompanied the reappearance of the moon transformed into grief over its gradual waning? In the ritual blessing for the new moon, the Talmudists (Sanhedrin 42a) still found an express parallel between the renewal of the moon and Messianic redemption: 'He speaks to the moon that it be renewed, a wondrous crown for those who were borne by me from the belly and *will one day like it grow young again* and glorify their maker.' But the shift of accent to the lessening of the moon, its changing phases, goes back to other conceptions. The Torah prescribes for the day of the new moon a special sin offering of a he-goat—but in this prescription it is not clear for what sin the offering is made. In a Talmudic explanation[2] we learn that God reduced the moon, whose light was originally equal to that of the sun. In answer to the moon's repeated complaints, God said: Offer up an atonement for Me, because I reduced the size of the moon.

This 'lessening of the moon' was interpreted by the Kabbalists as a symbol of the *Shekhinah*'s exile. The *Shekhinah* itself is the 'holy moon,' which has fallen from its high rank, been robbed of its light and sent into cosmic exile. Since then, exactly like the moon itself, it has shone only with reflected light. With the

---

[1] *Der kleine Versöhnungstag*, Vienna, 1911, by Armin Abeles, whose valuable remarks are in some need of correction. One of the oldest testimonies from Safed is that of Solomon Alkabez in *Menoth ha-Levi*, Venice, 1585, 9a: 'Now that the Temple is destroyed, there are pious men who in place of the sin offering on the day of the new moon, fast the preceding day.' This was probably written about 1750, but the custom seems to have been known in Germany by the middle of the fifteenth century; cf. *Leket Yosher*, by Joseph ben Moses, ed. Freimann, Berlin, 1903, I, pp. 47 and 116.

[2] Hullin 60b.

Talmudic explanation, which relates only to the designation of the moon as the 'lesser light' in the first chapter of Genesis, the Kabbalists connected their knowledge of the changing phases of the moon, which seemed to indicate that until the Messianic redemption the moon (and the *Shekhinah* as well) would time and time again sink back into utter lightlessness and want. Only in redemption would the moon be restored to its original state, and in support of this belief a verse from Isaiah (30 : 26) was cited. Meanwhile, no cosmic event seemed to the Kabbalists to be more closely connected with the exile of all things, with the imperfection and the taint inherent in all being, than this periodic lessening of the moon.

Here, then, we find a striking convergence of two themes which were to dominate the Kabbalah from this time on: the catastrophe of exile, and the regeneration of the light after its total disappearance, taken as a promise that all things would one day be rectified in redemption. But since, as we have seen, the day of the new moon could not very well be shorn of its festive character, Solomon Alkabez, Moses Cordovero, and their group, following an older pious custom, introduced the day preceding the new moon as a fast day, devoted principally to meditation on the great themes of exile and redemption. It is interesting to note that, contrary to many conjectures that have been voiced on the subject, no notice whatever is taken of this day in the oldest authentic texts of the Lurianic Kabbalah.[1] But Abraham Galante, a disciple of Cordovero, tells us that it was (c. 1570) the generalized custom in Safed for men, women, and school children to fast on this day and to spend the whole day in penitential prayer, confession of sins, and flagellation.[2] The name 'Lesser Day of Atonement' is attested for the first time in this circle.[3] We cannot be sure whether they chose this name because of the atonement due on *yom kippur katan* for the sins committed each month, or

[1] Nothing is said of this in the authentic writings of Vital, of his son Samuel Vital, or of Jacob Zemach.

[2] The texts in S. Schechter, *Studies in Judaism*, II, pp. 294 and 300. Cf. also the sources mentioned in Note 1, p. 151.

[3] It is first mentioned in Elijah de Vidas, friend of Cordovero, who wrote in Safed in 1575. Cf. his *Reshith Hokhmah*, Gate of Holiness, IV. Hizkiya de Silva maintains, *Pri Hadash* to the *Orah Hayyim* No. 417 (which, however, was written more than a hundred years later), that the name had been introduced by Cordovero himself.

because they drew a parallel between the scapegoat, sent out into the wilderness as a sin offering on *yom kippur*, and the he-goat which, as we have seen, was also sacrificed on the day of the new moon. The first explanation seems the more likely.[1]

The highly diversified liturgies that were composed for this day all reflect a convergence of the two themes we have discussed. 'I am the moon and thou art my sun'—these words from a prayer[2] state the motif that was varied over and over. And since the total disappearance of the moon symbolizes the ultimate darkness and horror of exile, certain Kabbalists believed this to be the ideal moment for 'meditation on the Messianic secret.'[3] The extremely detailed ritual for this day, developed in the *Hemdath Yamim*, is one of the most characteristic documents of the Sabbatian Kabbalah, whose strict asceticism derived from an awareness that the Messiah's reign had already begun, but that he was engaged in a tragic mission to the impurest depths of exile. The hope of redemption, then, was to be confirmed precisely at its most difficult and paradoxical turning point, namely, the exile of the redeemer himself.[4]

VI

The two categories of rite that I have just been discussing are related in substance. For the 'sacred marriage' is always a ceremony in which redemption is anticipated, in which the exile of the *Shekhinah* is at least momentarily annulled or attenuated. It is a very different matter with the innumerable rites calculated to resist the powers of the 'other side,' to exorcise the demons and destructive forces. Here magical conceptions and rites that had existed long before the Kabbalah were simply revived in new forms (and often enough even the forms were not new).

[1] This is the explanation given by Isaiah Horowitz in *Shne Luhoth ha-Berith*, 1648, 120b: Thus the days of the past month are 'purified' as they enter the new moon. The whole long passage, which also speaks of the 'Lesser Day of Atonement,' would seem by its style to have been taken from a manuscript of Cordovero.

[2] In Joseph Fiametta's *'Or Boker*, Venice, 1741, 5a.

[3] *Hemdath Yamim* on the day of the new moon, Vol. II, ed. Venice, 1763, 12a.

[4] On the Sabbatian character of this ritual, cf. my article in the quarterly *Behinnoth*, VIII (Jerusalem, 1955), pp. 15–16.

The custom I shall now describe is rather extreme in character, but I believe that it illustrates the process by which such 'antidemonic' rites—which later gained almost universal acceptance—developed among the Kabbalists. Until quite recently (and occasionally to this day) Jewish burials in Jerusalem were often marked by a strange happening. Before the body was lowered into the grave, ten men danced round it in a circle, reciting a Psalm which in the Jewish tradition has generally been regarded as a defense against demons (Ps. 91), or another prayer. Then a stone was laid on the bier and the following verse (Gen. 25 : 6) recited: 'But unto the sons of the concubines, which Abraham had, Abraham gave gifts, and sent them away.' This strange dance of death was repeated seven times. The rite, which in modern times has been unintelligible to most of the participants, has to do with Kabbalistic conceptions about sexual life and the sanctity of the human seed. Here we have an entire myth, the object of which is to mark off the act of generation from other sexual practices, which were interpreted as demonic in nature, and especially from onanism.

According to Talmudic tradition, demons are spirits made in the Friday evening twilight, who, because the Sabbath has intervened, have received no bodies. From this later authorities drew the inference (which is perhaps implicit in the Talmudic sources) that the demons have been looking for bodies ever since, and that this is why they attach themselves to men. This entered into combination with another idea. After the murder of Abel by his brother, Adam decided to have no further dealings with his wife. Thereupon female demons, *succubi*, came to him and conceived by him; from this union, in which Adam's generative power was misused and misdirected, stem a variety of demons, who are called *nig'e bne Adam*, 'Spirits of harm that come from man.'[1] The Kabbalists took up these old conceptions of demonic generation in pollution or other, chiefly onanistic, practices. They are systematized in the *Zohar*, which develops the myth that Lilith, queen of the demons, or the demons of her retinue, do their best to provoke men to sexual acts without benefit of a woman, their aim being to make themselves bodies from the lost seed. As far as I know, it has not yet been established whether Jews or Christians first developed these detailed theories concerning

[1] Cf. *Midrash Tanhuma*, ed. S. Buber, I, pp. 12 and 20, and *Zohar*, II, 231b.

succubi and *incubi*. Today neither seem very eager to claim authority for them. They were known among the Jews of the sixth century, as we learn from certain Aramaic exorcisms. In any event, they were well developed by the time the *Zohar* took them up at the end of the thirteenth century, and they play a considerable part in the Zoharic picture of man's relations with the 'other side.' To the Kabbalists, the union between man and woman, within its holy limits, was a venerable mystery, as one may judge from the fact that the most classical and widely circulated Kabbalistic definition of mystical meditation is to be found in a treatise about the meaning of sexual union in marriage.[1] Abuse of a man's generative powers was held to be a destructive act, through which not the holy, but the 'other side,' obtains progeny. An extreme cult of purity led to the view that every act of impurity, whether conscious or unconscious, engenders demons.

Abraham Sabba,[2] an early sixteenth-century Kabbalist who had come to Morocco from Spain, was first to establish a strange connection between this conception and a man's death. All the illegitimate children that a man has begotten with demons in the course of his life appear after his death to take part in the mourning for him and in his funeral.

For all those spirits that have built their bodies from a drop of his seed regard him as their father. And so, especially on the day of his burial, he must suffer punishment; for while he is being carried to the grave, they swarm around him like bees, crying: 'You are our father,' and they complain and lament behind his bier, because they have lost their home and are now being tormented along with the other demons which hover [bodiless] in the air.[3]

According to others, the demons claim their inheritance on this occasion along with the other sons of the deceased and try to harm the legitimate children. Those who dance seven times round the dead man do so in order to form a sacral circle, which will prevent these unlawful children from approaching the deceased,

---

[1] In Joseph Gikatila's *'Iggereth ha-Kodesh* (c. 1300), later attributed to Moses Nahmanides.

[2] Abraham Sabba, *Tseror ha-Mor*, Venice, 1576, 5a.

[3] *Hemdath Yamim*, 1763, II, 98b, and Bezalel ben Shelomo of Kobryn, *Korban Shabbath*, Dyhernfurth, 1691, 18c. A similar explanation already occurs in Hayim Vital, e.g., in *Sha'ar ha-Kavvanoth*, Jerusalem, 1873, Fol. 56b–c.

sullying his corpse, or doing other harm. Hence the verse from Genesis about the 'sons of the [demonic] concubines,' whom Abraham sent away lest they harm Isaac, his legitimate son. A similar rite, in which the bier is set down in the ground seven times on the way to the cemetery,[1] has the same purpose. Most important of all, the Kabbalists strictly forbade the children, and especially the sons, of the deceased from escorting him to his last resting place. In his lifetime, it was held, a pious man should expressly forbid 'all his children' to follow him to his grave; by so doing, he will keep his illegitimate demonic offspring away and, in case any of them should nonetheless get through to his grave, prevent them from endangering his true children, begotten in purity.

Characteristic in this connection is the following report of Johann Jakob Schudt, director of the Frankfort Gymnasium (high school) about the Jews of that city. In 1717 he wrote:[2]

They firmly believe that if a man's seed escapes him, it gives rise, with the help of *mahlath* [a female demon] and Lilith, to evil spirits, which however die when the time comes. When a man dies and his children begin to weep and lament, these *shedim*, or evil spirits, come too, wishing, along with the other children, to have their part in the deceased as their father; they tug and pluck at him, so that he feels the pain, and God himself, when He sees this noxious offspring by the corpse, is reminded of the dead man's sins. It is known to me that Jews in their lifetime sternly ordered their children not to make the slightest plaint or weep until the dead body in the cemetery had been purified by washing, cleansing, and the cutting of the finger- and toenails, because these unclean spirits are thought to have no further part in the body, once it is cleansed.

Another noteworthy rite is connected with similar conceptions. Especially in a leap year, the Kabbalists fasted on Monday and Thursday of certain weeks in the wintertime, in order to 'correct,' by special prayers and acts of penance, the taint which a man inflicts on his true form by nocturnal pollution and onanism. This rite is called *tikkun shovavim*. The first letters of the sections of Torah read in the synagogue on the corresponding

---

[1] *Ma'abar Yabbok*, Mantua, 1623, 66–7 of the second section (Chapters 29–30).

[2] Schudt, *Jüdische Merckwürdigkeiten*, IV, Appendix, p. 43.

Sabbaths form the word *shovavim*, the 'ill-bred,' obviously referring to the 'ill-bred' sons of man,[1] whose return to the sphere of
the holy this rite is thought to favor. We have evidence that this
rite was practiced in Austria in the fifteenth century, though the
sexual aspect is not explicitly mentioned.[2] The Kabbalists took it
over and elaborated on it.[3]

But it is not only in unlawful sexual practices that Lilith takes
a hand. Even legitimate union between man and wife is en-
dangered by her, for here too she tries to infringe on the domain
of Eve. Accordingly, we find widespread observance of a rite
recommended by the *Zohar*, the purpose of which was to keep
Lilith away from the marriage bed:

'In the hour when the husband enters into union with his wife,
he should turn his mind to the holiness of his Lord and say:

> Veiled in velvet—are you here?
> Loosened, loosened [be your spell]!
> Go not in and go not out!
> Let there be none of you and nothing of your part!
> Turn back, turn back, the ocean rages,
> Its waves are calling you.[4]
> But I cleave to the holy part,
> I am wrapped in the sanctity of the King.

'Then for a time he should wrap his head and his wife's head
in cloths, and afterwards sprinkle his bed with fresh water.'[5]

Understandably enough, rites of this kind occur chiefly in
connection with the sexual sphere. They embody the darker
aspects of Kabbalistic ritual, reflecting man's fears and other
emotional states. Unmistakably mythical in origin, they must be
regarded as scarcely inferior in importance and in influence to
those other rites in which the Kabbalists turned their face not
toward the 'other side,' but toward the holy and its realization on
earth.

[1] Luria already employed this name for these demonic creatures of desire;
cf. *Sha'ar Ruah ha-Kodesh*, 1912, 23a.

[2] In *Sefer Leket Yosher*, I, p. 116.

[3] Isaiah Horowitz, *Shne Luhoth ha-Berith*, 1648, 306b, Mordecai Yaffe,
Lebush ha-'Orah, No. 685. A complete ritual of this kind is developed in
Moses Zakuto, *Tikkun Shovavim*, Venice, 1716, and similar works, widely
read at the time.

[4] Lilith's actual dwelling place is at the bottom of the sea.

[5] *Zohar*, III, 19a.

5. The Idea of the Golem

SOME forty years ago Gustav Meyrink published his fantastic novel, *The Golem*.[1] By taking up a figure of Kabbalistic legend and transforming it in a very peculiar way, Meyrink tried to draw a kind of symbolic picture of the way to redemption. Such literary adaptations and transformations of the golem legend have been frequent, particularly in the Jewish and German literature of the nineteenth century, since Jakob Grimm, Achim von Arnim, and E. Th. Hoffmann. They bear witness to the special fascination exerted by this figure, in which so many authors found a symbol of the struggles and conflicts that were nearest their hearts.[2] Meyrink's work, however, far outdoes the rest. In it everything is fantastic to the point of the grotesque. Behind the façade of an exotic and futuristic Prague ghetto Indian rather than Jewish ideas of redemption are expounded. The alleged Kabbalah that pervades the book suffers from an overdose of Madame Blavatsky's turbid theosophy. Still, despite all this muddle and confusion, Meyrink's *Golem* has an inimitable atmosphere, compounded of unverifiable depth, a rare gift for mystical charlatanism, and an overpowering urge to *épater le bourgeois*. In Meyrink's interpretation, the golem is a kind of Wandering Jew, who every thirty-three years—it would seem to be no accident that this was the age of Jesus when he was crucified—appears at the window of an inaccessible room in the Prague ghetto. This golem

---

[1] Trans. Madge Pemberton, London, 1928.

[2] Cf. Beate Rosenfeld, who has investigated these interpretations in *Die Golemsage und ihre Verwertung in der deutschen Literatur*, Breslau, 1934.

is in part the materialized, but still very spooky, collective soul of the ghetto, and in part the double of the hero, an artist, who in the course of his struggles to redeem himself purifies the golem, who is of course his own unredeemed self. This literary figure, which has achieved considerable fame, owes very little to the Jewish tradition even in its corrupt, legendary form. An analysis of the main Jewish traditions concerning the golem will show how little.

By way of defining the climate of this investigation, I should like first of all to present the legend in its late Jewish form, as vividly described in 1808 by Jakob Grimm in the romantic *Journal for Hermits.*[1]

> After saying certain prayers and observing certain fast days, the Polish Jews make the figure of a man from clay or mud, and when they pronounce the miraculous Shemhamphoras [the name of God] over him, he must come to life. He cannot speak, but he understands fairly well what is said or commanded. They call him golem and use him as a servant to do all sorts of housework. But he must never leave the house. On his forehead is written *'emeth* [truth]; every day he gains weight and becomes somewhat larger and stronger than all the others in the house, regardless of how little he was to begin with. For fear of him, they therefore erase the first letter, so that nothing remains but *meth* [he is dead], whereupon he collapses and turns to clay again. But one man's golem once grew so tall, and he heedlessly let him keep on growing so long that he could no longer reach his forehead. In terror he ordered the servant to take off his boots, thinking that when he bent down he could reach his forehead. So it happened, and the first letter was successfully erased, but the whole heap of clay fell on the Jew and crushed him.

II

In investigating the golem as a man created by magical art, we must go back to certain Jewish conceptions concerning Adam, the first man. For obviously a man who creates a golem is in some sense competing with God's creation of Adam; in such an act the creative power of man enters into a relationship, whether of emulation or antagonism, with the creative power of God.

Strangely enough, the etymological connection between Adam,

---

[1] Taken from Rosenfeld, p. 41.

the man created by God, and the earth, Hebrew *'adamah*, is not expressly mentioned in the story of the Creation in Genesis. Moreover, the linguistic connection has been contested by Semitic scholars. Nevertheless, this etymological connection is very much stressed in the Rabbinical and Talmudic commentaries on Genesis. Adam is a being who was taken from the earth and returns to it, on whom the breath of God conferred life and speech. He is a man of the earth but also—as the late Kabbalists put it in a daring etymology, derived from an ingenious pun on Isaiah 14 : 14—the 'likeness of the most high,' namely, when he fulfils his function by freely choosing the good.[1] This Adam was made from the matter of the earth, literally from clay, as one of the speakers in the Book of Job (33 : 6) expressly points out, but from the finest parts of it. Philo wrote: 'It is conceivable that God wished to create his man-like form with the greatest care and that for this reason he did not take dust from the first piece of earth that came to hand, but that from the whole earth he separated the best, from pure primal matter the purest and finest parts, best suited for his making.'[2] The Aggadah has a similar conception, which it expresses in any number of variants. 'From what is clearest in the earth He created him, from what is most excellent in the earth He created him, from what is finest in the earth He created him, from the [future] place of divine worship [in Zion] He created him, from the place of his atonement.'[3] Just as according to the Torah a portion of dough is removed from the rest to serve as the priest's share, so is Adam the best share that is taken from the dough of the earth, that is, from the center of the world on Mount Zion, from the place where the altar would stand, of which it is said: 'An altar of earth thou shalt make unto me' (Ex. 20 : 24).[4] This Adam was taken from the center and navel of the earth, but all the elements were combined in his creation. From everywhere God gathered the dust from which Adam was to be made, and etymologies interpreting the word Adam as an abbreviation of his

[1] Menahem Azariah of Fano, *'Asarah Ma'amaroth*, Venice, 1597, in *Ma'amar 'Em Kol Hay*, II, 33. *'Eddameh* in Isa. 14 : 14 has the same consonants as *'adamah*.

[2] *De opificio mundi*, 137.

[3] From an unknown source in *Midrash ha-Gadol* on Genesis, ed. M. Margolioth, Jerusalem, 1947, p. 78.

[4] *Genesis Rabbah*, XIV, 2, ed. Theodor, p. 126.

elements, or of the names of the four cardinal points from which he was taken, gained wide currency.[1]

In the Talmudic Aggadah a further theme is added. At a certain stage in his creation Adam is designated as 'golem.' 'Golem' is a Hebrew word that occurs only once in the Bible, in Psalm 139 : 16, which Psalm the Jewish tradition put into the mouth of Adam himself. Here probably, and certainly in the later sources, 'golem' means the unformed, amorphous. There is no evidence to the effect that it meant 'embryo,' as has sometimes been claimed. In the philosophical literature of the Middle Ages it is used as a Hebrew term for matter, formless *hylé*, and this more suggestive significance will appear in the following discussion. In this sense, Adam was said to be 'golem' before the breath of God had touched him.

A famous Talmudic passage[2] describes the first twelve hours of Adam's first day:

Aha bar Hanina said: The day had twelve hours. In the first hour the earth was piled up; *in the second he became a golem*, a still unformed mass; in the third, his limbs were stretched out; *in the fourth the soul was cast into him*; in the fifth he stood on his feet; in the sixth he gave [all living things] names; in the seventh Eve was given him for a companion; in the eighth the two lay down in bed and when they left it, they were four; in the ninth the prohibition was communicated to him; in the tenth he transgressed it; in the eleventh he was judged; in the twelfth he was expelled and went out of Paradise, as it is written in Psalm 49 : 13: And Adam does not remain one night in glory.

Important for us in this remarkable passage is what it tells us about the second and fourth hours. Before the soul, *neshamah*, was cast into him and before he spoke to give things their names, Adam was an unformed mass. No less interesting is the further development of this motif in a midrash from the second and third centuries. Here Adam is described not only as a golem, but as a golem of cosmic size and strength, to whom, while he was still in this speechless and inanimate state, God showed all future generations to the end of time. The juxtaposition of these two motifs, between which there is an obvious relationship of tension

[1] Cf. Louis Ginzberg, *Legends of the Jews*, V, p. 72; Max Förster, 'Adams Erschaffung und Namengebung,' *Archiv für Religionswissenschaft*, XI (1908), pp. 477–529.
[2] Sanhedrin 38b.

if not of contradiction, is exceedingly strange. Even before Adam has speech and reason, he beholds a vision of the history of Creation, which passes before him in images.

Rabbi Tanhuma said in the name of Rabbi Eleazar [Eleazar ben Azariah]: In the hour when God created the first Adam, He created him as a golem, and he was stretched out from one end of the world to the other, as it is written in Psalm [139 : 16]: 'Thine eyes did see my golem.' Rabbi Judah bar Simeon said: While Adam still lay as a golem before Him who spoke and the world came into being, He showed him all the generations and their wise men, all the generations and their judges, all the generations and their leaders.[1]

It would seem as though, while Adam was in this state, some tellurian power had flowed into him out of the earth from which he was taken, and that it was this power which enabled him to receive such a vision. According to the Aggadah, it was only after the fall that Adam's enormous size, which filled the universe, was reduced to human, though still gigantic, proportions. In this image—an earthly being of cosmic dimensions—two conceptions are discernible. In the one, Adam is the vast primordial being of cosmogonic myth; in the other, his size would seem to signify, in spatial terms, that the power of the whole universe is concentrated in him.

And indeed, we find this latter conception in one of the fragments—so rich in archaic, mythical motifs—that have come down to us from the lost *Midrash Abkir*. Here we read:

Rabbi Berakhya said: When God wished to create the world, He began His creation with nothing other than man and made him as a golem. When He prepared to cast a soul into him, He said: If I set him down now, it will be said that he was my companion in the work of Creation; so I will leave him as a golem [in a crude, unfinished state], until I have created everything else. When He had created everything, the angels said to Him: Aren't you going to make the man you spoke of? He replied: I made him long ago, only the soul is missing. Then He cast the soul into him and set him down and concentrated the whole world in him. With him He began, with him He concluded, as it is written [Psalm 139 : 5]: thou hast formed me before and behind.[2]

---

[1] *Genesis Rabbah*, XXIV, 2, ed. Theodor, p. 230. *Ibid.*, XIV, 8, p. 132. In this latter passage on Gen. 2 : 7 we actually read: 'He put him [Adam] down as a golem extending from earth to heaven and cast a soul into him.'

[2] *Yalkut Shim'oni* to Gen. No. 34.

One is amazed at the audacity with which the Aggadic exegete departs from the Biblical version and begins Creation with the material making of man as a golem in whom the force of the whole universe is contained, but who receives his soul only at the end of Creation. Not the second and fourth hour of Adam's life, as in the account previously quoted, but the whole work of Creation lies between man in his amorphous state and man as an animated being. And whereas in the previous version earth for him was gathered from the whole world, here the whole world is concentrated in him.

Another mythical deviation from the Biblical story of Creation is also of importance for our purposes. Whereas in Genesis it is only when God breathes life into him that Adam becomes *nefesh hayah*, a living soul (Gen. 2 : 7), the old Jewish tradition contains several references to a tellurian earth-spirit, dwelling in Adam.

Here as so often the Aggadah goes back to ideas far removed from the Biblical text. A similar example is the story that a woman was created before Eve, which may, it is true, have originated as an attempt to resolve the contradiction between Genesis 1 : 27, where man and woman were created at the same time, and 2 : 21, where Eve was made from Adam's rib. According to a midrash[1] which, to be sure, is not quoted in this form before the ninth or tenth century, a woman was first made for Adam from the earth (and not from his flank or rib). This was Lilith, who irritated the Lord of Creation by demanding equal rights. She argued: We [Adam and I] are equal, because we both come from the earth. Whereupon they quarreled, and Lilith, bitterly disgruntled, uttered the name of God and fled to embark on her demonic career. In the third century this story seems to have been known in a somewhat different form, without the demonic Lilith. This version speaks of a 'first Eve,' created independently of Adam and hence no relation of Cain and Abel, who quarreled for possession of her, whereupon God turned her back into dust.[2]

But to get back to the soul, it is maintained, surprisingly enough, in traditions from the second century, that Genesis

---

[1] In the *Alphabet of Ben Sira*, ed. M. Steinschneider, 1858, 23a.

[2] *Genesis Rabbah*, XXII, 8, ed. Theodor, p. 213. Apparently the idea that Eve was created 'in the same way' as Adam but independently of him was current in the Jewish sources of Ophite Gnosticism, as Hippolytus (V. 26) records.

1 : 24: 'Let the earth bring forth living soul,' refers to the spirit (*ruah*) of the first Adam, which accordingly is not a pneuma blown into him, but an earth-spirit, a vital potency dwelling in the earth. I feel certain that this conception is related to gnostic ideas, which, though taken over by heretics, were originally Jewish—a fact that has often, oddly enough, been denied or disregarded. In his *Philosophoumena* (V. 26) Hippolytus speaks of a Judeo-Christian system of Ophite gnosis, probably from the middle of the second century; his source is a *Book of Baruch* by an otherwise unknown Justinus. According to this Justinus there were three original principles: the good God; *Elohim*, as father of all created things (the function assigned to God in Genesis); and *Edem*, called also Israel and Earth, who was half virgin and half snake. The name *Edem* seems to spring from a confusion, by Jewish heretics who had forgotten their Hebrew, between the words *'adamah*, Earth, and *'Eden* (written *Edem* in the Septuagint). Justinus' *Edem* has features of both, though her principal characteristics are those of *'adamah*. As Lipsius says, she is a mythological personification of the earth.[1] Here Adam is identified with *Edem*, just as he is with *'adamah* in the midrash.[2] In this version Paradise, the Garden, which here in good Jewish style is distinguished from Eden, is the totality of the angels who are allegorically referred to as the 'trees' in Paradise. 'But after Paradise had been born from the mutual love of *Elohim* and *Edem*, the angels of *Elohim* took some of the best earth, that is, not of the animal part belonging to *Edem*, but of the human and noble parts of the earth,' and from it formed man. Here, just as in the contemporaneous tradition of the above-quoted midrash, Adam's soul, unlike the *neshamah*, or pneuma, of the Bible, which is breathed into Adam by God, comes from the virgin Earth or *Edem*[3]—and again as in the midrash Adam is made from the best parts of the earth.

Still in line with the basic meaning of *Edem* as Earth, this version goes on to speak of a mythical marriage (*gamos*) between

[1] Richard Lipsius, *Der Gnostizismus*, Leipzig, 1860, 76. The connection with the Hebrew *'adamah* is also seen correctly in W. Scholz, *Dokumente der Gnosis*, 1909, p. 24, while Leisegang, for example, sees only the connection with the Biblical Eden.

[2] *Pirke Rabbi Eliezer*, XII.

[3] The same occurs again in Hippolytus, X, 15: 'the psyche of Edem, whom the mad Justinus also calls Earth.'

Earth and *Elohim*. Adam is their 'eternal symbol,' 'the seal and monument of their love.' Thus tellurian and pneumatic elements were combined in Adam and his descendants, for, as Justinus says, *Edem*-Earth 'brought her whole power to *Elohim* as a dowry, when they were married.' It strikes me as probable that this tellurian soul of Adam stems from older Jewish speculation (quite possibly it forms the basis of the midrash about Adam's vision of future generations while he was still a golem) and subsequently, through heretical Jewish gnostics, came to the Naassenes and Ophites, who welcomed it because it fell in with their own notions of *psyche* and *pneuma*.

Such ideas about a marriage between God and Earth were to reappear at a later day, in the Spanish Kabbalah, for example. Still, they play no part in the late conceptions of the golem. But in the countries where the golem began his career in the Middle Ages, particularly in Germany, we come across the story that God and Earth concluded a formal contract concerning the creation of Adam (it occurs, for example, in a late recension of the *Alphabet of Ben Sira*). God demands Adam for a thousand years as a loan from Earth, and gives her a formal receipt for 'four ells of earth,' which is witnessed by the Archangels Michael and Gabriel and lies to this day in the archives of Metatron, the heavenly scribe.[1]

III

The idea that such an act of creation might be repeated by magic or other arts that are not exactly defined had a different origin, namely, the legends recorded in the Talmud concerning certain famous rabbis of the third and fourth centuries.

[1] The text of the contract in N. Brüll, *Jahrbücher für jüdische Geschichte und Literatur*, IX (1889), p. 16. Cf. also the passage from the *Midrash ha-Ne'elam* in *Zohar Hadash*, 1885, 16b, according to which heaven, earth, and water were God's builders, but all of them were unable to give Adam soul, until 'God and earth joined to make him.' God's exclamation 'Let us make a man' was addressed not to the angels but to the earth, which brought forth Adam's golem (here simply 'body'). For the notion of the contract we have a parallel in a midrash of unknown origin, in *Yalkut Shim'oni* I, 41, where God makes a contract with Adam providing that David is to be granted seventy years of life (which Adam cedes from his own allotted 1,000 years). God and Metatron both sign the contract.

Rava said: If the righteous wished, they could create a world, for it is written [Isa. 59 : 2]: 'Your iniquities have separated between you and your God.' The implication is that if a man is saintly without sins, his creative power is no longer 'separated' from that of God. And the text continues as though its author wished to demonstrate this creative power: 'For Rava created a man and sent him to Rabbi Zera. The rabbi spoke to him and he did not answer. Then he said: You must have been made by the companions [members of the Talmudic Academy]; return to your dust.' The Aramaic word here rendered by 'companions' is ambiguous. According to some scholars Rabbi Zera's sentence should be interpreted to mean: 'You must come from the magicians.' In the Talmud this passage is immediately followed by another story: 'Rav Hanina and Rav Oshaya busied themselves on the eve of every Sabbath with the *Book of Creation*—or in another reading: with the instructions [*halakhoth*] concerning creation. They made a calf one-third the natural size and ate it.'[1]

Thus the creative power of the righteous is limited. Rava is able to create a man who can go to Rabbi Zera, but he cannot endow him with speech, and by his silence Rabbi Zera recognizes his nature. This artificial or magical man is always lacking in some essential function. We are not told how he was created, unless we are to infer from another legend about the Sabbath-calf that the methods of Hanina and Oshaya were later known to Rava. The setting of the one legend is Palestine, of the other Babylonia.

It seems likely—and so it was always assumed in the Jewish tradition—that this creation involved magic, though in a perfectly permissible form. The letters of the alphabet—and how much more so those of the divine name or of the entire Torah, which was God's instrument of Creation—have secret, magical power. The initiate knows how to make use of them. Bezalel, who built the Tabernacle, 'knew the combinations of letters with which heaven and earth were made'—so we read in the name of a Babylonian scholar of the early third century, the most prominent representative of the esoteric tradition in his generation.[2] The letters in question were unquestionably those of the name of

---

[1] Sanhedrin 65b. The last section is repeated in 67b, where the procedure is termed 'permissible in any case' and distinguished from forbidden black magic, though no precise reason is given.

[2] Berakhoth 55a.

God,[1] for it was generally held by the esoteric Jewish thinkers of the time that heaven and earth had been created by the great name of God. In building the Tabernacles, Bezalel had been able to imitate the Creation on a small scale. For the Tabernacle is a complete microcosm, a miraculous copy of everything that is in heaven and on earth.

A similar tradition concerning the creative power of letters forms the basis of the following midrash on Job 28 : 13, in which what is said in Job of wisdom is applied to the Torah: 'No one knows its [right] order, for the sections of the Torah are not given in the right arrangement. If they were, everyone who reads in it might create a world, raise the dead, and perform miracles. Therefore the order of the Torah was hidden and is known to God alone.'[2]

This brings us to the text that played so important a part in the development of the golem concept: the *Book Yetsirah* or *Book of Creation*. It is uncertain which reading of the above-mentioned legend about the Sabbath-calf is correct, whether it should really be taken as a reference to the brief but baffling *Book Yetsirah*, which has come down to us, or whether the rabbis derived their thaumaturgic instructions from some other, otherwise unknown 'instructions for [magical] creation.' That the *Book Yetsirah* should be mentioned in this passage does not strike me as quite so impossible as numerous authors have assumed. We do not know the exact date of this enigmatic text, which sets forth the meaning or function of the 'thirty-two ways of wisdom,' that is, of the ten *sefiroth* or original numbers, and of the twenty-two consonants of the Hebrew alphabet. We can only be sure that it was written by a Jewish Neo-Pythagorean some time between the third and the sixth century.[3]

A few passages in this book are of crucial importance for our context. The idea of the golem is, to be sure, unrelated to the conception of the ten *sefiroth* as set forth in this book, nor does it owe

[1] Correctly understood by L. Blau in *Altjüdisches Zauberwesen*, Budapest, 1898, p. 122. Blau, however, was unacquainted with the parallel passage in the *Greater Hekhaloth*, IX, where the significance of the letters is stated explicitly.

[2] *Midrash Tehillim* to Psalm 3, ed. S. Buber, 17a. Rabbi Eleazar, who transmitted this tradition, lived in the third century. Cf. above, Chapter 2, p. 37.

[3] Cf. my article 'Jezirabuch' in *Encyclopaedia Judaica*, IX (1932), 104–11. As I shall explain elsewhere, I now (1960) incline toward the earlier dating.

anything to the later Kabbalistic symbolism of the *sefiroth*. Significant for the creation of the golem were the names of God and the letters, which are the signatures of all creation. These letters are the structural elements, the stones from which the edifice of Creation was built. The Hebrew term employed by the author in speaking of the consonants as 'elementary letters' undoubtedly reflects the ambivalence of the Greek word *stoicheia*, which means both letters and elements.

Concerning these elements and their function in Creation, we read in the second chapter: 'Twenty-two letter-elements: He outlined them, hewed them out, weighed them, combined them, and exchanged them [transformed them in accordance with certain laws], and through them created the soul of all creation and everything else that was ever to be created.' And further:

How did He combine, weigh, and exchange them? A [which in Hebrew is a consonant] with all [other consonants] and all with A, B with all and all with B, G with all and all with G, and they all return in a circle to the beginning through two hundred thirty-one gates—the number of the pairs that can be formed from the twenty-two elements—and thus it results that everything created and everything spoken *issue from one name*.

Both the context and linguistic usage make it clear that what is meant by this name, from which all things issue, is the name of God and not 'any group of consonants combined into a name.'[1] Thus at every 'gate' in the circle formed by the letters of the alphabet there stands a combination of two consonants, which in line with the author's grammatical notions correspond to the two-letter roots of the Hebrew language, and through these gates the creative power goes out into the universe. This universe as a whole is sealed on all six sides with the six permutations of the name YHWH, but every thing or being in it exists through one of these combinations, which are the true 'signatures' of all being, as has been said in a formulation suggestive of Jacob Boehme.[2]

The *Book Yetsirah* describes in broad outlines, but with certain astronomico-astrological and anatomical details, how the cosmos was built—chiefly from the twenty-two letters, for after the first

---

[1] As L. Goldschmidt explains in *Das Buch der Schöpfung*, 1894, p. 84, and, following him, several recent translators.

[2] Johann Friedrich von Meyer, *Das Buch Jezira*, Leipzig, 1930, p. 24.

chapter no mention is made of the ten *sefiroth*. Man is a microcosmos attuned to the great world. Each letter 'governs' a part of man or a realm of the great world. The summary, dogmatic exposition tells us nothing of how the things and processes not mentioned here came into being. Though the treatise is presented as a theoretical guide to the structure of creation, it may quite conceivably have been intended also as a manual of magical practices, or at least as a statement of general principles, to be supplemented by more detailed instructions—perhaps oral—concerning the application of these principles to other things. The affinity between the linguistic theory set forth in the book and the fundamental magical belief in the power of letters and words is obvious.

We know from the medieval commentaries on the book, some philosophical, some magico-mystical, that it was interpreted in both ways. Whether the tradition of the French and German Jews, who read the book as a manual of magic,[1] is in keeping with its original intention may indeed be questioned. But the end of the book seems to point strongly in this direction, and certainly does not argue to the contrary. In this conclusion insight into the creative power of the linguistic elements is attributed to Abraham as the first prophet of monotheism:

When our Father Abraham came, he contemplated, meditated, and beheld,[2] investigated and understood and outlined and dug and combined and formed [i.e. created],[3] *and he succeeded.* Then the Lord of the World revealed Himself to him and took him to his bosom and

---

[1] This view was current not only among the Jewish esoterics of France and Germany, but is to be found in Rashi's commentary on the Talmudic tale about Rava's 'man.' In general Rashi (d. 1103 in Troyes) reflects a much older learned tradition.

[2] This strong emphasis on Abraham's meditations is lacking in certain old texts (Saadya's, for example) of the book.

[3] This verb 'formed' (*ve-tsar*) is present in the text at the end of the commentary of Judah ben Barzilai, ed. Halberstamm, p. 266, but is lacking (mistakenly no doubt) at the bottom of p. 99. Saadya (ed. Lambert, p. 104) also read it, though in his version the order of the verbs is different. In the text of the book, this verb form is used throughout in connection with the creation of individual things and has the meaning of 'created.' Judah ben Barzilai (p. 266) artificially interprets away the clear meaning of the two verbs ('he combined the letters and created') which are used here both of God's and of Abraham's activity. According to him, the words have different meanings for Abraham and for God. But the text offers no basis for such an interpretation.

kissed him on the head and called him His friend [another variant adds: and made him His son] and made an eternal covenant with him and his seed.

Medieval or modern commentators wishing to disregard the magical tendencies of the book found all manner of edifying reflections with which to explain away this conclusion. But the strange 'he created and he succeeded' does not refer merely to Abraham's successful speculative efforts, but explicitly to his operation with letters, in which he repeats above all the words employed by God in His creative activity. It seems to me that the author of this sentence had in mind a method which enabled Abraham, on the strength of his insight into the system of things and the potencies of letters, to imitate and in a certain sense repeat God's act of creation.

This view is supported by the fact that the old manuscripts of the *Book of Creation* not only bore the title *Hilkhoth Yetsirah* (suggested by the above-mentioned reading of the Talmud passage about the Sabbath-calf, unless it is the other way around and the Talmud refers to this title) but also bear at the beginning and end the additional title: 'Alphabet of Our Father Abraham,' *'Othioth de-'Abraham Avinu.* Judah ben Barzilai, who at the beginning of the twelfth century, in southern France or Catalonia, wrote his compendious commentary, in which he cites many old variants tells us, moreover,[1] that the title bore the addition: 'Each man who looks at it [i.e., who contemplatively immerses himself in it],[2] his wisdom is beyond measure'—that is, comparable to the creative wisdom of God!

Thus it seems to me that the German Hasidim who commented on the book in the thirteenth century were not too far from the literal meaning of the text when they said that Abraham had created beings by a magical process described, or at least suggested, in the *Book Yetsirah*. In mystical circles and at least among the German Hasidim, the verse from Genesis (12 : 5) to the effect that Abraham and Sarah took 'the souls they had made in Haran' with them on their journey westward was always interpreted as a

[1] Commentary on the *Book Yetsirah*, ed. Halberstamm, pp. 100 and 268. Actually such a text is in the British Museum MS of the *Book Yetsirah*; cf. Margoliouth's catalogue, No. 600 (Vol. II, p. 197).

[2] In the Hebrew of the oldest esoteric texts from the Talmudic period, the verb *tsafah* always has this meaning of a profound contemplative vision.

reference to this magical creation.[1] Here of course we have a problem. Whether formulated as early as must at least be envisaged as possible, or only in the medieval development of the ideas about the golem, such an exegesis involves a distinct deviation from the traditional exegseis of Genesis 12 : 5. In the exoteric Aggadah the 'souls' made by Abraham and Sarah are interpreted as proselytes to the faith in the One God among the men and women of their generation. A commentary dating from the second century runs: 'Are we to believe that Abraham could make souls? Why, if all the creatures in the world gathered together to make a single gnat and put a soul into it, they would not succeed!'[2] No more than a man make a gnat, can demons, according to another tradition,[3] make anything smaller than a grain of barley. But those who favored the thaumaturgic interpretation of the *Book Yetsirah*, and believed that a man or golem could be created with its help, interpreted Genesis 12 : 5 (in which *nefesh*, 'souls,' can also mean persons or, as in the *Book Yetsirah*, even 'human organisms') as the outcome of Abraham's study of the book. This was to adopt the interpretation so indignantly rejected in the older sources.

If this exegesis of Genesis 12 : 5 is an old one, the polemical question of the midrash—'Are we to believe that Abraham could make souls?'—may quite possibly have been directed against its currency in esoteric circles. But even if it was new to the Middle Ages, it certainly antedated the ritual of which we shall speak below. This interpretation still tells us nothing about the nature of the persons so created, except that Abraham took them along; so they must, like the man created by Rava, have been able to move. They are not symbolic condensations of magic ritual, for they physically accompany Abraham on his journey. This exegesis

---

[1] Thus in Eleazar of Worms, *Hokhmath ha-Nefesh*, 1876, 5d, who took the verse to mean that Abraham and Shem, son of Noah, (and not Sarah!) had busied themselves with the *Book Yetsirah*. We find a similar notion in the unprinted end of Pseudo-Saadya on the *Book Yetsirah*, MS Munich, 40, Fol. 77a, where it is also said: 'As someone demonstrates his power to the people, so did Abraham, and created persons, *nefashoth*, in order to demonstrate the power of God, who conferred [creative] force on the letters.'

[2] *Genesis Rabbah*, XXXIX, 14, ed. Theodor, pp. 378–9, and the parallels there noted. The passage on the impossibility of creating a gnat already occurs in the Tannaitic *Sifre* to Deut. 6 : 5, ed. Finkelstein, p. 54.

[3] Sanhedrin 67b.

should then be taken rather as an imitation of the Talmudic story about Rava, inspired by the definitely thaumaturgic conclusion of the *Book Yetsirah*. I regard this latter explanation as more plausible than any other. Judah ben Barzilai, who had excellent old sources at his disposal, was not yet acquainted with this explanation, or he would surely have mentioned it at the end of his commentary along with the other Aggadoth there quoted. But regardless of the age of this exegesis of Genesis 12 : 5, I believe that the present interpretation of the last lines of the *Book Yetsirah* follows necessarily from the text itself.

If Jewish esoterics as early as the third century—in case the *Book Yetsirah* really comes from this period—believed Abraham to be capable of such miraculous creation on the strength of his insight into the *hilkhoth yetsirah*, we shall be justified in drawing a parallel between these views and certain others held at roughly the same time. Such a comparison seems to throw new light on a number of important matters that have hitherto remained obscure. Graetz was the first to assume, on the basis of cosmogonic parallels, that the orthodox Jewish gnosis or esotericism of the *Book Yetsirah* was in some way connected with certain conceptions recorded in the *Pseudo-Clementines*.[1] These books, which contain a good deal of very interesting Jewish and semi-Jewish (Ebionite) material, are a strange Jewish-Christian-Hellenistic hodge-podge, composed in the fourth century—the period of Rava and his golem—from older sources.

In the semi-gnostic chapters of the 'homilies' on Simon Magus we find[2] a striking parallel to the above-mentioned conceptions of the Jewish thaumaturges and to the likewise semi-gnostic ideas of the *Book Yetsirah*. Simon Magus is quoted as boasting that he had created a man, not out of the earth, but out of the air by theurgic transformations (*theiai tropai*) and—exactly as later in the instructions concerning the making of the golem!—reduced him to his element by 'undoing' the said transformations.

First, he says, the human pneuma transformed itself into warm nature and sucked up the surrounding air like a cupping glass. Then,

---

[1] H. Graetz, *Gnostizismus und Judentum*, Krotoschin, 1846, pp. 110–15. H. J. Schoeps, *Theologie und Geschichte des Judenchristentums*, 1949, p. 207, seems to take an attitude of great reserve toward these relationships, but does not go into the matter in detail.

[2] *Homilia*, II, 26, Rehm, p. 46.

he transformed this air that had taken form within the pneuma into water, then into blood . . ., and from the blood he made flesh. When the flesh had become firm, he had produced a man, not from earth but from air, so convincing himself that he could make a new man. He also claimed that he had returned him to the air by undoing the transformations.

What here is accomplished by transformations of the air, the Jewish adept does by bringing about magical transformations of the earth through the influx of the 'alphabet' of the *Book Yetsirah*. In both cases such creation has no practical purpose but serves to demonstrate the adept's 'rank' as a creator. It has been supposed that this passage in the *Pseudo-Clementines* came, by ways unknown, to the alchemists, and finally led to Paracelsus' idea of the *homunculus*.[1] The parallel with the Jewish golem is certainly more striking. The 'divine transformations' in the operation of Simon Magus remind one very much of the creative 'transformations' (*temuroth*) of letters in the *Book Yetsirah*.

IV

The conceptions here set forth account for the medieval idea of the golem which made its appearance among the German and French Hasidim. Here we have a strange convergence of legend and ritual. The members of the strong esoteric movements that sprang up among the Jews in the age of the crusades were eager to perpetuate, if only in rites of initiation which gave the adept a mystical experience of the creative power inherent in pious men, the achievement attributed to Abraham and Rava and other pious men of old in apocryphal legends, some of which seem to have been current even before the eleventh century.

[1] Jacoby in *Handwörterbuch des deutschen Aberglaubens*, IV, 289. That such conceptions have remarkable parallels in early Christian apocrypha is demonstrated by the widespread legends about the childhood of Jesus, in which it is related that he made birds of clay, which flew off. Oskar Dähnhardt, in *Natursagen*, II (*Sagen zum Neuen Testament*), 1909, pp. 71–6. gathered the rich material concerning these conceptions, which go back to the second century. In medieval Arabic and Jewish treatments of this motif, the magical component makes its appearance just as in the stories of golem-making. According to the early medieval Hebrew (anti-Christian) *Toledoth Yeshu*, Jesus demonstrated his claim to be the son of God by making birds of clay and uttering the name of God over them, whereupon they lived, stood up, and flew off into the air.

I should like to make a few brief remarks that are important for an understanding of this development. The golem—beginning with the end of the twelfth century the name appears in a number of texts in the sense of a man-like creature, produced by the magical power of man[1]—starts out as a legendary figure. Then it is transformed into the object of a mystical ritual of initiation, which seems actually to have been performed, designed to confirm the adept in his mastery over secret knowledge. Then in the whisperings of the profane it degenerates once more into a figure of legend, or one might even say, tellurian myth. The early Hasidim and later some of the Kabbalists were very much concerned with the nature of this golem. Man is an earthly being, but has a magical power. The problem might be formulated as follows: does he with this magical power create a purely magical being, or is it a being related to the tellurian origins of man? It seems to me that both of these conflicting possibilities were at work in the development of the medieval golem conceptions.

Still another preliminary remark is in order. The Hasidim seem to have regarded the magic effected by application of the instructions found in, or read into, the *Book Yetsirah* as a natural faculty with which man within certain limits is endowed. Creation itself, in this view, is magical through and through: all things in it live by virtue of the secret names that dwell in them. Thus magical knowledge is not a perversion, but a pure and sacred knowledge which belongs to man as God's image. This view, which predominates in the following records, instructions, and legends, must be rigorously distinguished from the specifically Kabbalistic

[1] First in the *Yetsirah* commentaries of Eleazar of Worms and Pseudo-Saadya, who belonged to the same circle; cf. *Leshonenu*, VI (Jerusalem, 1935), p. 40. In the same periodical, XII (1944), pp. 50-1, J. Tishby pointed to a passage in the paraphrased translation, probably done in the twelfth century, of Judah Halevi's *Kuzari*, IV, 25, which, to his mind, may account for the shift to the new usage of the word 'golem.' Here it is stated, in a discussion of the *Book Yetsirah*, that if man had the same power as God (for whom the idea of a thing, its name, and the thing itself are one), 'he could by his word create bodies [*gelamim*] and achieve the power of God in creation, which is quite impossible.' The use of 'golem' in the sense of body is very common in the twelfth and thirteenth centuries. Tishby believes, however, that the special context of this passage may have provoked the shift to the new usage of the Hasidim. But since the Hasidim read the *Kuzari* in the usual translation of Judah ibn Tibbon (1176), in which the word 'golem' is not used, this explanation does not strike me as very likely.

view of magic underlying, for example, the *Zohar*. For here[1] magic is represented as a faculty first manifested in the fall of Adam and originating in the corruption of man, in his bond with the earth from which he came. The *Zohar* describes this magical knowledge, which is obviously not identical with that of the *Book Yetsirah*, as a knowledge concerning the leaves of the Tree of Knowledge. The leaves of the Tree of Death, with which Adam veils his nakedness, are the central symbol of true magical knowledge. Magic makes its appearance as a knowledge serving to veil Adam's nakedness, which resulted when his garment of heavenly light was removed from him. It is a demonized magic, which came into being with the earthly corporeity resulting from the fall and is bound up with the existence of the body. As long as Adam had his garment of light, his *kothnoth 'or*—literally, garments of light—which an esoteric midrash from the middle of the second century attributed to him in place of the *kothnoth 'or*—garments of skin—of Genesis 3 : 21,[2] his spiritual essence excluded the magical relationship pertaining to the realms of the Tree of Knowledge and of Death to earth-bound nature. It strikes me as possible that the latest forms of the golem conception, with their accent on danger and destructiveness, on the tellurian aspect of the golem, were in part influenced by these conceptions of Kabbalistic magic, but in the present state of our knowledge we cannot be sure. In any event, this conception of magic plays no part in the early history of the golem.

The oldest medieval testimonies to the magical interpretation of the *Book Yetsirah* are to be found in Judah ben Barzilai at the end of his commentary on the book (p. 268). It can be demonstrated beyond a doubt that these pages were read at least by Eleazar of Worms, and they were probably known to the whole group of Rhenish Hasidim at the turn of the twelfth century. They include a fragment about Abraham and a highly remarkable apocryphal version of the Talmudic passage about Rava and Zera, which deviates extensively and in a very characteristic way from

---

[1] Cf. primarily *Zohar*, I, 36b, 56a.

[2] Rabbi Meir in *Genesis Rabbah*, XX, 12, ed. Theodor, p. 196. This thesis of the Jewish esoterics seems to be connected with Origen's famous spiritualist interpretation, later sharply attacked by Jerome, to the effect that the 'garments of skin' were the material body. This thesis occurs frequently in Kabbalistic literature.

the original Talmudic story. Since the author shows elsewhere (p. 103) that he also knows the authentic form of the story, it is clear that, as he says in the beginning of his commentary, he is actually copying out 'old recensions' of the *Book Yetsirah*, at the end of which he found these fragments. Little notice has been taken of them,[1] but in our context it will be worth while to quote them in their entirety:

When our Father Abraham was born, the angels said to God: Lord of the World, you have a friend in the world and you mean to keep something hidden from him? God replied forthwith [Gen. 18 : 17]: 'Am I indeed hiding something from Abraham?' and he took counsel with the Torah and said: My daughter, come, and we shall wed you to my friend Abraham. She said: Not until the Gentle One [i.e., Moses] comes and takes [the Hebrew word can also mean 'marries'] the Gentle One [the Torah]. Thereupon God took counsel with the *Book Yetsirah* and said the same thing to it and handed it down to Abraham. He sat alone and meditated (*me'ayyen*] on it, but could understand nothing until a heavenly voice went forth and said to him: 'Are you trying to set yourself up as my equal? I am One and have created the *Book Yetsirah* and studied it: but you by yourself cannot understand it. Therefore take a companion, and meditate on it together, and you will understand it.' Thereupon Abraham went to his teacher Shem, son of Noah, and sat with him for three years, and they meditated on it until they knew how to create a world. And to this day there is no one who can understand it alone, two scholars [are needed], and even they understand it only after three years, whereupon they can make everything their hearts desire. Rava, too, wished to understand the book alone. Then Rabbi Zera said to him: It is written [Jer. 50 : 36]: 'A sword is upon the single, and they shall dote,' that is to say: A sword is upon the scholars who sit singly, each by himself, and concern themselves with the Torah.[2] Let us then meet and busy ourselves with the *Book Yetsirah*. And so they sat and meditated on it for three years and came to understand it. As they did so, a calf was created to them and they slaughtered it in order to celebrate their conclusion of the treatise. As soon as they slaughtered it, they forgot it [i.e., their understanding of the *Book Yetsirah*]. Then they sat for another three years and produced it again.

[1] A brief reference to this passage may be found in L. Ginzberg, *Legends of the Jews*, V, p. 210.

[2] These lines, taken over from another Talmud passage (Berakhoth 63b), are not at all inappropriate here. The word *baddim*, originally meaning 'liars,' is taken in the sense of *bodedim*, 'those who sit alone.'

I believe this passage to be the origin of the Hasidic view that the creation of the golem was a ritual. This is half implied in the passage itself, when on conclusion of their study the rabbis wish to celebrate, as it was the custom to celebrate on concluding a Talmudic treatise. In this form of the legend, the magical creation appears as confirmation and conclusion of the study of the *Book Yetsirah*. Moreover, we are told in what is unmistakably a reinterpretation of the original Talmudic story about Hanina and Oshaya (who are here confused with Rava and Zera) that this creation must serve no practical purpose. The moment they slaughter the calf to eat it at their celebration, they forget everything they have studied! Here then an entirely new motif is developed from the Talmudic form of the legend. This creation of a golem is an end in itself, a ritual of initiation into the secret of creation. Thus it is no longer surprising that the instructions about the making of a golem should originally have appeared as the conclusion of the study of the *Book of Creation*, exactly as Eleazar of Worms tells us at the end of his commentary on the book. Such a ritual at the conclusion of the study of the book was perhaps known to later circles, who were not deeply interested in the idea of a golem. The Moroccan philosopher Judah ben Nissim ibn Malka, a kind of freelance Kabbalist, reports in his Arabic commentary on the *Book Yetsirah* (c. 1365) that students of the book were given a magical manuscript named *Sefer Raziel* and consisting of seals, magical figures, secret names, and incantations.[1]

The apocryphal version of the story in Judah ben Barzilai is closely related to a version which we find in an obscure late midrash, probably from the twelfth century.[2] Here again the study confers world-creating power, but it is carried on not by two, but by three scholars:

When God created His world, He first created the *Book of Creation* and looked into it and from it created his world. When he had completed His work, he put it [the *Book Yetsirah*] into the Torah and

---

[1] George Vajda, *Juda ben Nissim ibn Malka, philosophe juif marocain*, Paris, 1954, p. 171. Vajda believes that the book was handed over at the beginning of the study, but this cannot be deduced with certainty from the text. Perhaps this step was taken in connection with an initiation at the conclusion of the study.

[2] 'Neue Pesikta,' in Jellinek's *Beth ha-Midrash*, VI, pp. 36–7.

showed it to Abraham, who however understood nothing. Then a heavenly voice went forth and said: Are you really trying to compare your knowledge with mine? Why, you cannot understand anything in it by yourself. Then he went to 'Eber and went to Shem, his teacher, and they meditated on it for three years, until they knew how to create a world. So likewise Rava and Rabbi Zera busied themselves with the *Book Yetsirah* and a calf was created to them, which they slaughtered, and Jeremiah[1] and Ben Sira also busied themselves with it for three years, and a man was created to them.

The author of this passage seems untroubled by the disproportion between the creation of a calf and the creation of a world. The knowledge of world creation is purely contemplative, while, as we shall see, the knowledge of the creation of a man, here attributed to Jeremiah and his son Ben Sira, suggests still other nuances of interpretation. The number of two or three adepts who study together and carry out the ritual of golem-making in common is not accidental. It seems to be based on a regulation in the Mishnah (Ḥagigah II, 1) to the effect that even if all other moral requirements for the study of a secret doctrine are met, a man must not concern himself with creation (that is, with the first chapter of the Bible and by extension with cosmogony in general) in the presence of more than two other persons. This prohibition seems to have been extended to the *Book of Creation*.

The end of the last quotation is the oldest reference so far known to us to the creation of a golem by Ben Sira and his father. We have at least three other accounts, which I shall quote here together, because of the light they throw on certain aspects of the golem conception.

a) In the preface to an anonymous commentary, known as Pseudo-Saadya, on the *Book Yetsirah*, we read a few lines about Abraham which are in agreement with those cited above.[2] The author then continues: 'It is said in the Midrash that Jeremiah and

---

[1] In Jellinek we read R. Hiya, which is no doubt a corruption, easily explained on graphical grounds, of Jeremiah.

[2] Edited by M. Steinschneider, *Magazin für die Wissenschaft des Judentums*, 1892, p. 83. In connection with the 'tradition,' communicated at the beginning of Steinschneider's text, about Abraham's study of the *Yetsirah*, cf. the exactly corresponding passage from Eleazar of Worms, *Sefer Rokeah* (*Hilkhoth Hasiduth*), reproduced by Ginzberg in his *Legends*, V, p. 210.

Ben Sira[1] created a man by means of the *Book Yetsirah*, and on his forehead stood *emeth*, truth, the name which He had uttered concerning the creature as the culmination of His work. But this man erased the *aleph*, by which he meant to say that God alone is truth, and he had to die.' Here it is clear that the golem is a repetition of the creation of Adam, concerning which we learn here for the first time that then too the name 'truth' was uttered. According to a well-known Talmudic saying (Shabbath 55a) 'truth' is the seal of God. Here it is imprinted on His noblest creation.

b) The version written down by students of Rabbi Judah the Pious of Speyer (d. 1217) in Regensburg is more explicit.[2]

Ben Sira wished to study the *Book Yetsirah*. Then a heavenly voice went forth: You cannot make him [such a creature] alone. He went to his father Jeremiah. They busied themselves with it, and at the end of three years a man was created to them, on whose forehead stood *emeth*, as on Adam's forehead. Then the man they had made said to them: God alone created Adam, and when he wished to let Adam die, he erased the *aleph* from *emeth* and he remained *meth*, dead. That is what you should do with me and not create another man, lest the world succumb to idolatry as in the days of Enosh.[3] The created man said to them: Reverse the combinations of letters [by which he was created] and erase the *aleph* of the word *emeth* from my forehead—and immediately he fell into dust.

As we see, Ben Sira's golem was very close to Adam; he was even endowed with speech, with which to warn his makers against the continuance of such practices. I shall have more to say below about this warning against idolatry and the example of Enosh. The golem is destroyed by the reversal of the magical combination of letters through which he was called into life and at the same time by the destruction, at once real and symbolic, of God's seal on his forehead. The seal seems to have appeared spontaneously on his forehead in the course of the magical process of creation, and not to have been inscribed by the adepts.

[1] According to a tradition which probably goes back to the early Middle Ages, Ben Sira is the son of the prophet; this was deduced from the fact that the names Sira and Yirmiyahu have the same numerical value, 271.

[2] MS of the *Sefer Gematrioth*, printed in Abraham Epstein, *Beiträge zur jüdischen Altertumskunde*, Vienna, 1887, pp. 122–3.

[3] The Targum and Midrash interpreted Gen. 4:26 as relating to the beginning of idolatry in the days of Enosh; cf. Ginzberg, *Legends of the Jews*, V, p. 151, with rich reference matter.

c) An interesting amplification of this passage is to be found in an early thirteenth-century text, originating with the early Kabbalists of Languedoc and clearly indicating the ties that must have existed between this group and the Hasidim of the Rhineland and northern France, In a pseudo-epigraphon attributed to the Tannaite Judah ben Bathyra, we read:[1]

The prophet Jeremiah busied himself alone with the *Book Yetsirah*. Then a heavenly voice went forth and said: Take a companion. He went to his son Sira, and they studied the book for three years. Afterward they set about combining the alphabets in accordance with the Kabbalistic principles of combination, grouping, and word formation, and a man was created to them, on whose forehead stood the letters *YHWH Elohim Emeth*.[2] But this newly created man had a knife in his hand, with which he erased the *aleph* from *emeth*; there remained: *meth*. Then Jeremiah rent his garments [because of the blasphemy: God is dead, now implied in the inscription] and said: Why have you erased the *aleph* from *emeth*? He replied: I will tell you a parable. An architect built many houses, cities, and squares, but no one could copy his art and compete with him in knowledge and skill until two men persuaded him. Then he taught them the secret of his art, and they knew how to do everything in the right way. When they had learned his secret and his abilities, they began to anger him with words. Finally, they broke with him and became architects like him, except that what he charged a thaler for, they did for six groats. When people noticed this, they ceased to honor the artist and came to them and honored them and gave them commissions when they required to have something built. So God has made you in His image and in His shape and form. But now that you have created a man like Him, people will say: There is no God in the world beside these two! Then Jeremiah said: What solution is there? He said: Write the alphabets backward on the earth you have strewn with intense concentration. Only do not meditate in the sense of building up, but the other way around. So they did, and the man became dust and ashes before their eyes. Then Jeremiah said: Truly, one should study these things only in order to know the power

[1] MS Halberstam, 444 (in the Jewish Theological Seminary in New York), Fol. 7b, and MS Florence, Laurentiana, Pl. II, Cod. 41, Fol. 200. The Halberstam MS, or a copy of it, is the source of the Latin translation in J. Reuchlin's *De arte cabalistica*, ed. 1603, col. 759.

[2] 'God is truth.' In the revision of the Kabbalistic book *Peli'ah* (c. 1350), in which this whole passage is copied, this important change is crossed out, leaving the more inoffensive older text (*'emeth* by itself!); cf. ed. Koretz, 1784, 36a.

and omnipotence of the Creator of this world, but not in order really to practice them.

In this Kabbalistic view of golem-making two contradictory motifs meet. Here the story is reinterpreted as a moralistic legend and the warning becomes more profound. To the Hasidim the creation of a golem confirmed man in his likeness to God; here, thanks to the daring amplification of the inscription on the golem's forehead, it becomes a warning; the real and not merely symbolic creation of a golem would bring with it the 'death of God'! The hybris of its creator would turn against God. This idea, barely hinted at in the second passage quoted, is clearly stressed by the anonymous Kabbalist.

The motif of warning against such creation, not so much because of the dangerous nature of the golem or of the enormous powers concealed in him as because of the possibility that it might lead to polytheistic confusion, connects these golem stories with the view of the origin of idolatry current in these same circles. For Enosh was said to have come to his father Seth and questioned him about his lineage. When Seth said to him that Adam had neither father nor mother but that God had created him out of the earth, Enosh went away and took a clod of earth and made a figure from it. Then he went to his father and said: But it cannot walk or speak. Then Seth said: God blew the breath of life into Adam's nose. When Enosh proceeded to do this, Satan came and slipped into the figure and so gave it an appearance of life. So the name of God was desecrated, and idolatry began when the generation of Enosh worshipped this figure.[1]

Here the conception of the golem converges with the speculation—in which Judaism, with its rejection of all idols, has always taken a hostile interest—on the nature of images and statues. In certain Jewish traditions cult images are indeed looked upon as a species of animated golem. Not wholly without justification, attempts have been made to relate the notion of living statues, widespread among non-Jews, with the golem legend, though such

[1] In a manuscript text of *Sefer Nitsahon*, from a Roman library, a copy of which by Adolf Posnanski I have read in Jerusalem, this tale is designated as a 'tradition of Rabbi Judah, the Pious.' In *Legends* I, p. 122, and V, p. 150, Ginzberg cites a similar text from a later so-called *Chronicle of Yerahme'el*, in which Enosh takes six clods of earth, mixes them, and forms a human figure from dust and mud.

parallels can apply of course only to the purely magical and not to the tellurian aspect of the golem.[1] The Jewish traditions concerning idolatry disclose one motif in particular, which is unquestionably connected with certain forms of the golem legend, namely, magical animation by means of the names of God.

We first encounter such a tradition in the Talmud (Sota 47a), where we are told that Gehazi cut one of the names of God into the muzzle of Jeroboam's bull idol (I Kings 12 : 28), whereupon the idol recited the first words of the Decalogue: 'I am thy God' and 'Thou shalt have no other.' A similar story is told about the idol which King Nebuchadnezzar (Dan. 3) had made. The king is said to have awakened it to life by putting on it the High Priest's diadem, stolen from the Temple in Jerusalem, on which was written the tetragrammaton YHWH. But Daniel, ostensibly wishing to kiss it, approached and removed the name of God, whereupon it fell lifeless to the ground.[2] In these tales the name of God, a sacred power, gives life to the cult images of polytheism. A conflicting view is that the devil, or—in anti-Catholic versions— Samael and Lilith had entered into such images. Both conceptions occur, for example, in the *Zohar*.[3] The legends recorded by Ahima'ats of Oria in his eleventh-century family chronicle show that a conception very close to the later forms of the golem legend was alive among the Italian Jews of the early Middle Ages, from whom the German Hasidim assuredly took many of their traditions. Ahima'ats tells of the magical miracles performed by

---

[1] Cf. Konrad Müller, 'Die Golemsage und die Sage von der lebenden Statue,' in *Mitteilungen der Schlesischen Gesellschaft für Volkskunde*, XX (1919), pp. 1–40. Müller, to be sure, had no more knowledge of the authentic Jewish traditions concerning the golem than did Hans Ludwig Held in his book *Das Gespenst des Golem; eine Studie aus der hebräischen Mystik*, Munich, 1927, where, pp. 104–16, we find material about living statues. Held's book shows great enthusiasm for the subject, but in all crucial passages the author substitutes inappropriate mystical meditations for the knowledge of Hebrew literature that he does not possess. It is pointless to take a polemical attitude toward this and similar elucubrations; it suffices to analyze the actual source material.

[2] *Cant. Rabbah*, to 7 : 9. So also in *Zohar*, II, 175a.

[3] In *Ra'ya Mehemna*, III, 277b, we are told that the generation that built the Tower of Babel fashioned idols. Samael and Lilith entered into these idols and spoke from them and so became gods. In *Tikkun* No. 66 of the *Tikkune Zohar* it is said, however (97b), that they had put the *shem meforash* into the mouths of these images, whereupon they began to speak.

Aharon of Bagdad, the *merkabah* mystic, and by Rabbi Hananel, who brought dead men back to life for a time by wedging a piece of parchment with the name of God under their tongue or sewing it into the flesh of their right arm. When the name is removed—in some stories on the pretext of a kiss, as in the legend of Daniel—the body falls back lifeless.[1]

The above-mentioned conflict between pure and impure powers in the cult images occurs also in connection with what to the Jewish mind is the worst of all idols, namely the golden calf. In one story, we are told that Samael, the devil, spoke from it.[2] The other thesis occurred in a lost midrash, several times quoted in medieval sources.[3] In a remarkable book which made its appearance after 1200 in the same circle as the conception of the golem, the magic of the *Book Yetsirah* is contrasted with that of the magicians. The anonymous author of the *Book of Life* contrasts Rava's method of creating a man with that of the magicians whose creation also, like that of the *Book Yetsirah*, employs earth as its basic element:[4]

The magicians of Egypt, who made creatures, were acquainted through demons or some other artifice with the order of the *merkabah* [the heavenly world and God's throne] and took dust under the feet of the order [suited to their undertaking] and created what they wished. But the scholars of whom it is said: 'N. N. made a man, etc.' knew the secret of the *merkabah* and took dust from under the feet of the [animal figures] of the *merkabah*, and spoke the name of God over it, and it was created. In this way Micah made the golden calf that could dance.[5]

---

[1] *Megillath 'Ahima'ats*, ed. B. Klar, Jerusalem, 1944, pp. 17 and 27–8.

[2] *Pirke Rabbi Eliezer*, XLV.

[3] Two recensions of the account from the Genizah in Cairo have been published by L. Ginzberg, one in *Ha-Goren*, IX (1923), pp. 65–6, and another in *Ginze Schechter*, I (1928), p. 243. They accord with the text used by the author of the *Sefer ha-Hayyim*, which is here translated. Saul Lieberman—*Yemenite Midrashim* (Hebrew), Jerusalem, 1940, pp. 17–18—was first to note that this midrash is the source of the strange, hitherto incomprehensible reference in the speech of the maker of the golden calf in the Koran, 20 : 95.

[4] I have translated from the MSS Munich, 207, Fol. 10d–11a (written in 1268), and Cambridge, Add. 643¹, Fol. 9a. M. Güdemann—*Geschichte des Erziehungswesens und der Cultur der Juden*, I, Wien, 1880, p. 169—omits the whole passage about the golden calf.

[5] A reference to the idolatrous Ephraimite mentioned in Judg. 17, whom the Midrash already credits with the making of the golden calf.

For like all Israel he had, in the exodus from Egypt, seen the *merkabah* in the Red Sea. But whereas the other Israelites had not concentrated on this vision, he did so, as is indicated in Song of Songs 6 : 12. When the bull in the *merkabah* moved to leftward,[1] he quickly took some of the dust from under its feet and kept it until the appropriate moment. And in the same way the magicians in India and the Arab countries still make animals of men, by conjuring a demon to bring them dust from the corresponding place and give it to the magician. He mixes it with water and gives it to the man to drink, whereupon the man is immediately metamorphosed. And our teacher Saadya also knows of such practices, which are carried out by angels or by the Name.

V

In the twelfth century at the latest a set procedure for golem-making developed on the basis of the conceptions set forth above. This procedure, if I am not mistaken, was a ritual *representing* an act of creation by the adept and culminating in ecstasy. Here the legend was transformed into a mystical experience, and there is nothing in the instructions that have come down to us to suggest that it was ever anything more than a mystical experience. In none of the sources does a golem created in this way enter into real life and perform any actions whatsoever. The motif of the magical servant or famulus is unknown to any of these texts[2] and does not make its appearance until much later when, as we shall see, the golem becomes a figure in Kabbalistic legend.

We possess four main sources of instructions for golem-making. I should like to discuss their principal features. The most precise instructions are given by Eleazar of Worms at the end of his commentary on the *Book Yetsirah*.[3] Revised and presented as a separate piece, they have come down to us in numerous manuscripts. The chapter is entitled *pe'ullath ha-yetsirah*, which probably means 'the practice, or practical application, of the *Book Yetsirah*,'

---

[1] This is read into Ezek. 1 : 10, where the bull in the *merkabah* looks leftward.

[2] After careful examination of the sources, I must withdraw my statement in *Eranos-Jahrbuch*, XIX, p. 151, Note 29, that this conception is first attested in Pseudo-Saadya.

[3] Only in the complete Przemyśl Edition, 1888, 15a, with the following tables of combinations.

though the 'practice of golem-making' would also be possible.[1]
Here as in the other texts Eleazar's complete tables of the combinations of the alphabet are lacking, but frequent reference is
made to them. In the first half of the seventeenth century the
Frankfurt Kabbalist Naphtali ben Jacob Bacharach had the
courage to include this text in a printed edition of one of his Kabbalistic works, though in revised form and accompanied by the
prudent explanation that the 'instructions' had been left incomplete, lest they be misused by unworthy persons.[2]

Eleazar's instructions specify that two or three adepts, joined
in the golem ritual, should take some virginal mountain earth,[3]
knead it in running water, and form a golem from it. Over this
figure they recite the combinations of the alphabet derived from
the 'gates' of the *Book Yetsirah*, which, in Eleazar's recension,
form not 231 but 221 combinations.[4] The characteristic feature
of this procedure is that not the 221 combinations themselves are
recited, but combinations of each of their letters with each consonant of the tetragrammaton according to every possible
vocalization (the Hasidim recognized the five vowels a, e, i, o,

[1] MS British Museum, Margoliouth 752, Fol. 66a; Cambridge Univ.
Libr. Add. 647, Fol. 18a–b; Jerusalem Univ. Libr., 8°, 330, Fol. 248; cf. on
this fragment my catalogue of Kabbalistic codices in Jerusalem *Kitve Yad
be-Kabbalah*, 1930, p. 75.

[2] '*Emek ha-Melekh*, Amsterdam, 1648, 10c–d; this passage is completely
translated into Latin from the excerpts from this work given in Knorr von
Rosenroth, *Kabbala denudata*, II (actually the third volume of the whole
work): *Liber Sohar restitutus*, Sulzbach, 1684, pp. 220–1.

[3] In his *Sefer ha-Shem*, MS Munich, 81, Fol. 127b, Eleazar also demands
virgin soil from the mountain for a magical cure effected with the 72-letter
name of God. I have found something similar in the medieval magical text
about the testing of a woman suspected of adultery, communicated in A.
Marmorstein, *Jahrbuch für jüdische Volkskunde*, II (1925), p. 381. On p. 11 of
Die Golemsage, B. Rosenfeld, whose medieval material on the subject is
otherwise taken entirely (including the mistakes) from my article 'Golem' in
Encyclopaedia Judaica, VII (1931), expresses the belief that this prescription
'probably has something to do with the view of the earth as the virginal
mother of Adam, which already occurs in the doctors of the Church and
later in medieval, particularly Middle High German, literature' (Köhler, in
Germania, VII, pp. 476 ff.). It may 'have reached the German Kabbalists
and have been transferred to the golem.'

[4] Saadya substituted '231 gates,' which is correct from the standpoint of
the theory of combination. As the tables in Eleazar of Worms show, the
German Hasidim arrived in a very complicated way at the 221 gates of their
text.

and u). This seems to have been the first step. It is possible that the procedure was limited to the recitation of all the possible combinations of two (in every conceivable vocalization) between one of the consonants, each of which according to the *Book Yetsirah* 'governs' a part of the human organism, and one consonant of the tetragrammaton. Not the printed texts, but several of the manuscripts give exact instructions about the order of these vocalizations. The result is a strictly formal recitative, both magical and meditative in character. One prescribed order of the alphabet produces a male being, another a female; a reversal of these orders turns the golem back to dust.[1] None of these instructions leave room between the act of animation and the act of transformation back into dust, for a pause during which the golem might exist outside the sphere of meditation.

The ritual character of this golem creation is particularly clear in the explanations of the so-called Pseudo-Saadya. The words of the *Book Yetsirah* (II, 4): 'So the circle [*galgal*] closes before and behind' were taken by him as a prescription. These words do not only tell us how God went about his creation, but also teach us how the adept should proceed when he sets out to create a golem. Commenting on this sentence, Pseudo-Saadya writes:[2]

They make a circle around the creatures and walk around the circle and recite the 221 alphabets, as they are noted [the author seems to have in mind such tables as we actually find in Eleazar of Worms], and some say that the Creator put power into the letters, so that a man makes a creature from virgin earth and kneads it and buries it in the ground, draws a circle and a sphere around the creature, and each time he goes around it recites one of the alphabets. This he should do 442 [in another reading 462] times. If he walks forward, the creature rises up alive, by virtue of the power inherent in the recitation of the letters. But if he wishes to destroy what he has made, he goes round backward, reciting the same alphabets from end to beginning. Then the creature sinks into the ground of itself and dies. And so it happened to R. I. B. E. [probably Rabbi Ishmael ben Elisha][3] with his students,

[1] So in the commentary to Chapter II, 5d.

[2] In addition to the text of the first edition of the *Book Yetsirah*, Mantua, 1562, with commentaries, I have used the MS of Pseudo-Saadya in the British Museum, No. 754 in Margoliouth's Catalogue of Hebrew Manuscripts, and the Munich MS Hebr. 40.

[3] This is the legendary hero of *merkabah* gnosis. But in the British Museum MS there is another abbreviation: R. Z., which probably refers to a Rabbi Zadok. Who is meant I do not know.

186

who busied themselves with the *Book Yetsirah* and by mistake went around backward, until they themselves by the power of the letters sank into the earth up to their navels. They were unable to escape and cried out. Their teacher heard them and said: Recite the letters of the alphabets and walk forward, instead of going backward as you have been doing. They did so and were released.

It strikes me as important that the golem is here buried in the earth, from which it rises. This might suggest a symbolism of rebirth, which would be perfectly in keeping with the nature of the whole as a ritual of initiation. Before his palingenesis the golem is buried! Of course, such an interpretation is not necessary and as far as I know this detail appears only in this one passage. The prescription that the earth of which the golem is made should be virginal (i.e., untilled) also favors the parallel with Adam, for he too was created of virgin soil. In the Munich manuscript of Pseudo-Saadya this passage is immediately followed by a second very detailed prescription, which is lacking in the printed version.[1] Here we read the following instructions: 'Take dust from a mountain, virgin earth, strew some of it all over the house, and cleanse your body. From this pure dust make a golem, the creature you wish to make and bring to life, and over each member utter the consonant assigned it in the *Book Yetsirah*, and combine it with the consonants and vowels of the name of God.' Circle 'as in a round dance,' and when the round is reversed, the golem returns to his original lifeless state.

We can gather indirectly from such instructions that the ritual culminates in ecstasy. The recitation of these rhythmic sequences with their modulations of vowel sounds would quite naturally induce a modified state of consciousness, and seems to have been designed for this purpose. This is made perfectly clear in a text which we possess in several manuscripts. It dates from the fourteenth century at the latest, but may well be older.[2] Here again we find technical prescriptions about the passage through all 231 gates. Then we read:

He should take pure earth of the finest sort and begin with combinations, until he receives the influx of inspiration, *shefa' ha-hokhmah*, and he should recite these combinations rapidly and turn the 'wheel'

[1] MS 40, Fol. 55b.

[2] MS Munich, 341, Fol. 183b; Cambridge Add. 647, Fol. 18b. (In this MS three golem recipes are combined!)

[of the combinations] as fast as he can, and this practice brings the holy spirit [that is, inspiration]. Only then [in such a state of mind!] should he undertake the [technical] part of golem-making.

These instructions show an unmistakable affinity to the yoga practices that had been disseminated among the Jews chiefly by Abraham Abulafia:

Then take a bowl full of pure water and a small spoon, fill it with earth—but he must know the exact weight of the earth before he stirs it and also the exact measurement of the spoon with which he is to measure [but this information is not imparted in writing.] When he has filled it, he should scatter it and slowly blow it over the water. While beginning to blow the first spoonful of earth, he should utter a consonant of the Name in a loud voice and pronounce it in a single breath, until he can blow no longer. While he is doing this, his face should be turned downward. And so, beginning with the combinations that constitute the parts of the head, he should form all the members in a definite order, until a figure emerges.

But it is forbidden to perform this operation too often. Its true purpose is: 'To enter into communion with His great Name.' The link between all this and Abulafia's Kabbalah (or its sources) is obvious.

It is in keeping with such a conception of the ecstatic nature of this vision of a golem when an important but anonymous Spanish author of the early fourteenth century explains that the process is not corporeal, but a 'creation of thought,' *yetsirah mahshavtith*. Abraham, he writes, 'almost succeeded in producing valuable creations, that is, creations of thought, and that is why he called his valuable book the *Book of Creation*.'[1] And a disparaging remark of Abulafia himself, the leading representative of an ecstatic Kabbalah in the thirteenth century, seems to imply a similar view of golem-making as a purely mystical process. He ridicules the 'folly of those who study the *Book Yetsirah* in order to make a calf; for those who do so are themselves calves.'[2]

An awareness of the inadequacy of the written instructions is discernible in several records of the later tradition. Naphtali Bacharach, for example, does not say what he omitted to prevent

[1] So in 'Questions of the Old Man,' *She'eloth ha-Zaken*, 97, Oxford MS. Neubauer, No. 2396, Fol. 53a.

[2] From Abulafia's *Ner 'Elohim*, quoted in my *Major Trends in Jewish Mysticism*, p. 384.

the misuse of his book. From parallels in the practical Kabbalah and in Abulafia's writings, one gathers that the omission may have concerned the intonation of the letter combinations, breathing technique, or certain movements of the head and hands that had accompanied the process. Hayim Joseph David Azulai, a famous Jerusalem Kabbalist of the eighteenth century, who was well acquainted with the traditions of the seventeenth-century school of Kabbalists in Jerusalem, said to Rabbi Jacob Baruch in Livorno (by word of mouth, it would seem) that in magic the 'corporeal combinations of letters as they first meet the eye are not sufficient.'[1]

[1] In Jacob Baruch's additions to the edition of Johanan Allemanno's *Sha'ar ha-Heshek*, Livorno, 1790, 37a. The similar remark which occurs in the novelistic version of the legends about the golem of the 'Great Rabbi Loew' of Prague is probably connected with this. This version, in which the golem takes on the entirely new function of combatting lies about ritual murder, is a free invention, written about 1909, and published in Hebrew by Judah Rosenberg (the author?), supposedly after an apocryphal 'Manuscript in the Library of Metz,' under the title: *The Miraculous Deeds of Rabbi Loew with the Golem*. Language and content both show it to be the work of a Hasidic author with a Kabbalistic education and (something unusual in these circles) novelistic leanings, writing after the ritual murder trials of the eighteen-eighties and nineties. Chajim Bloch's book, *Der Prager Golem*, Berlin, 1920, is a German version of this text, whose wholly modern character escaped the deserving, but quite uncritical, author. Nor is Held's opinion, that these versions are 'the only authentic documents to have come down to us' (*Gespenst des Golem*, p. 95), exactly indicative of critical understanding. He was surely fascinated by the following remark in Bloch's text (p. 59), which falls in very well with his own interpretation of the golem as man's double: 'Some regarded the golem as a "ghost" of Rabbi Loew.' In the Hebrew text of course there is no sign of this sentence, so welcome to such authors as Meyrink and Held. Toward the end of this Hebrew novel there are nineteen apocryphal 'utterances of Rabbi Loew on the nature of the golem,' which in reality, even if they were invented fifty years ago, do no less honor to the Kabbalistic frame of mind than to the imagination of the author. Here we read in § 17 (cf. *Nifla'oth Maharal 'im ha-Golem*, Pyotrkow, 1909, p. 73): 'One cannot study the letters of the *Book Yetsirah* as they are printed and make a man or living creature with them. Those who merely learn the combinations from the book can do nothing with them. First, because of the many corruptions and gaps in the text, and moreover, because everything depends on one's own spontaneous interpretations. For a man must first know to which 'lights' each letter points, then he will spontaneously know the material forces in each letter. All this can be studied; but when one has studied it all well, everything depends on one's intelligence and piety. If a man is worthy, he will achieve the influx [of inspiration] that enables him

From these testimonies on the practice of golem-making we learn chiefly two things:

1. As has been stressed above, it is without practical 'purpose.' Even where what is described seems to be on the border between a psychic experience (shared, it is true, by several adepts) and an objective manifestation of the golem, this 'demonstration' had no other purpose than to demonstrate the power of the holy Name. When rigorously interpreted, even the following statement in Pseudo-Saadya's commentary on *Yetsirah* (II, 5) remains within these limits: 'I have heard that Ibn Ezra made such a creature in the presence of Rabbenu Tam, and said: See what [power] God put into the holy letters, and he said [to Rabbenu Tam]: Go backward;[1] and it returned to its former state [as lifeless earth].' Even this report describes nothing more than a half-legendary initiation of the famous French Talmudist Rabbenu Tam (i.e., R. Jacob ben Me'ir, Rashi's grandson, who died in 1171) by the philosopher Abraham ibn Ezra, who travelled through Western Europe in the middle of the century, and whom the German and French Hasidim always revered as a great religious authority.[2] Here again the golem, no sooner created, is dissolved again into dust: with the initiation of the Talmudist it has served its purpose, which is purely psychic.

2. Golem-making is dangerous; like all major creation it endangers the life of the creator—the source of danger, however, is not the golem or the forces emanating from him, but the man

---

[1] It is clear from the context that this is an invocation, not to the golem but to Rabbenu Tam, who took part in the ritual. The whole story is told only in order to illustrate the act of going backward in destroying the golem.

[2] The mystical leanings of Abraham ibn Ezra were evidently clearer to them than to us, and in any case, they saw no contradiction between them and his other—grammatical, exegetical, and theological—interests. As late as 1270 Abraham Abulafia had before him a commentary of ibn Ezra on the *Yetsirah*, which he characterized as 'philosophical and in part mystical.'

---

to compose and combine the letters, in such a way as to produce a creature in the material world. But even were he to write down the combinations, his companion will be unable to do anything with them unless, through his own insight, he achieves the necessary concentration of thought. Otherwise the whole remains for him like a body without soul. Bezalel had the highest insight in these matters, and for him it would have been a little thing to create a man or living creature. For he even knew the right meditations concerning the letters with which heaven and earth are made.'

himself. The danger is not that the golem, become autonomous, will develop overwhelming powers; it lies in the tension which the creative process arouses in the creator himself. Mistakes in carrying out the directions do not impair the golem; they destroy its creator. The dangerous golem of later legends represents a profound transformation of the original conception, in which, as we have seen, a parallel with Adam was clearly present, but in which this tellurian element was not regarded as a source of danger.[1] And yet the danger incurred by the creator of a golem, at least as described by Pseudo-Saadya, is not entirely without such implications. For here the man himself returns to his element; if he makes a mistake in applying the instructions, he is sucked in by the earth.

There is another question to which we obtain no conclusive answer, namely: could golems speak? The Talmudist Rava was unable to confer speech on his artificial man. But even in the later ritual, muteness is not as essential as has often been supposed.[2] It was not always the rule, and apparently both conceptions were current among the German Hasidim. We do not know where the notion of a golem endowed with speech, as in the story about Ben Sira, first made its appearance.[3] The legends

---

[1] It is a mistake to read a reference to such a destructive power of the golem in the passage of *Midrash ha-Ne'elam* in *Zohar Hadash*, 1885, 21c, saying in connection with Gen. 6 : 11: 'By this is meant the golem that destroys everything and brings about its ruin.' Here 'golem' is used in the sense of an irreligious, soulless man, as also, in another passage of the same *Midrash ha-Ne'elam*, printed in *Zohar*, I, 121a: 'Rabbi Isaac said, No one sins, unless he is a golem and no man, which is to say: one who takes no account of his sacred soul and whose whole activity is like that of an animal.' The sacred soul is the divine part, in contrast to the mere vital soul. But is this usage connected with that of the Hasidim? Indeed, Joseph Gikatila wrote in the 'Garden of Nut Trees' (*Ginnath 'Egoz*, Hanau, 1615), 33c (which was written c. 1274, shortly before the *Midrash ha-Ne'elam*): 'The body with the vital spirit that dwells in it, called *nefesh*, by virtue of which the body is able to move back and forth, is called golem.' Since otherwise 'golem' means only 'body' in philosophical usage, this more precise use of the term may have been influenced by the language of the German Hasidim. Cf. my further remarks in the text about the question of the 'soul' in the golem.

[2] I myself expressed such an opinion in my 'Golem' article in *Encyclopaedia Judaica*, VII (1931).

[3] Thanks to a strange typographical error, the golem of Ben Sira was associated with the Hay ibn Yaktan of Avicenna (Hebrew: Ben Sina), which, in the famous philosophical poem of Ibn Tofeil, is described as a kind of

about Ben Sira are far older than the twelfth century, although their association with golem-making is first attested for this period. Possibly this motif first made its appearance in Italy. In the speculative discussions of the Kabbalists, in any case, the golems of Rava and Ben Sira are taken as examples of the alternative possibilities.

It is Pseudo-Saadya who puts golems on the highest plane. He says that recitation of the alphabets of the *Book Yetsirah* has the God-given power to produce such a creature and to give it vitality, *hiyyuth*, and soul, *neshamah*.[1] No other Kabbalistic source goes so far. In distinguishing between the pneumatic element of the soul and the purely vital element, he implies at least that such a golem could do more than merely move, so placing him on a level with the golem who warned Ben Sira that his activities might bring about the death of God.

Clearly Eleazar of Worms is more cautious than our other sources from the same school of Judah the Pious. In commenting on the verse: 'Knowledge and speech in Him who lives forever' (in an old hymn of the merkabah gnostics) he declares expressly that man has true knowledge (*da'ath*, which also means gnosis) by which he can make a new creature with the help of the *Book Yetsirah*, but that even with the help of the Name of God, he cannot endow his creature with speech.[2] With a significant restriction, this opinion is shared by the *Book Bahir* from the second half of the twelfth century. Here (§ 136) the Talmudic story about Rava is related, but with the following addition:

Rava sent a man to Rabbi Zera. He spoke to him and he did not answer. But if not for his sins, he would have answered. And what would have enabled him to answer? His soul. But has man a soul that he might transmit [to such a creature]? Yes, for it is written in Genesis 2 : 7: 'He blew into his nostrils the breath of life—thus man has a soul

[1] To *Yetsirah*, II, 5. Exactly as in the British Museum MS.

[2] From Munich MS, Hebr. 346, cited in my *Reshith ha-Kabbalah*, Jerusalem–Tel-Aviv, 1948, p. 231.

philosophical golem, brought into being by *generatio aequivoca*. In Isaac ibn Latif's *'Iggereth Teshubah* (*Kobetz 'al Yad*, I, p. 48), Ibn Sina's name is misprinted. Thus Ben Sira became the creator of Yehiel ben Uriel, that is, Hay ibn Yaktan. This misled A. Epstein, *Beiträge zur jüdischen Altertumskunde*, 1887, p. 124, into erroneous combinations concerning Ben Sira's golem.

of life' [with which he might confer language][1] were it not for sins, through which the soul ceases to be pure; and this impurity is the dividing line between the righteous and God. And so also it is written [Ps. 8 : 6]: 'Thou madest him only a little lower than God'.[2]

According to this passage, sinless beings would be able to transmit the soul of life, which includes the power of speech, even to a golem. Thus the golem is not mute by nature, but only because the souls of the righteous are no longer pure. In contrast to this conception, which possibly opens up eschatological perspectives for a new and improved golem, Isaac the Blind (c. 1200) contents himself with observing that the golem was speechless because Rava could give him no *ruah*.[3] What this author means by *ruah* is uncertain. Possibly it is taken in the sense of pneuma, the higher, spiritual soul.

Elaborating the statement of Eleazar of Worms, a Kabbalist at the turn of the fourteenth century goes so far as to say that although a golem has an animated form, he is still dead, because his creator can give him no knowledge of God or speech. 'Upon the real man God imprinted the seal *emeth*.'[4] For several Kabbalists who accepted the *anima rationalis* of the philosophers, the power of speech was inseparable from reason. Thus Bahya ben Asher (1291) says of Rava: 'He was able to give his creature a motor soul, but not the rational soul which is the source of speech.'[5] This is in keeping with the view prevailing among the Kabbalists that speech is the highest of human faculties, or, to quote J. G. Hamann, the 'mother of reason and revelation.'

But there were other Kabbalists who dissociated speech from reason. In one piece from the middle of the thirteenth century,

[1] My explanation of the passage in the complete translation of the *Book Bahir*, Berlin, 1923, p. 150, should be amended accordingly.

[2] This interpretation of the passage in Ps. as a reference to man's inability to give the golem speech occurs also in a text of the German Hasidim, which I have published in *Reshith ha-Kabbalah*.

[3] In his commentary on the *Yetsirah*, MS Leiden, Warner 24, Fol. 224b.

[4] Simeon ben Samuel, *Hadrath Kodesh*, at the beginning (printed in 1560 in Thiengen under the title *Adam Sikhli*). The author employs the term 'golem', but his use of the word is colored by the philosophical meaning 'matter' in contrast to living form. In the final letters of Gen. 2 : 7 about the life breath, the author finds the word *hotam*, seal.

[5] In Bahya's commentary on the Torah, Gen. 2 : 7, Venice, 1544, 11d, and in his *Kad ha-Kemah*, ed. C. Breit, II, 103b.

entitled 'Epitome of the Things According to Which the Masters of the *Merkabah* Operated,' a Spanish Kabbalist writes:[1]

> When the rabbis say: a childless man is like a dead man, this means: like a golem [lifeless matter], without form. Consequently pictures that are painted on a wall are of this nature, for although they have the form of a man, they are called only *tselem*, image [here in the sense of reflection, derived from *tsel*, shadow] and form. When Rava created a man, he made a figure in the form of a man by virtue of the combinations of letters, but he could not give him *demuth*, the real likeness of a man. For it is possible for a man, with the help of mighty forces, to make a man who speaks, but not one who can procreate or has reason. For this is beyond the power of any created being and rests with God alone.'

Here then, contrary to the opinion put forward by Bahya and so many others, the golem has speech, but neither language nor sexual urge.[2]

Among later Kabbalists, two important authorities, each in a different way, expressed themselves about the specific kind of vitality conferred on the golem. About 1530 Me'ir ibn Gabbai expressed the opinion that a magically produced man has no spiritual soul, *ruah*, for he is—and he cites the Talmud passage in authority—speechless. But he has the lowest degree of soul, *nefesh*, for he can move and has vitality.[3] Moses Cordovero takes a different view of the question in 1548. According to him,[4] a 'new creature' of this kind—Cordovero, like all the Sefardic Kabbalists of the sixteenth century, avoids the term golem, which seems at that time to have been in use only among the

[1] MS 838 of the Jewish Theological Seminary in New York, Fol. 35b.

[2] I have thus far found this conception in no other authentic Kabbalistic text. It is all the more interesting that it should recur in the utterances, mentioned in Note 1, p. 189, of a modern author inclining toward Kabbalism, which he puts into the mouth of the 'Great Rabbi Loew' of Prague. Here we read in § 9: 'The golem had to be made without generative power or sexual urge. For if he had had this urge, even after the manner of animals in which it is far weaker than in man, we would have had a great deal of trouble with him, because no woman would have been able to defend herself against him.' Small wonder that this motif should have played an important part in the literary treatment of the legend in modern fiction.

[3] Ibn Gabbai, *'Avodath ha-Kodesh*, II, 31.

[4] In his *Pardes Rimmonim*, XXIV, 10. This is the source of Abraham Azulai's remarks on the subject in his *Hesed le-Abraham*, IV, 30, written c. 1630.

German and Polish Jews—has no soul of any degree, neither *nefesh* nor *ruah* nor *neshamah*; he has, however, a special kind of vitality, *hiyyuth*, which Cordovero puts higher than the animal soul. How, Cordovero asks, could men, even aided by the alphabets of the *Book Yetsirah*, have drawn any of these three degrees of soul down to such a creature? According to him it is impossible. What actually happens, in his view, is as follows: When the adepts put the earth together and, as a result of their occupation with the *Book Yetsirah*, a creature in the form of man comes into being, this creature's parts [like those of all created beings] strive upward, toward their source and their home in the upper world, whence all tellurian things come or in which they have their prototype. Upon these elements there shines a light appropriate to their specific rank in the scale of the elements; it is not *nefesh* nor *ruah* nor *neshamah*, but a pure naked vitality which, because of the nature of the elements here joined, is above the animal level and comes closer to the source of light than does an animal. On the other hand, a golem does not die in the strict sense, as an animal dies, but simply returns to its element, the earth. Consequently Rabbi Zera, in the Talmud, had no need to kill him, because his elements disintegrated of their own accord. So it is that one who 'kills' a golem is not liable to punishment and transgresses no commandment of the Torah.

Here then we have a truly tellurian creature, which, though animated by magic, remains within the realm of elemental forces. A tellurian soul, very similar to that which animated Adam in the midrash discussed at the beginning of this study, flows into him from the earth. Adam-golem, as we have seen, was endowed not with reason but with a certain elemental power of vision, and man has a similar power to endow his golem with elemental forces, or, as Cordovero says, 'lights that shine into the elements.' So also in the Kabbalistic development of the golem, the tellurian and magical elements converge in a way that is specifically defined. The purely theoretical speculation of the Kabbalists about the meaning and nature of golems may thus be said to prepare the way for, or run parallel to, the development in which, reverting from the purely mystical realm to that of Kabbalistic legend, the golem once again becomes the repository of enormous tellurian forces which can, on occasion, erupt.

VI

The Safed Kabbalists of the sixteenth century speak of golems as of a phenomenon situated in the remote past; their discussion of the matter is purely theoretical. Occasionally a set of instructions for golem-making made its appearance among them; the readers were explicitly forbidden to experiment along these lines, but nowhere do we find any direct reference to such activities among them.[1] One of the manuscripts of Cordovero's commentary on the *Book Yetsirah* concludes with a kind of appendix, quoting ancient passages about the creation of a man by means of the *Yetsirah*. But even here it is stressed at the outset: 'No one should imagine that anyone still has the power to achieve practical results with this book. For it is not the case; the magical sources are stopped up and the Kabbalah on the matter has vanished.'[2] Another characteristic statement is that of Joseph Ashkenazi, who came to Safed from Prague and Posen. In his treatise fulminating against the Jewish philosophers, he speaks of golem-making not as an actual practice, but as something known only from tradition. He uses the term 'golem' current among the German Jews: 'We find [in the old text] that man can make a golem, who receives the animal soul by the power of his [i.e., his master's] word, but to give him a real soul, *neshamah*, is not in the power of man, for it comes from the word of God.'[3]

Among the German and Polish Jews, however, the conception of the golem reverted to the realm of living legend. And whereas in the twelfth and thirteenth centuries such legends related primarily to persons of Jewish antiquity, prominent contemporaries became golem makers in the later development. When the common people took up the old stories and descriptions of the ritual, the nature of the golem underwent a metamorphosis. Once again he became an autonomous being, and for the first time

[1] So in Abraham Galante (c. 1570), who in his commentary, *Zohore Hammah* to *Zohar*, I, 67b, gives a prescription which in its technical details deviates sharply from the old recipes. Indeed the *Zohar* text itself in this passage mentions the principle, frequent in Kabbalistic literature, of the destructive power implicit in a reversal of the alphabets.

[2] So in the MS which Hirschensohn described in 1887 in No. 31 of the first volume of the Jerusalem periodical *Ha-Zvi*, on a separately printed page (No. 27 of his list of MSS).

[3] Cf. *Tarbiz*, XXVIII (1958-9), p. 68.

acquired practical functions. He also took on new features, deriving from other conceptions.

The first report of this new development is of great interest. Transmitted by a famous Spanish rabbi of the first half of the fourteenth century, it is still quite in the esoteric tradition. In reference to the Talmudic passage about Rava, Nissim Girondi in Barcelona writes: 'The scholars in Germany who busy themselves almost daily with demonology take this passage as their foundation. They insist that this [i.e., the production of such a man] must take place in a vessel.'[1] But there is no mention of a vessel in any of the accounts of golem-making that have come down to us, unless this vessel should be identified with the bowl full of water and earth that we have encountered in one of our prescriptions. This, however, strikes me as unjustified. In my opinion the 'vessel' employed by the German golem makers should be taken as a retort. This would be extremely interesting, for it would mean that long before Paracelsus the Jews associated the retort, indispensable to the alchemist makers of homunculi, with their golem. Nissim Girondi was in contact with prominent scholars from Germany, and he is a cool-headed, reliable witness. His testimony proves that such stories were told about certain German Hasidim. Have we then here, among the Jews, an early form of the conception which found its classical expression in Paracelsus' instructions for making a homunculus?

According to Jacoby, Paracelsus' homunculus was an 'artificial embryo, for which urine, sperm, and blood, considered as vehicles of the soul-substance, provided the *materia prima*.'[2] At the end of forty days the homunculus began to develop from the putrefaction of this raw material. But such use of sperm was unknown to the Jews. Golems continued to be made of earth and water, and even in the later reports only clay or mud are mentioned. I have been unable to determine whether there is any reliable evidence of instructions for the making of a homunculus

---

[1] In his *Hiddushim* to Sanhedrin 65b.

[2] In *Handwörterbuch des deutschen Aberglaubens*, IV (1932), 286 ff. In *Das Gespenst des Golem*, pp. 118 and 123, Held describes two processes of Paracelsus, both from *De natura rerum*, one for the homunculus, and another for palingenesis, which indeed seem very closely related. Paracelsus' extravagant claims in regard to the gifts of his homunculi are not, to be sure, in line with the golem conception.

before Paracelsus.[1] It was only long after Paracelsus that the practice was attributed to earlier authorities, such as the physician, mystic, and reputed magician Arnaldus of Villanova; and such attributions appear to be legendary. I am far from certain that the interpretations of the homunculus as a symbol of rebirth after death or as an embryonic form of the philosopher's stone, as recently advanced by Ronald Gray, are correct.[2] But if they are, they suggest a profound connection with the symbolism of the golem, which, in one of the prescriptions recorded above, is buried in the earth as *materia prima* and rises up out of it.[3]

Paracelsus, it is true, also gave the name of homunculi to the golem-like figures of wax, clay, or pitch employed in black magic to inflict injury on enemies. By a combination of these two meanings, the homunculus became in legend the demonic servant, who seems to have made his first appearance in certain traditions of the seventeenth century. A similar metamorphosis took place among the Jews, but earlier. The golem as his maker's magical man of all work is known to none of the old traditions. This conception made its appearance only in the fifteenth and sixteenth centuries when the famous scholars among the German Hasidim, who developed the theory and ritual of the golem, became objects of popular legend. The oldest record of it known to us occurs in a manuscript from the first half of the sixteenth century, relating (among other things) much older legends about the German Hasidim. It is here that Nehemiah Brüll found the story to the effect that Samuel the Pious (father of Judah the Pious, the central

---

[1] In *Handwörterbuch, loc. cit.,* Jacoby promises a monograph on the homunculus, to appear in *Archive de l'Institut Grandducal de Luxembourg, section des sciences naturelles, nouvelle série, tome XII.* Unfortunately this monograph never appeared, and in the place indicated there is only a résumé containing less than the article in the *Handwörterbuch.*

[2] Ronald Gray, *Goethe the Alchemist,* Cambridge, 1952, pp. 205–20, especially pp. 206–8. Cf. also C. G. Jung, *Paracelsica,* 1942, p. 94, on the personification of the Paracelsian 'Aquaster' in the homunculus.

[3] This early contact of the golem with the homunculus motif would be still better attested if in Pseudo-Saadya to *Yetsirah,* II, 4, the word 'creature' (that is, one made by magic) were explained by the gloss 'homunculus.' But there is no such thing either in the MS that I was able to consult or in the first edition of 1562, 95b (although B. Rosenfeld, p. 18, quotes it from there). In the printed edition we find a meaningless והמסת corrupted from וכריאות in the MS. Only in the Warsaw edition of 1884(!) is this replaced by the word 'homunculus.'

figure among these Hasidim) 'had created a golem, who could not speak but who accompanied him on his long journeys through Germany and France and waited on him.'[1]

In the sixteenth century legends of this kind became very popular among the German Jews. About 1625 Joseph Solomon Delmedigo quotes the above-mentioned story about Abraham ibn Ezra and goes on to say:

It is also related of Solomon ibn Gabirol [the famous poet and philosopher of the eleventh century] that he created a woman who waited on him. When he was denounced to the government [evidently for magic], he proved that she was not a real, whole creature, but consisted only of pieces of wood and hinges, and reduced her to her original components. And there are many such legends that are told by all, especially in Germany.[2]

Along the same lines, we read in a report published in 1614 by Samuel Friedrich Brenz that the Jews had a magical device 'which is called *Hamor Golim* (!); they make an image of mud resembling a man, and whisper or mumble certain spells in his ears, which make the image walk.'[3]

This is a far cry from the golem ritual discussed in the preceding section. 'Here we discern the influence of a different realm of ideas, those concerned with the making of an automaton. The breaking down of the golem into its separate components clearly suggests a mechanical golem, a notion that appears nowhere else in the tradition. The servant motif is also connected with the mechanical man and no doubt has its source in the automaton legends of the Middle Ages,' which in turn harked back to ancient tales, such as those related in Lucian's *Liar*.[4]

In the late forms of the legend, which arose in seventeenth-century Poland, a new element appears; the servant becomes dangerous. This new golem is mentioned by German students of

---

[1] *Jahrbücher für jüdische Geschichte und Literatur*, IX (1889), p. 27. See also the text from a Hasidic MS of the same period, quoted by me in *Tarbiz*, XXXII (1963), p. 257.

[2] Delmedigo, *Matsref la-Hokhmah*, Odessa, 1865, 10a.

[3] Cf. Rosenfeld, p. 39, where *Hamor Golim* is correctly explained as a Hebrew translation (by an ignoramus!) of the Yiddish 'leimener goilem,' which then as now was a popular pejorative term for simpleton.

[4] Rosenfeld, *op. cit.*, p. 17. On the 'sorcerer's apprentice,' see also Note 1, p. 203.

Jewish lore as early as the seventeenth century, but it does not figure in Hebrew literature until almost a hundred years later. In both cases the sources are legends about Rabbi Elijah Baal Shem,[1] rabbi of Chelm, who died in 1583. His descendants told their children almost the same stories that Christian Judaists had heard two generations earlier from German Jews. Johann Wülfer wrote in 1675 that there were in Poland 'excellent builders who can make mute *famuli* from clay inscribed with the name of God.'[2] He seems to have heard of the matter from several sources, but could find no eyewitnesses. A more explicit account of Rabbi Elijah's activities—the earliest thus far known to us—was written in 1674 by Christoph Arnold.[3]

After saying certain prayers and holding certain fast days, they make the figure of a man from clay, and when they have said the *shem hamephorash* over it, the image comes to life. And although the image itself cannot speak, it understands what is said to it and commanded; among the Polish Jews it does all kinds of housework, but is not

---

[1] The epithet in itself means that he was regarded as expert in the 'practical Kabbalah' (magic). 'Baal shem' means literally one who is master of the name of God, who knows how to employ it. In the *Sha'ar ha-Yihudim*, Lemberg, 1855, 32b, he is referred to as R. Eliyahu Baalshem Tov.

[2] Wülfer in his *Animadversiones* to Sol. Zevi Uffenhausen's *Theriaca Judaica*, Hanover, 1675, p. 69.

[3] Letter to J. Christoph Wagenseil at the end of his *Sota hoc est Liber Mischnicus de uxore adulterii suspecta*, Altdorf, 1674, pp. 1198–9. In my translation I have in part made use of Schudt's German translation in his *Jüdische Merckwürdigkeiten*, Frankfurt a. M., 1714, Part II, Book VI, pp. 206 ff., which, according to B. Rosenfeld, p. 39, was taken from W. E. Tentzel's *Monatliche Unterredungen von allerhand Büchern*, I, 1689, p. 145. Schudt abridged slightly. The main passage runs in the original: 'Hunc [scil. golem] post certas preces ac jejunia aliquot dierum, secundum praecepta Cabbalistica (quae hic recensere nimis longum foret) ex . . . limo fingunt . . . Quamvis sermone careat, sermonicantes tamen, ac mandata eorundem, satis intelligit; pro famulo enim communi in aedibus suis Judaei Polonici utuntur ut quosvis labores peragat, sed e domo egredi haud licet. In fronte istius nomen scribitur nomen divinum Emeth . . . Hominem hujusque modi Judaeum quempiam in Polonia fuisse ferunt, cui nomen fuit Elias Baal Schem . . . Is, inquam, ancillatorem suum in tantam altitudinem excrevisse intelligens, ut frontem ejus non amplius liceret esse perfricanti; hanc excogitavit fraudem, ut servus dominum suum excalcearet . . . [et dominus] literam Aleph in fronte digito deleret. Dictum, factum. Sed homo luteus, in rudem materiam cito resolutus, corruente mole sua quae insanum excreverat, dominum in scamno sedentem humi prostravit ut fatis ac luto pressum caput non erigeret.'

allowed to leave the house.[1] On the forehead of the image, they write: *emeth*, that is, truth. But an image of this kind grows each day; though very small at first, it ends by becoming larger than all those in the house. In order to take away his strength, which ultimately becomes a threat to all those in the house, they quickly erase the first letter *aleph* from the word *emeth* on his forehead, so that there remains only the word *meth*, that is, dead. When this is done, the golem collapses and dissolves into the clay or mud that he was . . . They say that a *baal shem* in Poland, by the name of Rabbi Elias, made a golem who became so large that the rabbi could no longer reach his forehead to erase the letter *e*. He thought up a trick, namely that the golem, being his servant, should remove his boots, supposing that when the golem bent over, he would erase the letters. And so it happened, but when the golem became mud again, his whole weight fell on the rabbi, who was sitting on the bench, and crushed him.

Zevi Ashkenazi, a descendant of this Rabbi Elijah, told a very similar story to his son Jacob Emden, who records it in his autobiography[2] and elsewhere in his works. 'When the rabbi'—after creating a mute man who waited on him as a servant—'saw that this creature of his hands kept growing larger and stronger by virtue of the Name which, written on parchment, was fastened to his forehead, he grew afraid that the golem might wreak havoc and destruction [in a similar account by the same author, we read: 'that he might destroy the world'].[3] Rabbi Elijah summoned up courage and tore the piece of parchment with the name of God on it from his forehead. Then he collapsed like a clod of earth, but in falling damaged his master and scratched his face.' Thus the accounts are identical, except that in one version the golem maker comes off with cuts and abrasions, while in the other, he loses his life.

Still more detailed is the report of another contemporary, who wrote in 1682 that, 'apart from speaking,' these creatures 'perform all sorts of human activities for forty days and carry letters like messengers wherever they are sent, even a long way; but if

---

[1] This remark is lacking in Schudt. It has no parallel in other accounts. Here the golem seems to be confused with a household spirit. From here it was taken over into Jakob Grimm's account.

[2] Jacob Emden, *Megillath Sefer*, Warsaw, 1896, p. 4.

[3] In Emden's *Responsa*, II, No. 82, In a different stylization the same tale occurs again in Emden's critique of the *Zohar*, *Mithpahath Sefarim*, Altona, 1769, 45a (mistakenly paginated as 35a).

after forty days the piece of parchment is not taken from their forehead, they inflict great damage upon the person or possessions of their master or his family.'[1] Here we have two new elements: for one thing, the period of service is limited to forty days, a motif which I have found in no Jewish source, but which may very well be authentic. It is interesting to note that in Paracelsus it takes forty days for the sperm, once enclosed in the retort, to develop into a homunculus. The other new feature is the dangerous character of the golem, mentioned in all the variants. This golem has prodigious strength and grows beyond measure. He destroys the world, or in any case does a good deal of damage. It seems to be the name of God that enables him to do so. But it is also, and in at least equal degree, the power of the tellurian element, aroused and set in motion by the name of God. Unless this tellurian force in held in check by the divine name, it rises up in blind and destructive fury. This earth magic awakens chaotic forces. The story of Adam is reversed. Whereas Adam began as a gigantic cosmic golem and was reduced to the normal size of a man, this golem seems to strive, in response to the tellurian force that governs him, to regain the original stature of Adam.

This brings us to the form in which Jakob Grimm found the golem legend. It must have been shortly before Grimm's day, toward the middle of the eighteenth century, that the Polish legend about the rabbi of Chelm moved to Prague and attached itself to a far more famous figure, 'the Great Rabbi' Loew of Prague (c. 1520–1609). Of course the Prague legend may have grown up independently, but this strikes me as very unlikely. In the Prague tradition of the early nineteenth century, the legend was associated with certain special features of the Sabbath Eve liturgy. The story is that Rabbi Loew fashioned a golem who did all manner of work for his master during the week. But because all creatures rest on the Sabbath, Rabbi Loew turned his golem back into clay every Friday evening, by taking away the name of God. Once, however, the rabbi forgot to remove the *shem*. The congregation was assembled for services in the synagogue and had already recited the ninety-second Psalm, when the mighty golem ran amuck, shaking houses, and threatening to destroy

---

[1] Johann Schmidt, *Feuriger Drachen Gifft und wütiger Ottern Gall*, Koburg, 1682, quoted in Schudt, *loc. cit.* Schudt's whole passage also occurs in Held, pp. 67–9.

everything. Rabbi Loew was summoned; it was still dusk, and the Sabbath had not really begun. He rushed at the raging golem and tore away the *shem*, whereupon the golem crumbled into dust. The rabbi then ordered that the Sabbath Psalm should be sung a second time, a custom which has been maintained ever since in that synagogue, the Altneu Schul.[1] The rabbi never brought the golem back to life, but buried his remains in the attic of the ancient synagogue, where they lie to this day. Once, after much fasting, Rabbi Ezekiel Landau, one of Rabbi Loew's most prominent successors, is said to have gone up to look at the remains of the golem. On his return he gave an order, binding on all future generations, that no mortal must ever go up to that attic. So much for the Prague version of the legend, which has gained wide currency.

Many legends about the making of golems by famous or not so famous rabbis and mystics were widespread among the Jews of Eastern Europe throughout the nineteenth century and are heard occasionally even now. Often they border on literary dilettantism, and in any case they have no bearing on the present study.[2] Still, it is interesting to recall that Rabbi Elijah, the *Gaon* (i.e., the genius) of Vilna (d. 1797), the outstanding Rabbinical authority among the Lithuanian Jews, owned to his student Rabbi Hayim, founder of the famous Talmudic academy of Volozhin, that as a boy, not yet thirteen, he had actually undertaken to make a golem. 'But when I was in the middle of my preparations, a form passed

---

[1] Cf. the midrash passage quoted in Note 1, p. 162, which would fall in with such an interpretation. Much has been written about this legend of Rabbi Loew, which has attracted many writers. Our first literary record of it is in 1837, when it was used by Berthold Auerbach. We have already stressed (Note 1, p. 189) that Judah Rosenberg's *The Miraculous Deeds of Rabbi Loew with the Golem* are not popular legends but tendentious modern fiction. For the versions current in Prague, cf. Nathan Grün, *Der hohe Rabbi Löw und sein Sagenkreis*, Prague, 1885, pp. 33–8, and F. Thieberger, *The Great Rabbi Loew of Prague*, London, 1955, pp. 93–6. It was later related in Bohemia that Goethe's ballad, *The Sorcerer's Apprentice*, was inspired by a visit of Goethe to the Altneu Schul in Prague; cf. M. H. Friedländer, *Beiträge zur Geschichte der Juden in Mähren*, Brünn, 1876, p. 16. Friedländer speaks of this as a 'well-known' tradition. I have never been able to find out whether there is anything in it.

[2] Such material, in part from the collections of the YIVO (Yiddish Scientific Institute), formerly in Vilna (now in New York), in B. Rosenfeld, pp. 23–5.

over my head, and I stopped making it, for I said to myself: Probably heaven wants to prevent me because of my youth.'[1] The nature of the apparition that warned Rabbi Elijah is not explained in the text. Held's suggestion that it was the rabbi's double, hence the golem himself, is profound but not very plausible.[2] Since we have limited our investigation to the Jewish traditions of the golem up to the nineteenth century there is no need to go into the modern interpretations put forward in novels and tales, essays and plays. The golem has been interpreted as a symbol of the soul or of the Jewish people, and both theories can give rise, no doubt, to meaningful reflections. But the historian's task ends where the psychologist's begins.

[1] In Rabbi Hayim's introduction to the commentary of the 'Vilna Gaon' on the *Sifra de-Tseni'utha*, a part of the *Zohar*, ed. Vilna, 1819.
[2] Held, *Das Gespenst des Golem*, pp. 155–61.

Index